Second Edition

Philosophy of Religion

WILLIAM J. WAINWRIGHT

University of Wisconsin, Milwaukee

Wadsworth Publishing Company
I(T)P® An International Thomson Publishing Company

Belmont, CA • Albany, NY • Boston • Cincinnati • Johannesburg
London • Madrid • Melbourne • Mexico City • New York
Pacific Grove, CA • Scottsdale, AZ • Singapore • Tokyo • Toronto

Philosophy Editor: *Peter Adams*
Assistant Editor: *Kerri Abdinoor*
Marketing Manager: *Dave Garrison*
Production Editor: *Kate Barrett*
Print Buyer: *Stacey J. Weinberger*

Copy Editor: *Adrienne Armstrong*
Cover Designer: *Cassandra Chu*
Compositor: *Scratchgravel Publishing Services*
Printer: *Transcontinental Printing*

Printed in Canada
1   2   3   4   5   6   7   8   9   10

For more information, contact Wadsworth Publishing Company, 10 Davis Drive, Belmont,
CA 94002, or electronically at http://www.wadsworth.com

International Thomson Publishing Europe
Berkshire House
168-173 High Holborn
London WC1V 7AA, United Kingdom

International Thomson Editores
Seneca, 53
Colonia Polanco
11560 México D. F. México

Nelson ITP, Australia
102 Dodds Street
South Melbourne
Victoria 3205 Australia

International Thomson Publishing Asia
60 Albert Street #15-01
Albert Complex
Singapore 189969

Nelson Canada
1120 Birchmount Road
Scarborough, Ontario
Canada M1K 5G4

International Thomson Publishing
Southern Africa
Building 18, Constantia Square
138 Sixteenth Road, P.O. Box 2459
Halfway House, 1685 South Africa

International Thomson Publishing Japan
Hirakawa-cho Kyowa Building, 3F
2-2-1 Hirakawa-cho
Chiyoda-ku
Tokyo 102, Japan

Library of Congress Cataloging-in-Publication Data

Wainwright, William J.
  Philosophy of Religion / William J. Wainwright. — 2nd ed.
     p.   cm.
  Includes bibliographical references and index.
  ISBN 0-534-52753-1
  1. Religion—Philosophy.   I. Title
BL51.W15   1998
210—dc21   98-23850

CONTENTS

Chapter 1   The Nature of God   1

Possible Worlds and the Concept of a Maximally Perfect Reality   4
Is the Concept of a Maximally Perfect Reality Coherent?   6
Is a Perfect Reality Personal?   9
God's Metaphysical Attributes and the Concepts of Timelessness and
    Impassibility   12
God's Knowledge and Power   22
Conclusion   29

Chapter 2   Arguments for the Existence of God   35

The Ontological Argument   35
The Cosmological Argument   42
The Design Argument   51
Appendix: Miracles   61

Chapter 3   The Problem of Evil   70

Are God and Evil Compatible?   72
The Greater Goods Defense   75
The Free Will Defense   82
Must God Choose the Best?   91
Gratuitous Evil   95
Conclusion   100

Chapter 4   Immortality   106

The Possibility of Immortality   107
Arguments for Immortality   111
Conclusion   117

Chapter 5   Mysticism and Religious Experience   120

The Nature of Religious Experience   121
Do Religious Experiences Have Cognitive Value?   125
Conclusion   138

Chapter 6   Anti-Evidentialism   142

Fideism   143
William James and the Will to Believe   159
Alvin Plantinga and Properly Basic Beliefs   164
Conclusion   170

Chapter 7   Is Theism the Best Explanation?
Assessing Worldviews   178

Cumulative Arguments   178
Comparing Rival Worldviews   182
Comparing Rival Religious Systems   187

Chapter 8   The Diversity of Religions   201

Relativism   202
The Devaluation of Propositional Truth and Belief   205
Religious Pluralism   206
Revelation and Rival Religious Systems   214
Conclusion   217

Conclusion   223

Index   227

PREFACE

Philosophy of Religion grows out of my conviction that current texts don't adequately reflect recent developments in the field.

There has been a remarkable resurgence of interest in philosophical theology over the past thirty years. Philosophers at midcentury were generally agreed that the traditional arguments for God's existence were unsound. Almost all of them were suspicious of theistic metaphysics, and many doubted whether religious language was meaningful. The current situation is very different. Important philosophers are now prepared to defend arguments for God's existence. Many argue that traditional concepts of the divine are not only meaningful but are also superior to alternatives. In their opinion, classical theistic metaphysics is still viable. Others have vigorously challenged these claims. The consequence has been a fruitful debate that has thrown new light on the concept of divine reality, the adequacy of arguments for its existence, and a number of related issues.

While important work is still being done on these problems, philosophers of religion have recently become interested in two other areas. The first is non-Western religions and the problems generated by religious diversity. Because Western religious traditions are theistic, philosophers of religion have usually equated religion with theism. This sort of parochialism is no longer tenable. Accurate knowledge of other traditions is readily available and their important texts have been translated. Philosophers who are familiar with this material realize that they can't responsibly dismiss the impressive intellectual achievements of nontheistic traditions like Buddhism and Advaita Vedānta, and non-Western forms of theism. But as our knowledge and appreciation of alternative religious systems increases, the following questions become urgent: How do we judge religious systems as a whole? Are there criteria for assessing religious worldviews? Can one religious system be said to be better than another?

The other new area of interest is the epistemic status of religious beliefs. Under what conditions is a person rationally entitled to a belief, and are these conditions sometimes met by religious convictions? Is it true that properly held religious beliefs must rest on evidence? If it isn't, what are the constraints on legitimate belief? Reflection on these questions has led to attacks on evidentialism, a renewed interest in the history of fideism, and (most important) more careful analysis of the nature of justified believing.

Many current texts fail to cover the more recent developments in philosophical theology. Those that do often oversimplify the issues involved in

v

assessing arguments for and against God's existence, doctrines of God's attributes, claims made for religious experience, and other standard problems in the philosophy of religion. Many widely read texts continue to ignore non-Western traditions, and few adequately discuss the problems involved in deciding between rival religious worldviews. None of the current texts adequately reflects the new interest in epistemic issues.

Philosophy of Religion is designed to remedy these deficiencies. It has three important features.

The Arguments

Most of the standard arguments in philosophy of religion are examined in this book. In presenting them, I have tried to avoid two common mistakes. The first is oversimplification. Arguments should be presented in detail sufficient for students to appreciate their complexity and power. Furthermore, some important arguments in philosophy of religion *hinge* on technical points, and are misrepresented when these points are ignored. The Free Will Defense and the ontological arguments are examples. The other mistake is unnecessary complexity. Technical issues aren't equally important. An overemphasis on technical precision causes most students to lose interest; even the best students find it difficult to see the forest for the trees.

Rival Religious Worldviews

Non-Western doctrines and arguments are discussed at various points throughout the book. For example, Advaitin arguments for the impersonality of the Absolute are discussed in Chapter 1. Hindu views of immortality are examined in Chapter 4, and Vedāntin accounts of the relation between the Absolute and the space-time world are explored in Chapter 7. Problems involved in adjudicating between rival religious worldviews are discussed at length in Chapters 7 and 8.

The Epistemic Status of Religious Belief

The current interest in the conditions under which religious beliefs are properly held is reflected in the discussions of Chapters 5, 6, and 7. For example, William Alston's account of Christian mystical practice is discussed in Chapter 5. Fideism and Alvin Plantinga's defense of the "proper basicality" of some religious beliefs are examined in Chapter 6, and Chapter 7 discusses "informal" reasoning.

Features of the New Edition

Philosophy of Religion has been substantially revised. For example, Chapter 1 includes a new section on God's timelessness, and a section on gratuitous evil has been added to Chapter 3. Chapter 5 now includes a thorough discussion of William Alston's seminal work on religious experience. Chapter 6's section on Alvin Plantinga and proper basicality has been expanded to include an examination of his recent influential work on proper epistemic functioning. Chapter 8 is new, and addresses three important responses to religious diversity, including the widely discussed views of John Hick. Almost every chapter of the second edition incorporates smaller changes that either clarify the arguments of the first edition or reflect recent developments. Finally, the suggestions for further reading at the end of each chapter have been extended and updated. The net result of these changes is a book that introduces the student to philosophy of religion as currently practiced by the leading specialists in the field.

This book, then, is designed to acquaint students with the current state of the debate in philosophy of religion, and to familiarize them with the issues that will concern philosophers of religion in the foreseeable future. I hope it will also make a contribution in its own right.

William J. Wainwright

To Mimi

The Nature of God

ACCORDING TO WILLIAM JAMES (1842–1910), religious life includes three beliefs:

> "that the visible world is part of a more spiritual universe from which it draws its chief significance;
>
> that union or harmonious relation with that higher universe is our true end," and
>
> that life can be transformed for the better by making proper contact with it.

Religious people believe that "prayer or inner communion with the spirit thereof—be that spirit 'God' or 'law'—is a process wherein work is really done, and spiritual energy flows in and produces effects, psychological or material, within the phenomenal world."

James thinks that religion also involves "a new zest which adds itself to life, and takes the form either of lyrical enchantment or of appeal to earnestness and heroism." It provides, he says, "an assurance of safety and a temper of peace, and, in relation to others, a preponderance of loving affections."[1]

Throughout history, men and women have turned to religion for comfort, strength, and assurance. Traditions like Buddhism, Christianity, and Islam give life depth and significance by explaining the nature of reality and our place in it, by assuring us of the possibility of victory over life's difficulties, and by providing means for achieving it.

Religion is rooted in human needs and yearnings—a conviction that ordinary life is flawed and that the powers of the "visible world" aren't sufficient to mend it. While suffering causes some to doubt the very existence of a "higher universe," it strengthens the convictions of many others. In Elizabeth Gaskell's novel *North and South*, a factory girl who is dying in miserable surroundings argues that this can't be all there is and that there must therefore be a "God to wipe away all tears from all eyes." The incompleteness and unsatisfactoriness of life—its inability to fully satisfy our yearnings or provide lasting happiness—lead many to hope or believe that the visible world isn't the whole of reality.

But religion isn't rooted only in needs and yearnings. The order and beauty of the world and even the fact that it exists at all seem to point to

1

something beyond it. Furthermore, saints, mystics, prophets, and many ordinary men and women believe they have actually glimpsed a sovereign good that transcends life's contingencies and provides an answer to the quest for meaning and happiness.

Religion is thus rooted in human needs, yearnings, and experiences. The strength of conviction, hope, and commitment varies considerably from person to person. But, for the devout, the higher universe is a matter of what Paul Tillich (1886–1965) calls "ultimate concern."

Ultimate concern is "total." The self as a whole is caught up in it, and every other concern becomes secondary. The object of a person's ultimate concern is experienced as holy—distinct from all profane or ordinary realities. It is also experienced as a mystery. No matter how much one knows about it, it eludes one's grasp. One appears to be caught up in something so charged with enormous power, so real and splendid that, in comparison, other things are empty and worthless. In short, the object of ultimate concern is experienced as overwhelming and supremely valuable. It thus demands total surrender and promises total fulfillment.[2]

Whether ultimate concern is necessary for any kind of religious attitude is a matter of dispute. Nevertheless, it *is* characteristic of the religious attitudes idealized in Christianity, Buddhism, Islam, and other major religious traditions.

Ultimate concern can, however, take different forms. It often takes the form of worship and then involves praise, love, gratitude, supplication, confession, petition, and so on. It can also take the form of a quest for the ultimate good. The object of this quest is a knowledge of the ultimate good or a union with it that transfigures us and overcomes our wrongness. These forms of ultimate concern may be combined or they may exist separately. Christianity, for example, combines both. In Buddhism, however, ultimate concern usually takes the second form but not the first.

The fact that ultimate concern is an aspect of religious attitudes may have an important implication. Perhaps nothing can be a completely appropriate object of these attitudes unless it is so great that we can conceive of nothing greater.

Why think this? It isn't sufficient for the object of these attitudes to be the greatest reality that actually exists, for the most perfect existing reality might be limited or defective. Suppose, for example, that the most perfect existing thing was wiser and better than other existing things but was ignorant of a number of matters and somewhat selfish. It would not be appropriate to surrender totally to a being of this sort. The defects or limitations of the most perfect existing thing might not be this striking. Nevertheless, if there is a possible reality that surpasses the most perfect existing thing, then the latter is limited or imperfect in comparison with the former. It thus seems that our admiration, concern, and commitment shouldn't be unconditional and without reservation. A *fully* appropriate object of ultimate concern must therefore be maximally perfect in the sense that it is the most perfect possible reality.

This conclusion isn't certain, and some philosophers doubt it. They grant that an appropriate object of ultimate concern must be greater than other *existing* beings. If it weren't, it wouldn't be ultimate. If another existing being was greater, our concern, loyalty, and commitment should be directed toward *it*. Suppose, though, that a being *is* greater than other existing beings, that it created heaven and earth, and that it is perfectly righteous. Suppose also that its power and knowledge are vastly greater than that of other existing beings although not as great as they could possibly be. While such a being would be the most perfect existing reality, it wouldn't be the most perfect possible reality. For we can conceive of something greater—a perfectly righteous creator of heaven and earth with *unlimited* power and knowledge. But isn't a most perfect existing reality of this kind an appropriate object of ultimate concern? It surely isn't *morally* wrong to worship it. Nor does it seem unfitting to totally commit ourselves to it, making it the object of our ultimate loyalty.

This is a plausible objection. Nevertheless, two things suggest that a *fully* appropriate object of ultimate concern must be the greatest possible reality.

Suppose a being has many perfections and is greater than other existing beings but that we can conceive of something greater. If the second being *had* existed, we ought to have given ourselves to *it* rather than the first. If we admit this, however, can we say that our commitment to the first is totally unreserved? Wouldn't this be like saying, "I love her unreservedly, but I might have met someone more beautiful and affectionate and, if I had, I would have loved her instead"? If one's love depends on not having met someone more lovable, is it truly unreserved? Similarly, is one's commitment to something unreserved if it depends on there not having been something more perfect?

The second point is this. Ultimate concern includes a number of attitudes—love, loyalty, and commitment but also reverence, awe, and admiration. Each is unreserved. Suppose something is greater than other existing beings but less great than some possible being. Even if unreserved love, loyalty, and commitment are appropriate, are unreserved reverence, awe, and admiration appropriate? Not clearly. I don't *unreservedly* admire a painting or a ball player if I think it would be possible for a painting or ball player to be better. Do I, then, unreservedly admire a being if I think a better being might have existed?

There are thus reasons for thinking that an appropriate object of ultimate concern must be maximally perfect. Classical Western theology has *explicitly* thought of God in this way. The notion is also *implicit* in many Asian views. Thus Rāmānuja (1017?–1137?) defines Brahman as the "sum of all noble attributes."

Some of the arguments discussed in this book depend on the notion of a maximally perfect reality and others do not. Chapter 2, for example, examines three arguments for God's existence. The first depends on the notion but the others don't.

The next section will clarify the concept of a maximally perfect reality by introducing a few technical notions. These notions will also be used at other points in the first three chapters. Section II will examine some difficulties in the concept of a maximally perfect reality, and the following sections will explore the concept's implications.

POSSIBLE WORLDS AND THE CONCEPT OF A MAXIMALLY PERFECT REALITY

A maximally perfect reality may be partially defined as a reality so great that no possible world contains anything surpassing it.[3]

Our definition uses the concept of a logically possible world. This concept is frequently employed in the philosophy of religion and is closely connected with notions of necessity, contingency, and impossibility. These notions play an important role in discussions of the divine nature and in two of the most important arguments for God's existence. Our discussion in this section will lead us to definitions of these notions.

What is meant by a logically possible world? Let us begin by considering the set S, consisting of all and only those propositions that are true. S includes "2 + 2 = 4," "Water freezes at 32 degrees Fahrenheit," "It is wrong to lie," "Green Bay lost the Superbowl in 1998," "Mice can't fly," and so on. This set is enormous. Indeed, for every meaningful proposition p, either p or its denial will be a member of S. For example, consider the following two meaningful propositions—"Germany lost the Second World War" and "St. Louis is the capital of Missouri." The first is a member of S. The second is not a member of S. Nevertheless, its denial is. Since Jefferson City is actually the capital of Missouri, our set includes "It is not the case that St. Louis is the capital of Missouri." Because S contains every proposition that is true and no proposition that is false, its members provide a complete and accurate description of the way things actually are. Let us call this "the actual world."

Now suppose we were to replace one or more members of S with their denials. Suppose, for example, that we replace "Water freezes at 32 degrees," "Mice can't fly," and "St. Louis is not the capital of Missouri," with "Water does not freeze at 32 degrees," "Mice can fly," and "St. Louis is the capital of Missouri." The new set of propositions S', generated by these replacements, describes a world that is unlike the actual world in a number of respects. If we were to make different replacements, we could generate descriptions of worlds that differed from those described by S or S'.

Some of the worlds whose descriptions are generated in this way will be possible and others will not. A world is impossible if its description includes a logically impossible proposition. Roughly, a logically impossible proposition is one that cannot be true because there is no conceivable set of circumstances in which it would be true. A proposition may be logically impossible because it violates principles of logic or mathematics. Examples would be "2 + 3 = 4" or self-contradictory propositions like "John is married and John is not married." There are also logically impossible propositions that do not violate these principles. Noncontroversial examples of such propositions are "Something is larger than itself" and "Some dogs are triangles." A more controversial example is "There is nothing morally objectionable about torturing a child." (If there are no conceivable circumstances in which it would be true that torturing a child is morally unobjectionable, then the proposition cannot be true and is thus logically impossible.)[4]

Logical impossibility must be distinguished from other kinds of impossibility. For example, many things are causally impossible. Given the causal laws that hold in our world, nothing can travel faster than the speed of light. Or an action may be impossible because it exceeds the powers of the agent. I cannot lift anything weighing 500 pounds or run a three-minute mile. None of these things, however, is logically impossible. I can coherently conceive of a world whose natural laws permit things to travel faster than light travels in our world, and I can coherently conceive of a world in which I am able to lift 500-pound weights and run a three-minute mile. Writers of fairy tales and science fiction are very good at describing things that are ruled out by the causal laws that hold in our world or by the limited capacities and powers of the things in it, but that are nevertheless logically possible.

A logically possible world, then, is a world whose description does not include a logically impossible proposition. The actual world is itself a logically possible world. But innumerable worlds that are logically possible are not actual. Some of these (like the ones partially described in *The Wizard of Oz* or *The Lord of the Rings*) will be very different from our own. Others will differ from the actual world in only a few respects.

The notion of a logically possible world is connected with the notions of necessity, contingency, and logical impossibility—notions that play an important role in the philosophy of religion.

Propositions can be divided into three classes:

1. Logically *necessary* propositions are true in all possible worlds. Examples are "2 + 2 = 4" and "Nothing can be larger than itself."

2. Logically *contingent* propositions are true in some possible worlds but not in others. Examples are "Tigers exist" and "Unicorns exist." The first is true in the actual world and in many other possible worlds, but isn't true in all of them. (Some possible worlds don't contain tigers.) "Unicorns exist" is false in our world, but there are possible worlds that contain unicorns. In those worlds, "Unicorns exist" is true.

3. Finally, a logically *impossible* proposition such as "2 + 3 = 4" is false in all possible worlds.

We are now in a better position to understand the concept of a maximally perfect reality. Something is maximally perfect only if no actual *or possible* reality is greater. Thus, to claim that something like God or Brahman is maximally perfect is to claim not only that nothing in the actual world surpasses it but also that nothing in any possible world does so. This is a very strong contention. The next section will examine some of the problems connected with it.

IS THE CONCEPT OF A
MAXIMALLY PERFECT REALITY COHERENT?

Critics sometimes argue that the concept of a maximally perfect reality is incoherent. If it is, then a maximally perfect reality isn't possible: either the object of the religious attitudes of Christians, Buddhists, and others doesn't exist, or it could be more perfect than it is.

There are three reasons for thinking that the concept is incoherent. Some critics argue that there are no standards in relation to which something could be said to be more perfect than everything else. Others contend that a maximally perfect reality would have logically incompatible properties. Still others maintain that some perfections have no maximum. According to them, the concept of a maximally perfect reality is ill-formed like the concept of the largest possible number or the longest possible line.

The Lack of Standards

Charles Crittendon (1933–) puts the first objection in this way: "Normally when we say that something is 'greatest,' 'best,' 'most perfect,' etc., we mean greatest of *a given kind:* greatest symphony, best tennis player . . . most perfect likeness. The kind in question dictates which characteristics count for or against something's being greater, better, more perfect than something else. . . . [Thus] the best ball point pen would be one which smudges least, lasts longest, looks nicest, and so on; the best tennis player would be the one who wins the most important matches or something of the kind."[5] But while one ball point pen or tennis player can be better than another, it makes no sense to say that my ball point pen is better than the winner of Wimbledon. There is no class that includes both within which meaningful comparisons could be made. If I were to say that my ball point pen is better than the winner of Wimbledon, I would invite the question "A better what?" There is no clear answer to this question. Comparisons presuppose standards, and standards are possible only when there is a common class within which things can be ranked as better or worse.

Just as there is no significant class of comparison that includes ball point pens and tennis players, there is no significant class of comparison that includes everything. To say that something is as good as, or better than, everything else is thus nonsense. The notion of a reality that nothing surpasses is therefore incoherent.

This objection rests on a mistake. That some reality, x, is at least as perfect as every other possible reality does not entail that there is a class of comparison within which everything can be ranked. What *is* entailed is that, for every other possible reality, y, there are classes of comparison that include both x and y; and in each of these x ranks at least as highly as y. This can be true even if there is no *single* class within which x can be compared with everything else.

For example, God might be more perfect than other minds in virtue of His greater wisdom and righteousness and might be more perfect than physical entities in virtue of such features as greater power, permanence, and beauty. If God is maximally perfect, then (1) every possible reality can be compared with God in *some* respect and (2) no possible reality is better than God in *any* respect. This does not imply that God is better than everything else in the *same* respect and thus doesn't imply that God and everything else can be included in a common class of comparison.[6]

The Incompatibility of Some Perfections

The second objection hinges on the fact that some perfections are logically incompatible. Immutability is the property something has if it cannot change in any respect. Incorporeality is the property of being bodiless. Both properties have been traditionally regarded as perfections, and both are incompatible with such perfections as being able to dance or play tennis well.

Why does this create a problem? A maximally perfect reality is sometimes described as a being that possesses all perfections. If some perfections are incompatible, then no possible being has all of them. Hence, no possible being is maximally perfect. There are two ways of responding to this objection.

First Response

One can distinguish between imperfections, "mixed" perfections, and "pure" perfections. Some imperfections are defects like blindness or unrighteousness. Others are limitations such as our inability to lift stones over a certain weight or the fact that our knowledge of the world can only be acquired piece by piece through time-consuming and difficult investigations. These properties are not defects since the fact that we are limited in these ways doesn't imply that we are imperfect specimens of humanity. Their possession does, however, imply that the human species is less perfect in these respects than are other species whose members can lift stones of any tonnage or whose knowledge of the world is intuitive and complete.

A mixed perfection is a property that makes something better but implies some defect or limitation. Repentance, for example, implies a defect (the moral failure that one repents). Being human or being corporeal implies limitations (susceptibility to physical damage, for example). A pure perfection, on the other hand, is a perfection that does not entail a defect or limitation. Being or actuality, goodness, love, power, knowledge, unity, and independence are sometimes mentioned as examples.

While theists have sometimes characterized a maximally perfect reality as a reality that possesses *every* perfection, they have implicitly meant "every *pure* perfection." Even if some perfections are mutually incompatible, pure perfections may be consistent with one another. If they are, the properties of a maximally perfect reality are mutually compatible.

Second Response

The concept of a maximally perfect reality is designed to pick out a *possible* reality that is at least as good as any other possible reality. If some perfections are incompatible, then a reality that possesses *all* perfections is not a *possible* reality and is thus not a maximally perfect reality. A maximally perfect reality would possess a set of mutually consistent perfections that are as good as, or better than, any other set of mutually consistent perfections. However, it would not possess *all* perfections if there are some that are incompatible.[7]

Both responses reject the assumption upon which the objection was based (that a maximally perfect reality must have all perfections). The first response insists that a maximally perfect reality need only have all *pure* perfections. The second insists that all that is needed is that it have an unsurpassable set of *mutually compatible* perfections.

The Lack of Intrinsic Maxima

The third problem is created by the fact that certain perfections seem to lack "intrinsic maxima" (upper limits). Some properties admit of degrees and some do not. The sky can be more or less cloudy, but a tree can't be more or less of a maple. A day can be more or less hot, but it cannot be more or less in July. Some "degreed properties" have intrinsic maxima and others do not. Being cloudy, for example, has an upper limit (being completely cloudy). Being large, on the other hand, is a degreed property that does not have an upper limit. No matter how large an object is, it is logically possible that something is larger.[8]

Many of the perfections that have been ascribed to a maximally perfect reality are degreed properties—for example, knowledge, power, righteousness, love, and happiness. One being can know more than another, or be more powerful, and so on. Some of these appear to have intrinsic maxima. The knowledge of every true proposition or the power to bring about every contingent state of affairs may be the intrinsic maxima of knowledge and power, respectively.[9] Perhaps, too, nothing could be more righteous than a being whose dispositions and behavior never deviate from the appropriate moral standards—who is, for example, perfectly truthful, just, and faithful. Happiness, however, seems to lack an intrinsic maximum. No matter how happy a being is, it seems possible for it (or some other being) to be even happier.[10]

The problem, then, is this. Most religions believe that a maximally perfect reality would be happy. But happiness doesn't seem to have an intrinsic maximum. Their notion of a maximally perfect reality is therefore incoherent. Why is this the case? To be maximally perfect, a thing must be happy. But happiness has no upper limit. Hence, it is possible that the maximally perfect reality, or some other thing, be even happier and thus more perfect in that respect. This statement is incoherent. It is impossible for something to be *more* perfect than a thing that is *maximally* perfect (as perfect as anything could possibly be). Two responses are again possible.

First Response

One might deny that happiness has no intrinsic maximum. Theists, for example, have traditionally believed that God's happiness consists in the possession and enjoyment of the highest good (namely, Himself). That is, God's happiness consists in His delight in His own nature, activity, and splendor. Perhaps a happiness of this kind could not be surpassed.

Second Response

One might also respond to the objection by adopting a suggestion made by Charles Hartshorne (1897–). Hartshorne argues that a maximally perfect reality should be understood as a reality that (1) cannot be surpassed with respect to properties which have maxima and (2) with respect to properties which do not have maxima, can only be surpassed by itself. Suppose, for example, that a maximally perfect reality would be powerful and joyous. Since power has a maximum, it would possess it. It would thus be impossible for anything to be more powerful. On the other hand, if there really is no upper limit to happiness, its happiness cannot be maximal. Nevertheless, because it is maximally perfect, its joy is so intense that even though *it* could be still happier, its joy could not be surpassed by the joy of any *other* possible being.[11]

Conclusion

If our discussion has been sound, then the concept of a maximally perfect reality is probably coherent. It is not, however, sufficient to determine our understanding of divine reality, for the concept doesn't tell us precisely *what* properties a maximally perfect reality would have. It does provide some direction. If a property (1) is a perfection and (2) no equal or greater perfection is incompatible with it, then a maximally perfect reality would presumably have it. Nevertheless, it may be difficult to determine whether these conditions are met in particular cases. For example, whether immutability should be ascribed to a maximally perfect reality depends upon whether change is an imperfection. It also depends upon whether immutability is compatible with such perfections as creative activity.

The remainder of this chapter will examine problems that arise when one attempts to determine precisely what properties a maximally perfect reality would have.

IS A PERFECT REALITY PERSONAL?

The difficulties in ascribing properties to a maximally perfect reality can be illustrated by considering the fundamental question of whether such a reality is personal or nonpersonal. Theists believe that, even though ultimate reality transcends all finite realities, it is more like a person than anything else. That is, they believe that ultimate reality should be understood as God—an infinitely wise, good, and powerful ruler of heaven and earth. Many important religious traditions, however, are nontheistic—for example, Advaita Vedānta and Buddhism. These traditions believe that ultimate reality is impersonal. They don't think of it as a god.

Advaita Vedānta's rejection of theism is a consequence of its emphasis upon ultimate reality's unity and incomprehensibility. Advaita believes that Brahman (the first principle) is an absolute unity. "Brahman is without parts or attributes . . . one without a second. In Brahman there is no diversity whatsoever." "All difference in Brahman is unreal."[12]

The Brahman contains no plurality and transcends every distinction. It thus has no properties. Why is this the case? If the Brahman had properties, we could *distinguish* between the Brahman and its properties. This would be incompatible with its absolute unity. Furthermore, since Brahman has no properties and since we can only understand things by grasping their properties, it is incomprehensible. "It is the reality beyond all thought . . . outside the range of any mental conception."[13]

If ultimate reality transcends *all* properties, it transcends the property of being a person. However, even if the Brahman is not *literally* a person, it might be more like a person than anything else. Why, then, does Advaita reject theism?

Persons are rational agents—beings who have beliefs about themselves and the world and act on the basis of their beliefs. Believing and willing are essential to personhood. The major theistic traditions, accordingly, describe ultimate reality as an omniscient mind and an omnipotent and active will. Advaita Vedānta is nontheistic because its emphasis upon the divine unity leads it to deny that Brahman is either a knower or a causal agent.

Knowledge presupposes a distinction between the knower and what it knows. Even self-knowledge involves a distinction between the self as knower and the self as known. Advaita concludes that thought and knowledge are incompatible with Brahman's unity: "all specific cognition such as seeing, and so on is absent."[14]

Why can't the Brahman be a causal agent? If the Brahman is maximally perfect, it must be unlimited. It is limited, however, if something exists outside it. The Brahman must therefore be identical with the whole of reality. But if the Brahman is identical with the whole of reality and if the Brahman contains no plurality, then reality as a whole must be an undifferentiated unity. The spacetime world, with its distinctions among times, places, and events, is therefore unreal. Since a real causal relation is a relation between two real things, Brahman is not the cause of the space-time world or the events in it. The Brahman is thus neither the world's creator nor its ruler. "The Lord's being a Lord, his omniscience, his omnipotence, etc., all depend on . . . ignorance; while in reality none of these qualities belong to the Self [Brahman]. . . . In reality the relation of ruler and ruled [creator and created] does not exist."[15] The Brahman is the "ground" of the world, but only in the sense that it is the real thing upon which people project the illusion of spatio-temporal reality.

(This is compared with the way in which a person who mistakes a rope for a snake projects the illusory idea of the snake onto the rope.)

Advaita does, however, contain what one might call "theistic elements." It describes Brahman as infinite, joyous consciousness (although the consciousness has no objects or contents and is thus "empty"). Advaita also admits that the idea of an omniscient and omnipotent cause of the space-time world is superior to most conceptualizations of ultimate reality—though, like all conceptualizations, it too must be transcended.

Nevertheless, because Advaita refuses to ascribe either knowledge or activity to ultimate reality, it is essentially nontheistic. The maximally perfect reality is not the God of the theistic traditions—all powerful, all knowing, all loving, the ruler of heaven and earth. It is, rather, an "infinite ocean" of empty, joyous consciousness—impersonal, inactive, and anonymous. Brahman is "pure consciousness and infinite bliss"—"beyond all attributes, beyond action."[16]

Some nontheistic traditions are devoid of theistic elements. According to Hīnāyana Buddhism, a person is simply a collection of interrelated experiences and body states called "dharmas." The dharmas are causally conditioned and transient. (They last for at most a few moments.) Consciousness is as conditioned and impermanent as the other dharmas. Furthermore, the realm of the transient and causally conditioned is the realm of suffering or unsatisfactoriness (duhkha). One cannot therefore construe a maximally perfect reality as a person. To do so would imply that it was impermanent, causally conditioned, and unhappy. Ultimate reality (Nirvāna) is not a substance, it is not conscious, and it does not act. It is more like a transcendent place or state than a transcendent person.

Our discussion illustrates the way in which one's understanding of a maximally perfect reality is determined by one's philosophical ideas and one's evaluations.

For example, we have seen how Advaita's emphasis upon the idea of absolute unity and Buddhism's analysis of personhood lead them to reject theism. One's evaluations are also important. Traditional thought places a high value on unity, permanence, and stability and a correspondingly low value on plurality, impermanence, and change. Persons appear to be complex, changing realities. An emphasis upon the values of unity, permanence, and stability may therefore lead one to deny that ultimate reality should be understood as a person.

These ideas and evaluations, however, are controversial. The Buddhist's analysis of personhood may be unable to account for the self's unity. Classical theists argue that God's unity, permanence, and stability do not entail impersonality. Some modern theists place a high value on change and complexity and ascribe them to the first principle. They believe, for example, that God's knowledge grows progressively richer and that He changes in response to His creatures.

One's understanding of the nature of a maximally perfect reality will also be influenced by one's attitude toward certain religious experiences. For example, Advaita Vedānta places a high value on "monistic mystical consciousness"—a joyous state of consciousness in which the mind is emptied of its contents and distinctions disappear. (The nature and implications of these and other mystical states of consciousness will be discussed in Chapter 5.) Advaita privileges this experience and treats it as a model of the unifying and transfiguring knowledge (jnāna) that is the goal of the religious quest. It is thus not surprising that Advaita views the appropriate object of religious attitudes as "one without distinctions"—neither a knower nor a doer and hence not a god.

But other types of religious experience have different implications. As we shall see in Chapter 5, some of these experiences seem to have a person as their object. An emphasis upon them usually leads to theistic interpretations of maximal perfection.

Even the basic claim that a maximally perfect reality is a kind of person is thus subject to dispute. Let us assume, however, that the dispute has been resolved in favor of theism and turn to problems connected with four perfections traditionally ascribed to God—timelessness, impassibility, omnipotence, and omniscience. Examining these problems will further illustrate the difficulties involved in working out the implications of the concept of a maximally perfect reality.

GOD'S METAPHYSICAL ATTRIBUTES AND THE CONCEPTS OF TIMELESSNESS AND IMPASSIBILITY

Many traditional theists believe that God has four "metaphysical attributes"—simplicity, immutability, timelessness, and impassibility. Modern theists often find these problematic. First, we will explain these attributes and discuss some objections to them. Then we illustrate the issues by examining two of the metaphysical properties (timelessness and impassibility) in more detail.

The Metaphysical Attributes

What is meant by God's "simplicity"? A thing's real or intrinsic properties are those such that a change in them involves a real change in the thing itself. For example, color and shape are real properties of physical objects. Intelligence or cowardliness are real properties of some persons. A thing's extrinsic properties, on the other hand, can change without the thing itself really changing. When Theaetetus was young, Socrates was taller. When the boy grew up, Socrates was shorter. Although he lost the property of being taller than Theaetetus, there was no real change in Socrates' height. "Being taller than Theaetetus" was thus one of his extrinsic properties.

The doctrine of divine simplicity states that each of God's real properties is identical with His other real properties and with His being or nature. For example, God's knowledge is identical with His power. Both are identical with His being. Just as "the morning star" and "the evening star" have different meanings but refer to the same thing (namely, the planet Venus), so "the wisdom of God" and "the power of God" have different meanings but refer to the same thing (namely, the infinitely perfect divine life or activity). As Augustine (354–430) says, "He Himself is His own greatness. Let the same also be said of the goodness, the eternity, the omnipotence of God, in fact of all those attributes which can be predicated of God when He is referred to as He is in Himself."[17]

Something is immutable if it can't change. God's immutability follows from His simplicity. When a thing (really) changes, it retains some real properties, loses some, and acquires others. This implies that some of its real properties aren't identical. (If two properties are identical, one can't have one without having the other. Hence, if x retains P throughout a change but loses Q and acquires R, then P, Q, and R are different properties.) Thus, if God's real properties are identical, God can't (really) change. God is immutably what He is. His being or nature, His all-embracing intellectual vision, and the creative act by which He brings everything into existence are necessarily unchanging. Augustine believes that immutability is entailed by God's perfection. "For what undergoes a change does not retain its own being, and what is subject to change, even though it may not actually be changed, can still lose the being which it had. And, therefore, only that which is not only not changed, but cannot undergo any change at all, can be called being in the truest sense without any scruple."[18]

Many theists believe God is timeless. As Anselm (1033–1109) exclaims, "Yesterday and today and tomorrow thou art; or, rather, neither yesterday nor today nor tomorrow thou art; but simply, thou art, outside all time."[19] God doesn't have temporal location or temporal extension. In this respect, He is like abstract objects such as numbers or propositions. It makes no sense to ask when the square root of four occurs or how long it lasts. Similarly, it makes no sense to ask for God's temporal location or the length of His temporal duration. Of course, God isn't an abstract object but an infinitely perfect life and activity. Nevertheless, one shouldn't think of this life and activity as being in time—not even as everlasting. God timelessly knows and wills that, for example, life emerges on this planet after certain events and before others. But while temporality is a property of *what* God knows and wills, it isn't a property of God's *act* of knowledge or will. The objects of His knowledge and the contents of His will are in time. God Himself is not.

Many traditional theists also think that God is "impassible." God creates, sustains, and governs the world. It depends on Him for its being and qualities. But nothing acts on God or causally affects Him. God doesn't depend on the world in any respect.

In short, classical theists often maintain that God is simple, immutable, timeless, and impassible. Other theists have attacked this doctrine. In their opinion, the metaphysical attributes are unscriptural, have little basis in religious life and experience, and are philosophically problematic.

Are these charges well founded? Although theistic scriptures assert that God is beginningless and endless, He is depicted as if He were in time. God is also depicted as changing, although His existence and character remain constant. For example, He first brings Israel out of Egypt and then reveals Himself on Mt. Sinai. Furthermore, the God of theistic scriptures not only acts upon His creatures but is also affected by them. He is moved to pity by their misfortunes, is angered by their sin, responds to their petitions, and so on. In short, the God who is described in scripture doesn't seem to have the metaphysical attributes.

But this argument is inconclusive. Theistic scriptures also depict God as seated on a throne, as jealous, and as repenting some of His actions. Even the most scripturally centered theists agree that some features of these pictures shouldn't be taken literally. This may also be true of those features that seem incompatible with God's possessing metaphysical attributes.

The second charge is also inconclusive since the doctrine does have roots in religious life and experience. Most religious traditions stress the imperfection of the temporal order. The space-time world is in constant flux—a realm of complexity, dependence, and constant change. Nothing is permanent or secure. All temporal values are threatened and ultimately lost. In human experience, complexity, change, time, and dependency are bound up with loss and imperfection. It therefore isn't surprising that religiously sensitive men and women often conclude that a maximally perfect reality must be free from complexity, change, time, and dependency.

Their intuitions are supported by the fact that many mystics claim they perceive a divine reality possessing metaphysical attributes. For example, some of them say they have *experienced* an undifferentiated unity that transcends distinctions, time, and change even though it is also somehow "active" and "stirring," the ground of mundane reality.

The intuitions and experiences supporting the doctrine of God's metaphysical attributes aren't conclusive. Nevertheless, they might be sufficient if there are no decisive objections to the doctrine.

Many modern theists think there *is* a decisive objection. God's personality is essential to theism. Persons think, act, and experience emotions. Being a person entails the possibility of understanding, of forming and carrying out intentions, of consciously interacting with other things, and (perhaps) of experiencing emotional states like joy or sorrow. If simplicity, immutability, timelessness, or impassibility are incompatible with these properties, they are incompatible with being a person and thus can't be ascribed to God.

Charles Hartshorne thinks the two sets of properties *are* incompatible. "To say, on the one hand, that God is love, to continue to use popular religious terms like Lord, divine will, obedience to God, and on the other to speak of an absolute, infinite, immutable, simple, impassible deity, is either a gigantic hoax of priestcraft, or it is done with the [mistaken] belief that the social connotations of popular language are ultimately in harmony with these descriptions."[20] To illustrate these issues, we will examine two metaphysical attributes that seem especially problematic to modern theists—timelessness and impassibility.

Is God Timeless?

Can God be timeless? The doctrine's critics think not. A timeless being couldn't know temporal events and it couldn't bring them about. It would thus be neither omniscient nor omnipotent. Since God *is* omniscient and omnipotent, He can't be timeless.

Timeless Knowledge

If God is timeless, His knowledge involves no before or after. Everything is embraced "at once" in an unchanging intellectual vision. Thus, speaking strictly, God didn't *foresee* the Second World War before its outbreak, *perceive* that it was going on between 1939 and 1945, and then *remember* it. God's knowledge that World War II occurs at a certain point in history is timeless. Sentences like "God knows that the Second World War will occur," "God knows that World War II is now occurring, " and "God knows that World War II occurred" should be interpreted as expressing a changing relation of World War II to God's timeless knowledge of its occurrence. There is no change in the divine knowledge itself.

This conception is problematic for two reasons. It may not be coherent. It also seems that types of knowledge which *ought* to be ascribed to an omniscient being can't be timeless.

Is a timeless knowledge of changing events coherent? The doctrine seems to imply that God's unchanging intellectual vision is simultaneous with everything that occurs. Since all events are present to God, they are simultaneous with His knowledge of them. (Just as what is present to me is simultaneous with my apprehension of it.) Nor is there any temporal distinction between one act of divine knowledge and another. The act by which God apprehends World War I is simultaneous with (or the same as) the act by which He apprehends World War II. Thus, World War I is simultaneous with God's knowledge of World War I, His knowledge of World War I is simultaneous with (or the same as) His knowledge of World War II, and His knowledge of World War II is simultaneous with World War II. It follows that World War I is simultaneous with World War II!

This popular argument isn't compelling. In the first place, if God is timeless, then *no* temporal terms apply to Him. God's knowledge doesn't precede or follow the events He knows. But it isn't simultaneous with them either. In the second place, the argument illicitly transfers properties of God's knowledge to its object. Suppose that my daughter tells me that she went to the movies yesterday rather than the day before yesterday as she had intended. There is no temporal distinction between my apprehension that my daughter went to the movies yesterday and my apprehension that she didn't go the day before yesterday, for a single mental act embraces both. It doesn't follow that yesterday is the day before yesterday, or that my daughter's going to the movies was simultaneous with her not doing so. Similarly, the fact that there is no temporal distinction between God's *knowledge* of World War I and His *knowledge* of World War II doesn't imply that there isn't a temporal distinction between the First and Second World Wars.

The second problem with timeless knowledge is this. If God is timeless, it seems that He can't know some things I know. God can timelessly know that at noon on January 20, 1998, I utter the sentence "It is now noon." He can also timelessly know that my department meeting starts at noon on January 20, 1998. But it seems that God can't know that it is *now* noon or that the meeting is *now* starting.[21] For knowing what time it is, or that an event is starting (or has started or will start), presupposes that the knower is in time. But, of course, I know things like these. It thus appears that I know things that God can't. If I do, God doesn't know everything and thus isn't omniscient.

Is this argument sound? Suppose that at noon on January 20, 1998, I glance at my watch and truly say, "The meeting is now starting." If God is timeless, He can't truly utter a sentence like "The meeting is now starting," for its use implies that the person who utters it is in time. (Its sense is, roughly, "The meeting is starting at the moment I utter this sentence.") The important question, however, is whether God can know *what* I know in knowing that the meeting is now starting.

God *can* timelessly know that my department meeting starts at noon on January 20, 1998. Is this sufficient to ensure that He knows what I know when (at noon) I know that my meeting is now starting? It might seem that it isn't. After all, I might know that my meeting starts at noon on January 20, 1998, and yet not know that the meeting is starting *now*. Hence, what *I* know in knowing the former can differ from what I know in knowing the latter. But this lack of equivalence appears to be a consequence of my ignorance of *other* facts about the temporal relations of events to each other. For example, I might be engrossed in my work, forget the time, and not realize that the meeting scheduled for noon is starting while I am working. God, on the other hand, timelessly knows the relation of each event to every other event. He thus knows what events occur at the same time, what events follow other events, and what events precede them. He therefore knows that the meeting begins at the moment I glance at my watch and utter the sentence "The meeting is now starting." And if I had been engrossed in my work and forgotten the time, He would know that the meeting begins while *that* is taking place. It seems, then, that what God knows in timelessly knowing that my meeting starts at noon on January 20, 1998, more or less *amounts to* what I know when (at noon) I know that the meeting is starting.

The general point is this: if the world is composed of substances, events, and the relations among them, then a timeless God's knowledge of the world's constituents can be complete. The *mode* in which God knows temporal happenings differs from that in which I know them, for I am in time and God isn't. But *what* we know (substances, events, and their relations) is the same.

Still, if God doesn't know events as we know them (that is, as past, present, or future), isn't there a sense in which His knowledge *is* limited? There is. But two observations help remove the sting from this concession. Consider, for example, not knowing what time it is now. Not knowing what time it is now is not knowing what one's position currently is in the temporal series—that is, not knowing where one is now temporally located (at noon, before noon, or after noon). This is clearly a limitation for *temporal* beings, for temporal beings have temporal locations. It is not clearly a limitation *for God* since God does not have a temporal location. Not knowing one's temporal location when one doesn't have one isn't a cognitive limitation.

The second observation is this: traditional theists believe that God can't experience pain or guilt. The former is incompatible with His infinite joy and the latter with His moral perfection. But if God can't experience pain or guilt, then, while he may know all *about* pain and guilt, He doesn't know what they *are like*. For knowing what pain and guilt are like requires direct acquaintance with them, and God's perfection rules this out. Similarly, if God isn't in time, then, while He can know all *about* time, He can't know what it is like to *experience* events as past, present, or future. Now traditional theists believe that the fact that God can't know what pain or guilt is like is consistent with His omniscience. It is thus difficult to see why they shouldn't conclude that the fact that God can't know what temporal existence is like is also compatible with His omniscience. God's inability to know what pain, guilt, and time are like is a *consequence* of His perfection and hence doesn't detract from it.[22]

Timeless Action

Many of the actions theists ascribe to God seem to imply that He is in time. For example, He forgives sin and threatens punishment. But forgiveness is *subsequent* to sin, and threats and warnings *precede* the behavior they are designed to avert.[23] If God is timeless, forgiveness, threats, and warnings must be divested of their temporal implications. One might say, for instance, that God timelessly knows that Peter sins at time t and timelessly forgives that sin. Again, while the *proclamation* of God's threat or warning (by means of prophecy, preaching, or the interior voice of conscience) temporally precedes the relevant behavior, God's *bringing about* the proclamation must be a timeless action.

But does this make sense? Isn't the concept of bringing something about inherently temporal? If it is, the notion of a timeless action collapses.

Critics contend that "x brings about a temporal state of affairs s" entails "x is temporally related to s and is thus temporally located." They support their contention by appealing to ordinary examples of "deliberate or intentional production" such as building a house, writing a letter, or forming a mental image of the Boston harbor, or to ordinary examples of "deliberate and intentional sustaining" such as "a single continuous singing action that sustains a single continuous sound."[24] These actions precede or are simultaneous with their effects and are thus temporally related to them. Examples like these aren't conclusive, however.

A builder is temporally related to the building she constructs, and a singer is temporally related to the sound he emits. However, other examples of production occur in which the producer *isn't* temporally related to what he or she produces. For example, consider Charles Dickens' relation to the events he narrates in *Oliver Twist*. Events in the novel are temporally related to each other. But the time of the novel isn't temporally related to the time in which Dickens exists and writes his novel. (Sikes' murder of Nancy doesn't occur at any time in the historical world, and thus doesn't literally occur before, at the same time as, or after the time at which Dickens wrote the novel.) The analogy with God's timeless action is imperfect. Dickens exists in *a* temporal order (though not the same temporal order as the one he creates). And the temporal order that God produces isn't fictional. Nevertheless, the example shows that causes aren't always temporally related to their effects. If they aren't, timeless divine actions may be possible.

Nor is it clear that our notion of action in inherently temporal. Where c is a conscious being and s is a temporal state of affairs, "c brings about s" can be interpreted as "if c wills s, then s, and c wills s."[25] Since the latter sentence doesn't clearly entail that c is temporal or stands in temporal relations to s, neither does the former. One could object that willing is itself temporal. But that it is isn't obvious. An act of will can't *follow* what is willed, and its object must be a contingent state of affairs. Both of these conditions can be met, however, by timeless acts of willing.

Critics also object that a timeless and immutable cause can't have a temporal and mutable effect such as the succession of events comprising the earth's evolutionary history. But this too is inconclusive. The objection illicitly transfers a property of the cause to its effect. Why, after all, can't God timelessly will that birds emerge after reptiles and before mammals? Why, in other words, can't the succession of events be part of the *content* of what God timelessly wills? That God's *act of will* is timeless doesn't obviously imply that the effect which is its *object* is timeless.

Is God Impassible?

The doctrine of impassibility asserts that God depends on nothing. God affects creatures. Created beings are causally dependent upon Him for their existence and properties. But creatures don't affect God. Neither His existence nor His real properties depend on the world. Critics believe that impassibility has two unacceptable consequences. If God isn't causally affected by the world, He can't know it and He can't be compassionate.

Impassibility and God's Knowledge

Consider an ordinary instance of knowledge such as my knowing that it is snowing heavily. My cognitive relation to the snowstorm has two important features.

Every relation has "its converse so that if A is related to B, B must be related to A."[26] Nevertheless, a relation can involve a real modification of one of its terms without involving a real modification of the other. For example, if I dislike the paintings of Grant Wood, then his paintings are disliked by me. But though this relation really modifies me, it doesn't really modify the paintings. Grant Wood's pictures are unaffected by my dislike. The same is true of my knowledge of the snowstorm. I know that it is snowing and the snowstorm is known by me. But while my knowledge really modifies me, it doesn't modify, or make a real difference to, the snowstorm.

My knowledge of the snowstorm has another important feature. It *depends* on the snowstorm. (I couldn't know that it was snowing if it wasn't snowing.) The snowstorm, on the other hand, doesn't depend on my knowledge of it.

What is true of my knowledge of the snowstorm seems to be true of any ordinary instance of knowledge. Knowledge involves a real modification of the knower but not of the known. Furthermore, it depends upon its object while its object doesn't depend upon it. If God is impassible, this can't be true of His knowledge of the world. God's real properties aren't dependent upon the world. Hence, either God's knowledge of creation isn't a real modification of His being, or His knowledge of the world doesn't depend on its object. In either case, God's knowledge is very different from ordinary knowledge.

Classical theists believe that God's knowledge of the world really modifies Him. But many deny that His knowledge depends on its object. God knows contingent states of affairs insofar as He causes them or brings them into being. For example, He knows that an earthquake will occur at such and such a time and place because He has decreed that it will do so. God's knowledge of contingent states of affairs is an aspect or consequence of His willing them. Hence, it doesn't depend on them.

This explanation accounts for God's knowledge of the contingent states of affairs He causes. Many theists, however, believe that some contingent states of affairs *aren't* caused by God. In their opinion, some human actions are "contra-causally free"—that is, they aren't determined by antecedent causal conditions *or* by God's decrees. But if free actions aren't determined by God's decrees, then God can't know them in knowing His decrees. In the case of free actions, God's knowledge appears to depend on an object He doesn't cause.[27]

In short, if creatures are contra-causally free, God's knowledge of their actions seems to depend on the actions that are the objects of His knowledge. This knowledge is a real modification of His being. Hence, God isn't completely impassible. *One* of His real properties (knowledge of free actions) depends upon the world.

Impassibility and God's Compassion

Many modern theists believe that God participates in the suffering of His creatures. God's knowledge of contingent states of affairs isn't the only divine property that depends on the world. His affective states also depend on it. God isn't aloof or unmoved by our distress but shares our griefs as we share the griefs of those we love. God's joy is therefore tempered by sympathetic sorrow. The degree and quality of His happiness is thus partly determined by the state of sentient creatures.

Charles Hartshorne expresses this well. Certain forms of independence are admirable. For example, it is desirable for one's moral character to be independent of circumstances. That is, it is desirable that one's will for the good remain constant regardless of the nature of the circumstances in which one finds oneself. Again, a superiority to "death and degeneration" is admirable. It is better to be independent of other things with respect to one's being. It is also better to have a wisdom and power that cannot fail and is thus independent of what may happen.

But other forms of independence aren't admirable. "The father that as little as possible depends upon the will and welfare of his child is an inhuman monster. . . . One should not simply agree to every whim of the child . . . but neither should one try to act and think and feel just as one would have acted or thought or felt had the child's joy been sorrow, or her sorrow joy, or her likes dislikes." Nor is there anything admirable about a happiness that is unaffected by the sorrows of others. We don't admire people who "can be equally happy and serene and joyous regardless of how men and women suffer around" them.

Human sympathies are limited. A *perfect* being, however, would be *maximally* responsive to the joys and sorrows of others. Hence, God *must* be affected by His creatures. Impassibility is incompatible with His perfection.[28]

But *can* a maximally perfect being be touched by suffering? As Friedrich von Hügel (1852–1925) points out, suffering is intrinsically evil and thus seems inconsistent with God's perfection. Furthermore, the belief that God's life includes sorrow is incompatible with a conviction that is deeply embedded in human religious consciousness—that the source and end of the world is unalloyed goodness and perfect joy. God, says von Hügel, is "Perfect Love, Unmixed Joy, Entire Delectation. . . . But if so we will not admit the presence of any Evil, be it sin or even only Sorrow, be they actual or even only potential, in Him Who thus dwarfs for us all our little human goodness and earthly joy by his utter Sanctity and sheer Beatitude."[29]

Nevertheless, Hartshorne has a point. All theistic traditions attribute compassion to God. Chapters in the Qurān, for example, begin with the words "In the name of Allah, the compassionate and merciful." Compassion, however, involves sharing others' suffering, and sympathetic suffering seems incompatible with unalloyed joy.

Classical theists have tried to solve this problem in several ways. Anselm argued that God is compassionate in the sense that He acts *as if* He felt compassion although He doesn't actually do so. That is, God acts as we do when we act compassionately, but He doesn't experience the feeling. "For when thou beholdest us in our wretchedness, we experience the effect of compassion. But thou dost not experience the feeling. Therefore, thou art both compassionate because thou dost save the wretched, and spare those who sin against thee; and not compassionate because thou art affected by no sympathy for wretchedness."[30] Hartshorne rightly objects that a compassion without feeling isn't real compassion.

Bernard of Clairvaux (1090–1153) maintained that while God can't grieve or suffer in His *own* nature, He became incarnate so that He might "learn by his own experience how to commiserate and sympathize with those who are . . . suffering and tempted." The divine nature is "passionless." Hence, insofar as He is divine, God only knows compassion intellectually. He doesn't *experience* it. By assuming human nature, however, God "learned mercy [compassion] in suffering."[31]

Bernard's solution is superior to Anselm's because it implicitly recognizes that compassion includes feeling or emotion. But Bernard's solution isn't available to non-Christians. Furthermore, the God of scripture and devotional practice appears to be compassionate in His *own* (divine) nature and not merely in the human nature He assumes in the Incarnation.

Thomas Aquinas (1225–74) has a more adequate solution. Love and joy are pure perfections. Hence, God literally has them although the mode in which He loves and rejoices differs from the mode in which we do so. (Human love and joy are often partly voluntary. We willingly embrace what we love or rejoice in. But they are also "passions"—externally induced modifications of our animal nature over which we have little control. God has no animal nature. His love and joy are wholly active, an expression only of His will.)

Anger and sorrow differ from love and joy because they entail suffering. Hence, even when these emotions are appropriate, they are only mixed perfections. They can therefore only be ascribed to God metaphorically. Nevertheless, anger and sorrow aren't *equally* metaphorical. Anger is ascribed to God because He produces effects similar to those that an angry person might produce. But no internal modification of God corresponds to anger in us. By contrast, God "is said to be saddened in so far as certain things take place contrary to what He loves and approves." While God doesn't literally grieve, there is something *in* God (an internal modification of God) that we apprehend as sorrow—namely, His love. That is, when our awareness of God's love is coupled with our recognition that creatures disobey God and suffer, we construe the divine love as sorrow.[32]

Like Bernard, Thomas implicitly recognizes that there is no compassion without sympathetic feeling or emotion. But unlike many modern theologians, Thomas thinks the emotion in question is simply love—not tender sorrow. This has two advantages. Love is compatible with unalloyed joy while sympathetic sorrow is not. Furthermore, love can be a purely active emotion—a spontaneous expression of the lover's own inner richness. By contrast, sympathetic sorrow is essentially a reaction rather than an action. Love thus coheres better with God's independence.

Thomas's solution is superior to Anselm's and Bernard's. Whether it is fully satisfactory depends on whether a compassion that doesn't literally involve sympathetic suffering is really compassion and thus adequately meets the demands of religious consciousness.

Conclusion

While the doctrine of God's metaphysical attributes is rooted in religious life and experience, there is a tension between these properties and the personal attributes ascribed to God by theism.

The doctrines of timelessness and impassibility illustrate the difficulty. They capture a number of religious intuitions and experiences. The doctrine of timelessness reflects a deep sense of God's unchanging perfection, a confidence that the divine can't be touched by loss, mutability, or decay, and an experience of a reality underlying the world's flux that eludes our spatial and temporal categories. The doctrine of impassibility is rooted in a sense of absolute dependence on a God who is wholly active and never passive, a conviction that suffering is incompatible with perfection, and an experience of ultimate reality as unalloyed joy or happiness. On the other hand, many think that these doctrines aren't consistent with other theistic beliefs and intuitions—that God knows and causes temporal events, for example, or that God is compassionate.

We have argued that a belief in divine timelessness is compatible with the conviction that God knows and causes temporal events. But we have also argued that if God is timeless, He probably can't know what it is like to experience events as past, present, or future. A type of cognitive experience is thus closed to Him. Whether this is consistent with His omniscience (and hence with His perfection) is debatable.

Our verdict on the doctrine of impassibility is similarly mixed. God's impassibility *may* be compatible with His compassion. Nevertheless, if some actions are contra-causally free, the doctrine of impassibility must be qualified. God's knowledge of free actions depends on them. Hence, *one* of His real properties depends on the world.

The doctrine of simplicity must also be qualified. Suppose that God's knowledge partly depends on other things. If all of God's real properties were identical with each other and with His being, then His knowledge would be identical with His other real properties and with His being. Thus, since His knowledge partly depends on other things, so would His being. No theist can accept this conclusion. Hence, God can't be absolutely simple.[33]

This section has discussed attributes that are controversial among theists. Some think God has the metaphysical attributes. Others do not. The next section examines two properties that almost all theists ascribe to God—omnipotence and omniscience.

GOD'S KNOWLEDGE AND POWER

Persons know and act. Hence, if a maximally perfect reality is *personal*, it possesses knowledge and power. Since its perfection is *maximal*, its knowledge and power are perfect. As the great Muslim theologian Al-Ghazzali (1059–1111) said, He is "powerful, almighty and all-subduing; inadequacy and weakness befall Him not. . . . He is Lord of the visible world and the invisible, and of power and might; His are dominion, subjugation, creation and command. . . . He knows all things that can be known, grasping all that happens from the limits of the earth to the highest heaven. . . . He knows the secrets and that which is more shrouded in secrecy than secrets . . . by a knowledge which is ancient from eternity."[34]

A maximally perfect reality is therefore "omniscient" and "omnipotent." But how should these notions be understood? Can we provide characterizations of God's power and knowledge that include all and only those things that ought to be ascribed to a perfect being? We will discuss some difficulties involved in this task in the following two subsections.

Omnipotence

Few theists think that God can perform logically impossible tasks. A state of affairs such as 2 + 2's equaling 5 is logically impossible. Hence, *no* one can bring it about. Necessary states of affairs such as 2 + 2's equaling 4 are logically possible, but they aren't "producible"; that is, they can't have causes. Thus, *no* agent can produce them. There are also states of affairs that are logically possible and producible but can't be produced *by God*. For example, the state of affairs consisting of my freely choosing to spend the evening reading Henry James can't be brought about by someone other than myself. (If it were brought about by someone else, then either the action wouldn't really be *my* action or it wouldn't be *free*.) Since the state of affairs consisting of my freely reading Henry James can't be brought about by someone other than myself, it can't be brought about by God.

Thus, omnipotence only includes the power to perform logically possible tasks. This isn't a real limitation. Since the tasks in question (bringing about a logically impossible state of affairs, producing an unproducible state of affairs, bringing about another person's free action) can't be performed by *any* possible being, no possible being could surpass God with respect to power by possessing the ability to perform them. Hence, these tasks aren't included within the scope of maximally perfect power.

God's *perfection* also makes certain things impossible for Him. For example, any being that can be appropriately called omnipotent has the power to create and lift stones of any weight, size, texture, and so on. But if it possesses this power, it can't create stones it is unable to lift. Nevertheless, because its "inability" to create stones that it can't lift is simply a consequence of its *unlimited* power to make and lift stones, it doesn't seem to be a real incapacity.[35]

A maximally perfect being also can't have powers whose possession or exercise entails a limitation or weakness. Thus God can't destroy Himself or divest Himself of His knowledge or power. Why not? A maximally perfect being is eternally wise and powerful. It also possesses these properties *essentially*. P is an essential property of something if and only if there are no possible worlds in which it exists and lacks P. For example, if there aren't any possible worlds in which Socrates exists and isn't human, "being human" is one of his essential properties. On the other hand, "being a philosopher" isn't an essential property of Socrates because there are possible worlds in which he has no interest in philosophy. Thus, if eternal wisdom and power are essential properties of a maximally perfect being, it has them in every possible world in which it exists.

Suppose, then, that a maximally perfect being *could* destroy itself or divest itself of its knowledge or power. If it could, there would then be possible worlds in which it does so. Therefore, it wouldn't be eternally wise and powerful *in those worlds*. But as we just saw, a maximally perfect being is eternally wise and powerful in *every* world in which it exists. Hence, it can neither destroy itself nor make itself ignorant or weak.

Can a maximally perfect being sin? Presumably not, for moral goodness also seems to be one of its essential properties. However, Nelson Pike (1930–) thinks this has an unacceptable implication.[36]

Suppose it is morally wrong for God to bring about a particular state of affairs. Suppose, for example, that *s* is an earthquake that causes much suffering and that God has no morally sufficient reason for producing or permitting it. If God is essentially good, He can't bring *s* about. But an *omnipotent* being surely has the power to bring about *any* sort of natural disaster. It therefore has the power to bring about *s*. (Though if it is good, it won't do so.) Hence, if God is essentially good, He isn't omnipotent.

Pike concludes that while God is good, He isn't *essentially* good. That is, He is good in our world, but there are logically possible worlds in which He isn't. Suppose, for example, that the name of the being who happens to be God is "Yahweh." It is necessarily true that *if* Yahweh is God, He doesn't sin. (No sinful being could be called "God.") But it isn't necessarily true that Yahweh *is God* or that Yahweh is sinless. Yahweh doesn't sin but He could sin if He wished to. Hence, there are possible worlds in which Yahweh acts badly (although because He does so, He isn't God in those worlds). Since Yahweh isn't good in every possible world in which He exists, His goodness isn't essential.

Nevertheless, we can rely on Yahweh's goodness. While it is logically possible that Yahweh sins, His nature or character provides "material assurance" that He won't. Yahweh's choices aren't constrained by ignorance or by nonrational factors such as sensual desires or nervous impulses. Since Yahweh has no motive or reason for acting wrongly, we can be fully assured that He won't.[37]

Should classical theists accept Pike's recommendation and abandon their belief in God's essential goodness? Probably not. According to Pike, Yahweh sins (and thus isn't God) in some possible worlds although He doesn't sin (and is God) in ours. But a being that isn't divine and even sins in some of the logically possible worlds in which it exists doesn't seem *maximally* perfect. Hence, if Pike is right, Yahweh isn't maximally perfect. But in that case, He isn't God.

It therefore seems that a maximally perfect being must be essentially good. If so, it can't bring *s* about even though beings who aren't essentially good can do so. God's power is thus limited by His goodness. But this limitation may not be as significant as it appears. While God can't bring earthquakes about when doing so would be morally wrong, He can bring about earthquakes of any magnitude when doing so would be morally permissible. God's inability to bring *s* about isn't, then, a consequence of a deficiency in His earthquake-producing powers but of His own inherent goodness. Hence, the limitation doesn't seem to involve real weakness.

In summary, God's power is subject to logical constraints. It is also limited by His own nature and perfections. The freedom of finite moral agents may impose a further set of restrictions; these will be discussed in Chapter 3.

Omniscience

The doctrine of omniscience raises several questions. For example, can a timeless being know what we know in knowing what time it is, or can an impassible being know what suffering is like? These questions were briefly addressed in the section on God's metaphysical attributes. This section discusses a more serious problem—God's knowledge of "future contingents."

A future contingent is something that hasn't yet occurred, is logically contingent, and isn't necessitated by its causal history. If we are contra-causally free, the decisions we will make tomorrow are future contingents. Future contingents create two problems. First, how can God know them? Second, is His knowledge of future decisions compatible with their freedom?

God's Knowledge of Future Contingents

There are three reasons for thinking that God can't know future contingents—that the future is indeterminate, that foreknowledge would involve "backwards causation," and that there is no basis for such knowledge.

The first difficulty is raised by philosophers who believe that the future isn't fully determinate. While the past history of the universe and the laws that govern it block out the rough shape of the future, the finishing strokes must be supplied by future decisions. Until they are made, the future is indeterminate. *No one* can know the future in all its details because as yet there isn't anything definite to know. At the present moment, the proposition that I or someone else freely decides to do something at some future time is neither true nor false (although it will become true or false once the decision is made). Since the proposition isn't yet true or false, not even God can now *know* that it is true or false. Hartshorne and others think that this limitation doesn't detract from God's perfection, however, since it is a necessary constraint on any knower.

This is doubtful, for the restriction does seem to involve imperfection. Most facts about persons depend upon facts about people's volitions. For example, my birth depended on the volitions of my parents, and these in turn depended upon the volitions of countless others. Thus, if God doesn't know future choices, He knows little about humanity's future. He is also ignorant of many facts about nature. For example, He doesn't know whether climatic conditions will be radically altered by nuclear war, since he doesn't know whether someone will press the button. A God who can't foresee choices won't be totally ignorant of the future. Like us, He can make estimates of the relative likelihood of alternative futures. Because His knowledge of nature's laws and the past is perfect, God's estimates will be much more accurate than ours. Nevertheless, His estimates will only be estimates. It is therefore probable that they will sometimes be mistaken. If they are, then the decisions God bases on them will be erroneous. God will thus be "constantly changing his mind and intentions . . . altering his measures, relinquishing his old designs, and forming new schemes and projections."[38] These limitations are incompatible with traditional theism and shouldn't be ascribed to a maximally perfect being without conclusive reasons for doing so.

The belief in the future's indeterminacy seems too controversial to provide a conclusive reason. The view is counter-intuitive. It certainly *seems* that propositions like "At *t* (some date in the future) I freely decide to go to the movies" is now either true or false even though neither I nor anyone else may know which. If it is, the future isn't indeterminate.

There is a second difficulty: some think that foreknowledge is impossible because it involves "backwards causation." If God knows our choices before we make them, His knowledge precedes them. But as we have seen, God's knowledge of free decisions depends on the object of His knowledge (the free decisions). Thus, future occurrences (our choices) are the cause of certain things in the past (God's foreknowledge). This seems impossible. Causes precede or accompany their effects. They don't follow them.

One can resolve this difficulty in three ways. If God is timeless, His knowledge of human volitions won't precede them. Hence, it won't involve backwards causation.

One might also appeal to God's "middle knowledge." Some think that God's knowledge isn't confined to what is logically possible and what actually occurs. He also knows what any possible person would freely decide to do in any circumstance in which the person might be placed. This is called "middle knowledge." Since God knows what persons would freely do if He created them and also knows who He will create and the circumstances in which He will place them, He knows what decisions will be freely made. But neither God's middle knowledge nor His knowledge of His creative intentions depend on the future. Hence, God's knowledge of future contingents doesn't involve backwards causation.[39]

The third response points out that a past fact can *depend* on another without being *caused* by it. Consider the fact that Julius Caesar was assassinated before I will have finished writing this chapter. This fact about the past depends upon my finishing the chapter (since it entails it). Yet it seems odd to say that finishing my chapter is a cause of it. Or consider my knowledge of necessary truths like $1 + 2 = 3$, or of abstract objects like numbers. My knowledge of these truths and objects depends upong them. They aren't its cause. (Necessary truths and abstract objects don't act or produce effects.) So the fact that God's foreknowledge *depends* on the future doesn't clearly entail that it is *caused* by it. If it doesn't, His foreknowledge needn't involve backwards causation.[40]

The third difficulty involves the question, How could God *know* future contingents? If God is in time, the future isn't immediately present to Him.

Furthermore, His knowledge of the future can't be grounded in His knowledge of the past or of His own intentions because future contingents aren't necessitated by the past or by God's decisions. There thus seems to be no *basis* for God's knowledge of the future. The problem can't be satisfactorily solved by appealing to middle knowledge, for God's knowledge of what people would freely decide to do in the different circumstances in which He might place them seems equally groundless. (As we shall see in Chapter 3, subjective conditionals describing how possible free persons would behave in various circumstances aren't made true by logical facts, nature's laws, the past, or God's decrees. Hence, God's knowledge of them isn't a consequence of His perfect knowledge of logical truths, nature's laws, the past, and His own intentions.)

One can respond to this difficulty in two ways. If God is timeless, there may be a sense in which the future *is* immediately present to him. One might also deny that God's knowledge of the future *needs* a basis. Some knowledge is groundless. For example, we are immediately aware of our own intentions, and of the truth of simple necessary propositions like $1 + 2 = 3$. Our knowledge of these things isn't based on something else such as inference, testimony, or the use of our senses. Perhaps God's knowledge of future contingents is similarly groundless. The answer to "How does God know the future?" may be "He just does."

Foreknowledge and Human Freedom

Many think that God's foreknowledge is incompatible with human freedom, for consider the following argument:

1. It is necessarily true that if God foreknows that something will occur, it will occur.

2. God's foreknowledge is necessary because it "is a thing which already *has*, and long ago *had* existence," and "in things which are past, their past existence is now necessary: having already made sure of existence . . . 'tis now impossible, that it should be otherwise than true, that that thing has existed."[41]

3. Necessary consequences of necessary facts are themselves necessary. Therefore,

4. What God foreknows is necessary. (From 1, 2, and 3.) Hence,

5. If God foreknows our decisions, they are necessary. (From 4.)

Some objections to the argument are misplaced. For example, people sometimes object that facts about the past aren't necessary because the denials of the propositions that express those facts are logically possible. Although this is true, it misses the point—namely, that since the future is logically *entailed* by unalterable facts about the past, it too is unalterable.

People also object that foreknowledge doesn't make things necessary. Foreknowledge isn't the cause of the future occurrence of contra-causally free decisions; but, on the contrary, their future occurrence is the cause of their being foreknown. This too is inconclusive. The fact that foreknowledge doesn't *make* our choices necessary doesn't imply that the existence of fore-knowledge may not *prove* that they are necessary.

One can solve the problem by denying that God literally *fore*knows any-thing. If God is timeless, His knowledge of contingencies that lie in *our* future isn't temporally related to them. Therefore, His knowledge of future contin-gents doesn't temporally precede them and so isn't past in relation to them. According to this solution, the argument is unsound because it mistakenly as-sumes that God's beliefs about future contingents come before them in time.

But even if God *is* in time, the argument may be unsound. Some facts about the past aren't necessary. A distinction should be made between facts about the past that don't logically include facts about the future and facts about the past that do. The fact that human beings existed in the first century of the Christian era is an example of the first. The fact that Julius Caesar died before I will have completed this chapter is an example of the second. Facts about the past that don't include facts about the future are unalterable. Once they have secured a hold on existence, no one can bring it about that they don't hold. However, some facts about the past that include facts about the fu-ture aren't necessary in this sense. It may be true that Julius Caesar died before I will have finished this chapter. Furthermore, this fact is a fact about the past. Nevertheless, until I complete the chapter, I have the power to bring it about that the fact *never held*. (This shouldn't be confused with a power to *alter* the past. I can't make it the case that "'Caesar died before I will have finished this chapter' was true but is no longer true." But I *can* make it the case that "'Cae-sar died before I will have finished this chapter' was never true." In other words, I can't *change* facts about the past but I have some power to determine what these facts are. Thus, if I can complete this chapter or abandon it, I have the power to either make it true that Caesar died before I will have finished the chapter or make it true that he died before I will have abandoned it.)[42]

Why is this important? God's "forebeliefs" (His beliefs about the future) are facts about the past that logically include facts about the future. Suppose Jones is my next-door neighbor. "Jones believes that I will travel to Antwerp next summer" doesn't entail "I will travel to Antwerp next summer"—for Jones may be mistaken. God, however, is essentially omniscient. It is logically impossible for Him to believe falsely. Hence, "God believes that I will travel to Antwerp next summer" does entail that I will do so. Thus, God's forebeliefs logically include facts about the future.

But as we saw, *some* facts about the past that logically include facts about the future *depend* upon the future. God's beliefs about what I will do may be facts of this kind. If they are, then even though God may believe that I will go to Antwerp next summer, and even though His beliefs cannot be mistaken, I have the power to bring it about that God never believed this. I can go to Antwerp next summer or stay home. If I go, God has always believed that I will go. If I don't, He has always believed that I won't. God's beliefs about what I will do thus *depend* upon what I will do. Hence, the fact that His beliefs about the future can't be mistaken doesn't show that my actions aren't free.

Is this solution acceptable? Some facts about the past that logically in-clude facts about the future depend upon the future but many don't. For example, "Jones finished his manuscript last year" entails "Jones won't be fin-ishing his manuscript next year." Thus, the fact that Jones finished his manu-script last year logically includes a fact about the future. In this case, however, the future fact depends on the past fact, not vice versa.[43] Again, if God is es-sentially omnipotent, it is necessarily true that if He has determined that I will scratch my ear tomorrow, I will scratch it. Here too, a past fact (God's prede-termination) logically includes a fact in its future (my scratching my ear) but doesn't depend on it.[44] Thus, the fact that God's forebeliefs logically include facts about the future isn't sufficient to show that they depend upon the fu-ture. Some facts about the past that include facts about the future depend on it but others don't.

Furthermore, ordinary beliefs about the future *don't* depend on the future. I have no power over other people's past beliefs. For example, if I don't go to Antwerp next summer, I bring it about that Jones's belief that I will do so is false. I don't bring it about that he never believed it.

On the other hand, human beliefs about the future *don't logically include it.* The fact that I have no power over the past beliefs of other people is therefore inconclusive. Nor is it obviously absurd to suppose that God's intuitive knowledge of future contingents depends upon what He knows—that His be-liefs about the future are made true by it. If they are, then each of us may have the power to (partly) determine what His beliefs will eternally be. The solu-tion we are discussing is controversial, but it may be correct.

In conclusion, future contingents present two problems—how God knows them and whether His knowledge of them is compatible with human freedom. The problems can be resolved by appealing to God's timelessness. If God is in time, His beliefs about future contingents may be groundless and they may depend upon events in His future. These consequences may be un-welcome. They aren't clearly incoherent.

CONCLUSION

The major religious traditions believe that the object of their devotion is worthy of unlimited admiration, total commitment, and unconditional sur-render. These attitudes are appropriate only if their object is maximally per-fect—so splendid that a greater object is inconceivable.

The nature of maximal perfection is controversial. Theists believe that knowledge and conscious activity are perfections and therefore ascribe them to ultimate reality. Because ultimate reality's perfection is maximal, theists also think that its knowledge and abilities are perfect. The ultimate is thus "omniscient" and "omnipotent." In addition, many traditional theists believe that ultimate reality is unitary (simple), timeless, immutable, and impassible.

In this respect, traditional theism resembles the major nontheistic traditions that also describe the ultimate as timeless, immutable, and so on.

The classical theist's conception of ultimate reality raises a number of questions. God's metaphysical attributes must be reconciled with His personality, and the notions of omnipotence and omniscience involve difficulties. Nevertheless, the theist's picture of maximal perfection seems roughly coherent.

But does the concept *apply* to anything? Are there reasons for thinking that a maximally perfect person *exists?* We shall examine this question in Chapter 2.

Notes

1. William James, *The Varieties of Religious Experience* (New York: The Modern Library, 1902), 475–76.

2. Paul Tillich, *Dynamics of Faith* (New York: Harper and Brothers, 1956), chapter 1.

3. A complete definition would add other conditions. Suppose, for example, that every possible being was very imperfect. Even if one of them was at least as perfect as every other, it would be absurd to call it maximally *perfect.* A maximally perfect being must not only be at least as perfect as every other possible being, but it must also be free from serious limitations and obvious imperfections.

4. Logical impossibility in this sense is sometimes called "broadly logical impossibility," and is distinguished from logical impossibility in a narrower sense. (A proposition is logically impossible in the narrow sense if and only if it violates principles of logic or mathematics.)

5. Charles Crittendon, "The Argument from Perfection to Existence," *Religious Studies* 4 (1968): 124.

6. See Thomas V. Morris, "The God of Abraham, Isaac and Anselm," *Faith and Philosophy* 1 (1984): 177–87. It should be noted that some traditional theists believe there *are* classes of comparison that include everything. Every existing entity has being, truth, and goodness and can be ranked according to the degree to which it has those qualities. Evil things have little being, truth, or goodness. God's being, truth and goodness, on the other hand, are infinite.

7. This response is inadequate if both of the incompatible properties are perfections a being needs to be appropriately called "perfect." Omniscience might be an example of such a property. The ability to ride a bicycle isn't.

8. For these distinctions and their relevance to the problem at hand, see William Mann, "The Divine Attributes," *American Philosophical Quarterly* 12 (1975): 151–59.

9. A state of affairs is contingent if it is logically possible that it obtain and logically possible that it does not obtain.

10. Love is another degreed perfection that might seem not to have a maximum. This isn't clear, however. A love that is a spontaneous expression of a

being's inner richness and splendor and embraces every existing being in proportion to its worth or dignity may be the intrinsic maximum of love. Theists have traditionally thought that God's love is like this.

11. Charles Hartshorne, *The Divine Relativity* (New Haven, Conn.: Yale University Press, 1948).

12. The first quotation is from *Shankara's Crest Jewel of Discrimination*, trans.
Swami Prabhavananda (New York: Mentor Books, 1970), 101. The second is from
The Vedānta Sūtras of Bādarāyana with the Commentary by Śaṅkara, trans. George
Thibaut (New York: Dover, 1962), part II, 158.

13. *Śaṅkara's Crest Jewel*, 93.

14. *Vedānta Sūtras*, part I, 281.

15. Ibid., part I, 329–30.

16. *Śaṅkara's Crest Jewel*, 62.

17. Augustine, *The Trinity*, trans. Stephen McKenna, in *The Fathers of the
Church*, vol. 18 (Washington, D.C.: Catholic University of America Press, 1963),
188.

18. Ibid., 177.

19. Anselm, *Proslogion* xix, in *Saint Anselm, Basic Writings*, trans. S. W. Deane
(LaSalle, Ill.: Open Court, 1962), 25.

20. Hartshorne, *Divine Relativity*, 26.

21. I am adopting an example of Patrick Grim ("Against Omniscience: The
Case from Essential Indexicals," *Nous* XIX [1985]: 151–80).

22. If the Christian doctrine of the Incarnation is true, God the Son (the second member of the Trinity) experiences pain and time. But He experiences them
insofar as He is man, not insofar as He is God. Furthermore, the Son can't experience
guilt.

23. See Richard Swinburne, *The Coherence of Theism* (Oxford: Clarendon
Press, 1977), 211–12.

24. Nelson Pike, *God and Timelessness* (New York: Schocken Books, 1970), 106,
111.

25. I am adopting a suggestion of Richard Sturch, "The Problem of Divine
Eternity," *Religious Studies* 10 (1974): 487–93.

26. Ibid., 107.

27. One response to this problem is that God's knowledge of free actions
doesn't depend on them but is instead a consequence of His knowledge of how
free creatures would behave in any set of circumstances in which He might place
them together with His knowledge of what circumstances He will place them in.
(For more on this, see the later section on God's knowledge of future contingents.)
This solution is unsatisfactory because it merely shifts the problem. As we shall see
in Chapter 3, the conditional propositions describing how free creatures would
freely act if they were placed in various circumstances don't depend on God. (God
doesn't make them true.) Hence, if God's knowledge of free actions depends upon
these conditionals, it depends upon something that is independent of His own being and activity. It may be misleading to call this dependence "causal" but it is a
real dependence nonetheless.

28. Hartshorne, *Divine Relativity,* 42–58.

29. Friedrich von Hügel, "Suffering and God," *Essays and Addresses on the Philosophy of Religion. Second Series* (London: J. M. Dent, 1930), 208–209.

30. Anselm, *Proslogion* viii, 13f.

31. Bernard of Clairvaux, *The Steps of Humility,* trans. George Burch (Notre Dame, Ind.: University of Notre Dame Press, 1963), chapter 3.

32. Thomas Aquinas, *On the Truth of the Catholic Faith, Book One: God,* trans. Anton C. Pegis (Garden City, N.Y.: Doubleday, 1955), chapter 9, no. 17. Thomas's distinction between God's anger and sorrow seems specious since both can be treated in the same way. For example, we can interpret God's anger as the way in which His justice is comprehended by those who reject Him (or recognize that His love is rejected).

33. There are other reasons for rejecting the doctrine of absolute simplicity. If God's creative acts are free, then there are logically possible worlds in which God exists but chooses not to create and logically possible worlds in which He creates different things. But if so, then not all of God's real properties are identical. For example, since God possesses the property of omnipotence in *all* of the logically possible worlds in which He exists but possesses the property of creating me in only some of them, "being omnipotent" can't be identical with "creating me." For very interesting defenses of the doctrine of simplicity, however, see William Mann, "Divine Simplicity," *Religious Studies* 18 (1982): 451-71 and Norman Kretzmann and Eleonore Stump, "Absolute Simplicity," *Faith and Philosophy* 2 (1985): 353–82. The qualified doctrine of impassibility does seem consistent with the doctrine of God's timelessness and immutability.

34. Al-Ghazzali, *The Foundations of the Articles of Faith,* trans. Nabih Amin Faris (Lahore, Pakistan: Sh. Muhammad Ashraf, 1969), 3–4.

35. C. Wade Savage, "The Paradox of the Stone," *The Philosophical Review* LXXVI (1967): 74–79.

36. Nelson Pike, "Omnipotence and God's Ability to Sin," *American Philosophical Quarterly* 6 (1969): 208–16.

37. Cf. Richard Swinburne, "Duty and the Will of God," *Canadian Journal of Philosophy* IV (1974): 213–17.

38. Jonathan Edwards, *Freedom of the Will* (New Haven, Conn.: Yale University Press, 1957), 253.

39. Cf. David Basinger, "Divine Omniscience and Human Freedom," *Faith and Philosophy* 1 (1984): 291–302.

40. It may, however, involve ontological dependence. Even determinists concede that God's forebeliefs are counterfactually dependent on what He foreknows. They admit, for example, that if I were not to go to Antwerp this summer, God would never have believed that I would. But they deny that there is any ontological dependence. God's foreknowledge ontologically depends on facts about the past (including His own decisions) that make my trip to Antwerp inevitable. Many indeterminists, on the other hand, maintain that God's forebeliefs *really* (that is, ontologically and not merely counter-factually) depend upon the future that He foreknows. (For more on the distinction between determinism and indeterminism, see Chapter 3.)

41. Jonathan Edwards, *Freedom of the Will,* 257.

42. Marilyn McCord Adams, "Is the Existence of God a 'Hard Fact'?" *The Philosophical Review* LXXVI (1967): 492–503, and William Rowe, *Philosophy of Religion* (Encino, Calif.: Dickenson, 1978), 162–65. For some of the difficulties involved in drawing this distinction clearly, see Joshua Hoffman and Gary Rosenkrantz, "Hard and Soft Facts," *The Philosophical Review* XCIII (1984): 419–34.

43. Paul Helm, "Divine Foreknowledge and Facts," *Canadian Journal of Philosophy* IV (1974): 305–15.

44. Note that while "Jones won't be finishing his manuscript next year" may not express a "substantive" fact about the future, "I will scratch my ear" does.

For Further Reading

Good discussions of Advaita Vedānta can be found in Eliot Deutsch, *Advaita Vedānta* (Honolulu: The University Press of Hawaii, 1973), Ninian Smart, *Doctrine and Argument in Indian Philosophy* (London: George Allen and Unwin, 1964); and M. Hiriyana, *Outlines of Indian Philosophy* (London: George Allen and Unwin, 1932). Stephen H. Phillips, *Classical Indian Metaphysics* (Chicago and La Salle: Open Court, 1995) provides an interesting account of a debate between a leading Advaitin and his realist opponents. Useful introductions to Buddhist thought are Edward Conze, *Buddhism: Its Essence and Development* (New York: Harper, 1959) and *Buddhist Thought in India* (Ann Arbor: The University of Michigan Press, 1967); and David Kalupahana, *Buddhist Philosophy: A Historical Analysis* (Honolulu: The University Press of Hawaii, 1976): and Paul Williams, *Mahāyāna Buddhism* (London and New York: Routledge, 1989).

For an excellent account of the traditional view of God's attributes see George H. Joyce, *Principles of Natural Theology* (New York: AMS Press, 1972), pages 276–478 and 524–56. Aspects of the traditional view are criticized by Charles Hartshorne, *The Divine Relativity* (New Haven: Yale University Press, 1948), Nelson Pike, *God and Timelessness* (New York: Schocken Books, 1970), Anthony Kenny, *The God of The Philosopher* (Oxford: Clarendon Press, 1979), and Alvin Plantinga, *Does God Have a Nature?* (Milwaukee, Wis.: Marquette University Press, 1980). Good general discussions of the divine attributes are provided by Richard Swinburne, *The Coherence of Theism* (Oxford, Clarendon Press, 1978), and Edward R. Wierenga, *The Nature of God: An Inquiry into Divine Attributes* (Ithaca, N.Y.: Cornell University Press, 1989). H. P. Owen surveys major views of God in *Concepts of Deity* (New York: Herder and Herder, 1971).

Readers interested in God's eternity should consult Nelson Pike, *God and Timelessness;* Nicholas Wolterstorff, "God Everlasting," in *God and The Good,* ed. C. Orlebeke and L. Smedes (Grand Rapids, Mich.: Eerdman's, 1975); Eleonore Stump and Norman Kretzmann, "Eternity," *The Journal of Philosophy* 78 (1981): 429–58, and "Eternity, Awareness, and Action," *Faith and Philosophy* 9 (1992): 463–82; and Brian Leftow, *Time and Eternity* (Ithaca, N.Y.: Cornell University Press, 1991).

Good discussions of omnipotence are found in George Mavrodes, "Some Puzzles Concerning Omnipotence," *The Philosophical Review* 72 (1963): 221–23; J. L. Cowan, "The Paradox of Omnipotence," *Analysis* 25 (Supplement) (1965): 102–08, and "The Paradox of Omnipotence Revisited," *Canadian Journal of Philosophy* 3 (1974): 435–45; James Cargile, "On Omnipotence," *Nous* 1 (1967): 201–05; Julian Wolfe, "Omnipotence," *Canadian Journal of Philosophy* (1971): 245–47; Peter Geach, "Omnipotence," *Philosophy* 43 (1973): 7–20; and W. S. Anglin, "Can God Create a Being He Cannot Control?" *Analysis* 40 (1980): 220–23. The reader should also consult the articles cited in footnotes 35, 36, and 37.

Important discussion of the problem of divine foreknowledge and human freedom are Nelson Pike, *God and Timelessness,* chapter 4; Alfred J. Freddoso's extensive introduction to Luis de Molina, *On Divine Foreknowledge (Part IV of the Concordia)* (Ithaca, N.Y.: Cornell University Press, 1988); William Hasker, *God, Time, and Knowledge* (Ithaca, N.Y.: Cornell University Press, 1989); and Linda Zagzebski, *The Dilemma of Freedom and Foreknowledge* (New York: Oxford University Press, 1991). John Martin Fischer's *God, Foreknowledge, and Freedom* (Stanford, Calif.: Stanford University Press, 1989) collects some of the best literature on the subject.

CHAPTER 2

Arguments for the Existence of God

HOW CAN GOD'S EXISTENCE be established? People sometimes appeal to the evidence of religious experience. Some think that God's existence is a presupposition of morality. In their view, morality makes sense only if theism is true. Others believe that theism or some other religious position provides the best overall explanation of the facts of human experience. Some of these views will be discussed in Chapters 5 and 7.

Most philosophers, however, have concentrated on three arguments—the ontological argument, the cosmological argument, and the argument from design. Ontological arguments attempt to show that God's nonexistence is impossible. Cosmological proofs isolate some general feature of a spatio-temporal universe (such as existence or change) and argue that God must be postulated to explain it. Design arguments contend that the world's order, beauty, and apparent purposiveness point to a designing intelligence.

The cosmological and design arguments are expressions of ordinary religious convictions. Anyone who thinks that God alone can explain why there is any world at all is implicitly employing a cosmological argument. A person who believes that the world's order, beauty, and goodness are indications of divine activity is using a design argument. Ontological arguments have been employed only by religious intellectuals. Nevertheless, they may be partly rooted in faith's conviction that God's nonexistence is somehow inconceivable. This chapter examines these three arguments.

THE ONTOLOGICAL ARGUMENT

The most popular form of the ontological argument derives God's existence from His logical possibility, necessary truths about His nature, and principles of logic. Roughly, the idea is that maximal perfection is incompatible with nonexistence. Something that doesn't exist, or might not have existed, isn't as perfect as it would be if its nonexistence was inconceivable. Hence, if a being is *maximally* perfect, it *must* exist.

Philosophers are sharply divided over the value of the argument. According to Immanuel Kant (1724–1804), "The attempt to establish the existence of a supreme being by means of the famous ontological argument . . . is . . . merely so much labour and effort lost; we can no more extend our stock of [theoretical] insight by mere ideas, than a merchant can better his position by adding a few noughts to his cash account."[1] Charles Hartshorne, on the other hand, believes that the ontological argument is "one of the greatest intellectual discoveries of all time."[2] We will set out the argument and then discuss objections to it.

The Argument

The ontological argument can be formulated as follows:

1. For any proposition p, if it is possible that p is necessarily true, p is necessarily true.

2. Necessarily, if God exists, it is necessarily true that He exists.

3. It is possible that God exists.

4. If it is possible that God exists, then it is possible that it is necessarily true that He exists. (From 2 and the principle that when one proposition necessarily implies another and the first is possible, the second is also possible.)

5. If it is possible that it is necessarily true that God exists, then it is necessarily true that God exists. (From 1.)

6. If it is possible that God exists, then it is necessarily true that He exists. (From 4 and 5.)

7. It is necessarily true that God exists. (From 3 and 6.) Hence,

8. God exists. (From 7 and the principle that whatever is necessarily true, is true.)

The argument is valid. Are its premises true? The first premise is an axiom in some systems of logic. It is also intuitively plausible. Premise 1 is equivalent to "If p isn't necessarily true, it isn't possible that it is necessarily true." (Where p and q are any propositions, "p implies q" is equivalent to "not-q implies not-p.") This proposition implies that contingent truths like "Hillary Clinton exists" and "I like Verdi's late operas" *couldn't* be necessary truths. This is surely right. How *could* Hillary Clinton's existence or my fondness for Verdi's late operas hold in all possible worlds? The general idea is that a proposition's "modal status" (whether it is necessary, or impossible, or logically contingent) is an *essential* feature of it. That is, it possesses that modal status in every possible world in which it exists. Thus, a proposition's modal status doesn't change from one possible world to another. Hence, if a proposition isn't necessarily true, there is no possible world in which it is necessarily true; or, what comes to the same thing, if there is a possible world in which it is necessarily true, it is necessarily true.

The second premise is also plausible. God's mode of existence differs from ours. Human beings exist contingently; there are logically possible worlds in which we don't exist. We also exist dependently. Without the appropriate causes, human life would not have emerged on this planet. A maximally perfect being, on the other hand, must be *self-existent*.

What does this mean? A self-existent being is essentially causeless; there is no possible world in which it depends on another for its existence. Its existence is also self-explanatory or intrinsically intelligible (though not necessarily intelligible *to us*); if we could grasp its nature, we would see *why* it exists. Since essential causelessness and intrinsic intelligibility are perfections, a maximally perfect being would possess them.

Yet if a maximally perfect being possesses these perfections (if, in other words, it is self-existent), it exists necessarily (in all possible worlds). Why is this the case? Suppose an essentially causeless being was *not* a logically necessary being. If it wasn't, then its existence would be contingent (since it isn't necessary) but uncaused (since it is essentially causeless). Hence, there would be no reason why it existed when it might just as well not have. Its existence would be an unintelligible brute fact and so *not* self-explanatory or intrinsically intelligible. Therefore, if a being is both essentially causeless and intrinsically intelligible (if, that is, it is self-existent), it must exist necessarily. So premise 2 is plausible. Maximal perfection entails necessary existence.

The first two premises are both therefore plausible. Is the third premise true? That is, is God's existence logically possible? The fact that "God exists" is a meaningful sentence isn't conclusive. ("Round squares exist" is meaningful, but round squares are impossible.)[3] On the other hand, that God's existence is logically possible seems intuitively obvious to many of us.[4] Our intuitions are supported by the fact that no one has deduced a logically impossible proposition from "God exists" and thus shown that the proposition is impossible. There are thus good, if not conclusive, reasons for the third premise.

The argument is valid, then, and its premises are plausible. Must we therefore accept its conclusion?

Objections

There is a formidable difficulty in accepting the ontological argument. The same pattern of reasoning can be used to establish the existence of *anything* provided that (1) it is necessarily true that if it exists, it exists necessarily and (2) its existence is logically possible. Hence, if we can construct coherent concepts of necessarily existing nondivine entities, we can prove that they exist.

Consider the following: (1) the concept of a "perfect island"—a necessarily existing island that possesses every feature that could be desired in an island, (2) the concept of a "perfect devil"—a necessarily existing, omnipotent, omniscient, and perfectly malignant being, and (3) the concept of what Clement Dore (1930–) calls a "near god," a necessarily existing being whose knowledge, power, and goodness are extensive but limited.

If these concepts are coherent (entail no logical impossibilities), then perfect islands, perfect devils, and near gods are logically possible. But their concepts include necessary existence. Hence, they exist. Thus, the same pattern of reasoning that establishes God's existence also establishes the existence of a variety of absurd entities. The objection indicates that the ontological argument must therefore be unsound.

Proponents of the ontological argument can meet this objection by showing that these absurd entities aren't really possible. There are two ways of doing this.

First Strategy: Perfect Islands, Perfect Devils, and Near Gods Don't Exist

The argument's critics admit that *if* a necessary being is possible, it exists. But this implies that if it *doesn't* exist, it *isn't* possible. If one can show that perfect islands, perfect devils, and near gods don't exist, one can therefore conclude that they aren't possible.

Thus, Henry More (1614–1687) argued that it is necessarily true that if a world contains a perfect devil, the universe is a bad whole—one in which evil outweighs good. (Since a perfect devil is omnipotent and omniscient, it can create a bad universe. Since it is perfectly malignant, it will want to do so.) But our universe contains more good than evil and thus isn't a bad whole. Hence, a perfect devil doesn't exist. If a perfect devil were possible, however, it *would* exist. (Since a perfect devil is a necessary being, it would exist in all possible worlds. It would thus exist in the actual world.) Hence, a perfect devil isn't possible.[5]

Similar arguments can be directed against the possibility of necessarily existing omniscient kangaroos, necessarily existing omnipotent gnomes, and perfect islands. For example, if a necessarily existing omnipotent gnome is possible, it exists. Hence, an omnipotent gnome exists. But it doesn't. Therefore necessarily existing omnipotent gnomes aren't possible.

One can establish the impossibility of many absurd entities in this way. However, one *can't* establish the impossibility of a maximally perfect being with an argument of this type unless one has fairly conclusive reasons for thinking it doesn't exist. There is thus a relevant difference between the ontological argument and many of its parodies. We know that the absurd entities "established" by the parodies don't exist and therefore aren't possible. We don't know that a maximally perfect being doesn't exist.

But the first strategy doesn't entirely dispose of the difficulty. We know that perfect devils and perfect islands don't exist. But do we know that a near god doesn't exist? Is the available evidence incompatible with the existence of a very wise, powerful, and good—but limited—being and thus with the existence of a near god? If it isn't, we can't argue from a near god's obvious nonexistence to its impossibility.

Second Strategy: Concepts of Perfect Islands, Perfect Devils, and Near Gods Are Incoherent

One way of showing that an entity is impossible is by showing that its concept is incoherent (entails a logical impossibility). For example, we know that round squares are impossible because we know that their concept entails a contradiction. Hence, if we can establish the incoherence of the concepts of such things as a perfect island or a perfect devil, we can conclude that the entities to which these concepts apply aren't possible.

For example, islands necessarily depend for their existence on many other things. They can't exist without surrounding water, earth, rock, and so on. An island that depends on nothing is inconceivable. But the existence of water, earth, rocks, and the like is contingent; some possible worlds don't contain them and hence don't contain islands. Therefore, no island can exist necessarily. The concept of a perfect island (a *necessarily existing island* with every desirable feature) is therefore incoherent.

It isn't as easy to show that the concepts of a perfect devil or a near god are incoherent. Some theists argue that malignancy is incompatible with omnipotence and omniscience. Moral evil is a consequence of ignorance, dependence, or weakness—nonrational factors that distort our moral perceptions and make it difficult to act on them. An omnipotent and omniscient being wouldn't be influenced by these factors. It would thus have no motive for acting badly. But an agent can't do something without a motive for doing it. Hence, an omnipotent and omniscient being can't act evilly.[6] If this argument is sound, the concept of a perfect devil (a necessarily existing, *omnipotent, omniscient, and perfectly malignant* being) is incoherent.

Some theists think that the concept of a near god is also incoherent. Necessary beings are either self-existent or dependently necessary. Self-existence has been discussed. An entity is dependently necessary if it exists in all possible worlds but, in each world in which it exists, depends on some other entity for its existence. Some theists believe that numbers, propositions, and values are dependently necessary. For example, the proposition "$2 + 2 = 4$" exists in every possible world because God *thinks* it in every possible world. Since near gods exist necessarily, they must be either self-existent or dependently necessary.

But near gods aren't self-existent. Why is this the case? If a being of kind K is self-existent, nothing else is needed to explain it; the existence of a being of that sort is self-explanatory or intrinsically intelligible. But near gods are essentially limited. So if a near god were self-existent, the existence of a being with limited wisdom, power, and goodness would be self-explanatory or intrinsically intelligible. Yet it can't be. When a being's wisdom, power, and goodness are limited, it is appropriate to ask why its capacities and attainments extend just so far and no further. Why, for example, it can lift 984,107 tons of matter but not 984,108 tons? Or why it knows geometry but not Sanskrit? Its limitations, in other words, don't appear to be *self*-explanatory; some *extrinsic* explanation seems called for. Since self-existent beings *are* self-explanatory, near gods can't be self-existent.[7]

But they can't be dependently necessary either. Why not? If a near god were dependently necessary, its existence would depend on that of *another* entity which exists in every world in which it does—that is, in every possible world. This necessary entity, in turn, would either be dependently necessary or self-existent. So to avoid an infinite regress of dependently necessary beings, each depending on its predecessor for its existence, we must postulate the existence of a self-existent being on which the near god's existence ultimately depends. The only plausible candidate for a self-existent being, however, is a maximally perfect being—in other words, God. Yet the supposition that the near god's existence depends upon God is incoherent. For, unlike propositions, numbers, values, and other abstract entities, near gods are concrete beings like hydrogen atoms, horses, minds, or angels. Now, given God's omnipotence and sovereignty, it is a necessary truth that God can prevent the existence of any concrete entity that is distinct from Himself. If He can, He can prevent a near god's existence. But if God *can* prevent a near god's existence, then there is a possible world in which He *does* so and (in that world) the near god doesn't exist. Therefore, since there is a possible world in which the near god doesn't exist, its existence isn't necessary at all and hence isn't *dependently* necessary.

So near gods can't be self-existent and they can't be dependently necessary. Since necessary beings are either self-existent or dependently necessary, near gods aren't necessary beings. The concept of a near god (a *necessarily existing limited* being) is thus incoherent.

If the arguments of this section are sound, the concepts of a perfect island, a perfect devil, and a near god are incoherent. Perfect islands, perfect devils, and near gods are therefore impossible. The concept of a maximally perfect being, on the other hand, seems coherent. (See Chapter 1.) There is thus a crucial difference between the ontological argument and its parodies.

God's Possibility and the Possibility of Other Necessary Beings

Are there better reasons for thinking that a maximally perfect being is possible than for thinking that its competitors (perfect devils, near gods, and so on) are possible? If there aren't, parodies of the ontological argument are as plausible as the argument itself.

The question is also important for another reason. If a maximally perfect being is possible, its competitors aren't. Conversely, if one of its competitors is possible, a maximally perfect being isn't possible.[8] Why is this the case?

As we saw in the last section, a maximally perfect being such as God could prevent the existence of every other concrete entity. But the existence of necessarily existing things isn't preventable. Hence, if God exists, no other necessarily existing concrete entity exists. (If it *did* exist, its existence would be unpreventable and so God couldn't prevent it.) Consider, then, the following argument.

1. If God's existence is possible, He exists in all possible worlds (that is, His existence is necessary). But as we have just seen,
2. If God exists in a world, no other necessarily existing concrete entity exists in that world. Hence,
3. If God exists in *all* possible worlds, no possible world contains other necessarily existing concrete entities. (From 2.)
4. If no possible world contains other necessarily existing concrete entities, other necessarily existing concrete entities are impossible. (If

something is possible, it exists in a possible world and vice versa.) Therefore,

5. If God is possible, other necessarily existing concrete entities are impossible. (From 1, 3, and 4.) On the other hand,

6. If other necessarily existing concrete entities are possible, God isn't possible. (From 5.)

The possibility of God and the possibility of God's competitors are thus mutually exclusive. If we have better reasons for thinking that God is possible than for thinking that His competitors are possible, the possibility of the latter can be dismissed. Conversely, if we have better reasons for thinking that one of God's competitors is possible, we should conclude that God isn't possible. Which is more plausible, then, God's possibility or the possibility of some of His competitors?

God's possibility seems intuitively obvious to many of us. But while perfect devils and near gods don't appear on their face to be logically impossible, neither do they appear on their face to be logically possible. Most of us probably have no clear intuitions either way. Hence the possibility of a maximally perfect being receives some support from our intuitions. The possibility of necessarily existing nondivine entities doesn't.

Furthermore, the concepts of a perfect island, a perfect devil, a near god, and so on, are obviously "cooked up."[9] The idea of maximal perfection isn't. Human beings are religious animals; and as humanity's religious consciousness evolves, its object is almost invariably construed as maximally perfect. It is tempting to conclude that an idea that is so deeply rooted in human nature, and that we spontaneously believe to be possible, is more likely to be coherent than an artificially constructed concept whose implications haven't been thoroughly explored.

Finally, God is not known to be nonexistent, and attempts to show that the concept of God is incoherent haven't succeeded. On the other hand, many of the cooked-up entities are clearly nonexistent (for example, a perfect devil). The concept of a perfect devil or a near god (and other things of that kind) may also be incoherent.

The case for God's possibility thus seems stronger than the case for the possibility of His competitors.[10]

Conclusion

The ontological argument makes three assumptions—the modal status of a proposition is a necessary feature of it (and hence a proposition that is possibly necessary, is necessary), a maximally perfect being would exist in all possible worlds, and the existence of a maximally perfect being is logically possible. The third assumption is the most controversial. If it is true, no other concrete object can exist necessarily. Perfect islands, perfect devils, and near gods are impossible, and parodies of the ontological argument that allegedly establish their existence are unsound. (They are unsound because they employ a false premise—namely, that the entities in question are logically possible.)

Still, the case for God's possibility *is* plausible and seems stronger than the case for the possibility of His competitors. The ontological argument thus provides some reason for thinking that God exists.

Why, then, do so many find the argument unconvincing? Three reasons are particularly important.

God's logical possibility could be *demonstrated* only by showing that He actually exists. (If something exists, it is logically possible that it exists.) Hence, no one who doubts the argument's conclusion has a *conclusive* reason for accepting its third premise. ("It is possible that God exists.") Several informal considerations *support* the premise. It seems intuitively plausible to a number of us. No one has deduced a logically impossible statement from "God exists," and the concept of God isn't "cooked up." But many think that this informal support is too weak to justify the confidence that such a complex concept contains no hidden incoherencies.

There are also problems with the second premise. ("If God exists, He necessarily exists.") Although it is deeply embedded in classical Western theology, theists themselves often doubt it. Some suspect that the concept of a necessarily existing *concrete* entity is incoherent. If it is, then not even God can exist in all possible worlds. Others doubt that necessary existence is a perfection. Other things being equal, knowledge or compassion makes things better than they would otherwise be. Is this true, however, of existence or even *necessary* existence? There are also theists who doubt whether God should be construed as a maximally perfect being. (See Chapter 1.) And yet if He isn't maximally perfect, why should we think He necessarily exists?

Nor will the argument convince anyone who thinks he or she has good reasons for rejecting the conclusion. The ontological argument *is* valid; *if* its premises are true, so is its conclusion. But it doesn't follow that we must *accept* the conclusion—only that we must accept it *or* reject one of the premises. Those who are convinced they have stronger reasons for denying God's existence than for thinking that His existence is possible, or for thinking that He would necessarily exist if He did exist, are rationally entitled to reject the argument.

Hence, while the ontological argument can't be dismissed, it is clear why theists themselves often view it with suspicion. It *is* valid. Those who find its premises persuasive thus have a reason for accepting its conclusion.[11] But the premises are controversial. Those who are convinced they have good reasons for denying that God exists have a right to reject the argument.[12] Those who believe that God exists, but think the premises are weak, will find it unpersuasive.

THE COSMOLOGICAL ARGUMENT

Cosmological arguments infer God's existence from characteristics that any spatio-temporal world would presumably have—contingent existence, for example, or causal interactions.

There are several types of cosmological argument. The first argues that infinite temporal regresses are impossible. If so, the world has a beginning. But nothing can *begin* to exist unless something *causes* it to exist. Hence, the world has a cause.

This argument is the standard proof of God's existence in Islam. It was also defended by important Jewish philosophers and by the Christian Bonaventura (1221–74). Most Western philosophers neglected it, however, because they weren't convinced that infinite temporal regresses are impossible. After all, why *couldn't* every event be preceded by an earlier one so that the chain of events goes back forever?[13]

The most influential medieval proponents of the cosmological argument didn't deny that infinite temporal regresses are possible. Thomas Aquinas is an example. He bases his five proofs of God's existence on features he thinks any spatio-temporal order would have—"motion" (change), causal activity, beings that are generated and decay, gradations of value (the fact that some things are better than others), and order. Aquinas admits that reason can't exclude the possibility of an infinite temporal regress of movers, or causes, or corruptible beings. Although revelation tells us that the world had a beginning, philosophy can't prove it.

Aquinas thinks, however, that God would be needed to explain the world even if it were beginningless. Things like change or causation aren't intelligible unless we suppose that God exists and is responsible for them. He argues, for example, that:

> It is certain, and evident to our senses, that in the world some things are in motion [change]. . . . [But] whatever is moved must be moved by another. If that by which it is moved be itself moved, then this also must needs be moved by another, and that by another again. But this cannot go on to infinity, because then there could be no first mover, and, consequently, no other mover, seeing that subsequent movers move only inasmuch as they are moved by the first mover; as the staff moves only because it is moved by the hand. Therefore, it is necessary to arrive at a first mover, moved by no other; and this everyone understands to be God.
>
> In the world of sensible things we [also] find there is an order of efficient causes. There is no case known (neither is it, indeed, possible) in which a thing is found to be the efficient cause of itself; for so it would be prior to itself, which is impossible. Now in efficient causes it is not possible to go on to infinity, because in all efficient causes following in order, the first is the cause of the intermediate cause, and the intermediate is the cause of the ultimate cause, whether the intermediate cause be several or one only. Now to take away the cause is to take away the effect. Therefore, if there be no first cause among efficient causes, there will be no ultimate, nor any intermediate, cause. But if in efficient causes it is possible to go on to infinity, there will be no first efficient cause, neither will there be an ultimate effect, nor any intermediate efficient causes. . . . Therefore it is necessary to admit a first efficient cause, to which everyone gives the name of God.[14]

Aquinas thinks that instances of change or causal activity can't be adequately explained by *earlier* changes or causal activities. In his opinion, that changes or causal activities *have* taken place (and are now over) can't explain why changes and causal activities are *now* taking place. The latter isn't intelligible unless we assume that the changes and causal activities that are now occurring are grounded in more perfect activities that are *occurring at the same time*. While these activities may themselves be grounded in still more perfect activities and those in even better activities, the chain as a whole depends on its first member. (Think of the way in which the motion of my pen is grounded in the motion of my hand, and how this is in turn grounded in my intention to move my hand. The last is basic. If I stop willing, my hand stops moving and so does the pen.)

Aquinas concedes that infinite *temporal* regresses are possible. Each change or causal activity could be preceded by an earlier one. He thinks, however, that series of *simultaneously* occurring changes or causes must have first members—an activity that is the source of change but isn't itself susceptible to change or a causal activity that is not, and could not be, derived from another. The ultimate ground of change ("the first mover") or causal activity ("the first cause") is God.

These cosmological arguments are historically important. Their plausibility, however, depends on assumptions that are no longer widely held. Ancient and medieval science, for example, thought in terms of hierarchies of simultaneously occurring causes of different ontological kinds. Effects at lower levels of being were explained by causal activities at higher levels of being. Ancient and medieval metaphysics also assumed that the less perfect can be explained only by the more perfect.[15]

Modern versions of the cosmological argument dispense with these assumptions. Most of them focus on contingent existence.

Something exists contingently if it is logically possible that it exists and logically possible that it doesn't. Modern versions of the cosmological argument attempt to show that the activity of a self-existent being is the only thing that can explain the existence of contingent being. For example, Samuel Clarke (1675–1729) argued that "an infinite succession . . . of merely dependent beings, without any original independent cause, is a series of beings, that has neither necessity nor cause, nor any reason at all of its existence, neither within itself nor from without." There must therefore "of necessity have existed from eternity, some one immutable and independent being" that is the cause of the others. Since this being "has existed from eternity, without any external cause of its existence, [it] must be self-existent, that is necessarily existing."[16]

Why must a being's existence be logically necessary if its activity is to adequately explain contingent being? John Hick (1922–) thinks that it needn't— "factual necessity" is sufficient.[17]

A factually necessary being is a contingent being that is essentially causeless. Since "being causeless" is one of its essential properties, there aren't any possible worlds in which it is caused. Hence, it *can't* have a cause. Asking for its cause is thus as misguided as asking for the name of a bachelor's wife.

Hick thinks that because God is factually necessary, His activity adequately explains the existence of contingent being. Although we can raise causal questions about trees, atoms, minds, or the space-time world as a whole, we can't raise causal questions about God. God *can't* have a cause, and thus the search for causes must stop with Him. God therefore provides a satisfactory ultimate explanation.

Hick is mistaken. Since a factually necessary being is logically contingent, it might not have existed. Why, then, *does* it exist? The question has no answer. Since a factually necessary being isn't self-existent, its existence isn't self-explanatory. But because it is essentially causeless, no *other* being can explain it. Its existence is thus contingent yet inexplicable. Therefore, a factually necessary being can't adequately explain contingent being. The question is "Why are there *any* contingent beings at all?" It isn't answered by postulating the activity of still another contingent being—not even an essentially causeless one.

The question could be answered by postulating the activity of a self-existent being. A self-existent being too is essentially causeless. But its existence is also logically necessary. (See the section on the ontological argument at the beginning of this chapter.) Hence, a self-existent being doesn't exhibit the feature we are trying to explain—namely, contingent existence.

We can formulate the cosmological argument as follows.

1. If something exists, its existence is either self-existent (and hence self-explanatory) or some other being causes it to exist.

2. A contingent being isn't self-existent. Therefore,

3. A contingent being is caused to exist by some other being. (From 1 and 2.)

Contingent beings are usually caused by other contingent beings. For example, my existence was caused by my parents, their existence was caused by their parents, and so on. But what about contingent beings as a whole?

4. Either the series of contingent beings has a first member (a contingent being that isn't caused by another contingent being) or it doesn't (the series is beginningless).

5. If the series has a first member, then a self-existent being exists and causes it. (From 3. Since the first member is *contingent*, another being causes it. By hypothesis, the first member isn't caused by a contingent being. Hence, it is caused by a self-existent being.)[18]

6. If the series of contingent beings doesn't have a first member (and is therefore beginningless), a self-existent being exists and causes the whole series. (From 3. Since the existence of the series is contingent, another being causes it. Since the cause of the series of contingent beings isn't part of the series, it isn't itself contingent.)

7. If contingent beings exist, a self-existent being exists that causes them. (From 4, 5, and 6.)

8. Contingent beings exist. Hence,

9. A self-existent being exists and causes contingent beings to exist. (From 7 and 8.)

The argument's most controversial features are the inference from 3 to 6 and its first premise. Why does a beginningless series of contingent beings need a cause for its existence to be intelligible? And why assume that the existence of everything *is* intelligible—that there *is* a reason for its existence? We now discuss these questions in detail.

Does a Beginningless Series Need a Cause?

Is the cosmological argument's inference from premise 3 to premise 6 sound? Many critics believe it isn't. Perhaps every contingent being *is* caused by some other being. It doesn't follow that the *series* of contingent beings is caused by another being. The series might be beginningless with each member being caused by a preceding member. If it were, each member would be explained (by a preceding member), and so the series as a whole would be accounted for. No further explanation would be required. Thus, a beginningless series of contingent beings may not need an explanation. Hence, we can't infer that it has a cause.

Paul Edwards (1923-) puts the point this way. Suppose five Eskimos arrive in New York. We wonder why they are there and are told that one of them "did not enjoy the extreme cold in the polar region and decided to move to a warmer climate." Her husband "loves her dearly and did not wish to live without her." Their child is with them because "he is too small and too weak to oppose his parents." The fourth "saw an advertisement in the *New York Times* for an Eskimo to appear on television." The fifth "is a private detective engaged by the Pinkerton Agency to keep an eye on Eskimo No. 4. . . . We have now explained in the case of each of the five Eskimos why he or she is in New York. Somebody then asks: 'All right, but what about the group as a whole; why is *it* in New York?' This would plainly be an absurd question. There is no group over and above the five members, and if we have explained why each of the five members is in New York we have *ipso facto* explained why the group is there." Edwards then concludes "it is just as absurd to ask for the cause of the series [of contingent beings] as a whole as distinct from asking for the cause of individual members." A whole is explained when its parts are explained. In a beginningless series in which each member is caused by a preceding member, nothing is left to explain. No further cause is needed.[19]

This common objection misses the point. The question isn't, "Why does this or that member of the series exist?" but "Why does *any* member of the series exist—that is, why is there a series *at all?*" The first question can be answered by pointing out that each member is caused by a preceding member. The second question can't. Since the causes in question are *members* of the series, they are *part* of what we are trying to explain.

If the series doesn't have an external cause, it is an inexplicable brute fact—something that might not have existed, but (for no reason) just happens to do so. Consider an analogy. That Jacob and Rachel begat Joseph satisfactorily explains Joseph's existence. That Isaac and Rebekah begat Jacob satisfactorily explains Jacob's existence. But if what puzzles us isn't Joseph's existence or Jacob's existence but human existence in general, these explanations aren't helpful. Even if we were to learn that every human being is begotten by other human beings, our question wouldn't have been answered, for we still wouldn't know why there are human beings in the first place. Similarly, if what puzzles us is that *any* contingent beings exist, we aren't helped by learning that one contingent being is caused by another, that by a third, and so on.[20]

Edwards's story is misleading. In the case of the Eskimos, no part of the question ("Why are the Eskimos in New York?") was left unanswered. But "Every contingent being is caused by another contingent being" doesn't answer the question "Why are there any contingent beings at all?" In Edwards's story, the explanations don't presuppose the fact they are trying to explain—the presence of the five Eskimos in New York. By contrast, those attempts to answer the question about the existence of contingent beings in general that appeal to the causal activity of contingent beings *do* implicitly rest on the fact they are trying to explain—namely, the existence of contingent beings. The two cases are therefore dissimilar.

In short, the existence of the series of contingent beings is puzzling whether the series is beginningless or not. If it isn't caused by a non-contingent being, it has no explanation. In effect, premise 3 asserts that contingent existence *does* have an explanation. Premise 3 thus implies premise 6. Even if there are an infinite number of contingent beings and each of these is caused by another contingent being, a self-existent being is the only thing that can explain the existence of contingent entities.

The Principle of Sufficient Reason

The modern cosmological argument's most problematic feature is its first premise. Why think that something's existence is either self-explanatory or explained by the activity of another being? Many seventeenth- and eighteenth-century philosophers thought this followed from the "principle of sufficient reason." The principle is sometimes stated like this:

> **PSR^1:** **For every contingent fact F, some other fact F' obtains such that, given F', F must obtain.**

PSR^1 implies that facts are either necessary or fully determined by other facts.

Classical theists can't accept the principle in this form. That God freely decided to create our world rather than some other world, or none, is a contingent fact. If PSR^1 is true, His decision is fully determined by other facts—either facts about His nature or facts about other things. Neither alternative is acceptable. If God's decision is fully determined by His nature, other choices aren't possible. God has to make that decision. Thus, His choice isn't free. If God's decision is fully determined by other things, His sovereignty and independence are compromised as well as His freedom. Classical theists must therefore insist that at least one contingent fact doesn't have a sufficient reason—namely, the fact that God freely decided to create our world.

However, classical theists can accept weaker versions of the principle. We can weaken the principle by narrowing its scope—restricting it to certain *kinds* of contingent facts. We can also weaken it by qualifying the demand for a *sufficient* reason—that is, a set of facts that *fully* determines what we are trying to explain.

For example, we can restrict the principle's scope to the *existence* of contingent entities:

PSR^2: **There is a sufficient reason for the existence of every contingent entity.**

PSR^2 doesn't entail that there is a sufficient reason for an entity's "accidental" properties (properties it might or might not have). Hence, it doesn't entail that there is a sufficient reason for an entity's freely deciding to do something.

One can also restrict the scope of the principle to contingent facts that "require" sufficient reasons:

PSR^3: **Every contingent fact that requires a sufficient reason has one.**

A contingent fact "requires" a sufficient reason if and only if (1) it is logically possible that it has a sufficient reason and (2) it is unintelligible if it doesn't have one. All contingent facts satisfy the first condition. Some may not satisfy the second.

Consider a case in which I have good strategic reasons for moving my pawn to king's 4 and freely decide to do so. If my decision is contra-causally free, it isn't fully determined by its causal antecedents.[21] But though my decision isn't determined by its causal antecedents, "My decision is determined by its causal antecedents" doesn't entail a logically impossible proposition. The first condition is therefore satisfied. The second isn't. My decision is intelligible because it expresses intelligible reasons and motives. (The move is strategically sound and I want to win the game.) Nevertheless, because these reasons and motives don't *determine* my decision, it doesn't have a sufficient reason.

One can also weaken the principle by dropping the demand that contingent facts have a *sufficient* reason. Charles Hartshorne thinks that whether or not things have sufficient reasons, nothing is "through and through *pure* chance." Reason discounts the possibility of something whose "inexplicability . . . would be infinite and total." "Mere chance, as an entire account of a being's existence," isn't admissible.[22] Hartshorne's remarks suggest the following principle:

PSR^4: **There is at least *some* reason for every contingent fact.**

While some contingent facts may lack causally sufficient conditions, PSR^4 implies that at least they have necessary conditions which partly explain them.

Each of the weaker principles is compatible with God's freedom. PSR^2 and PSR^3 don't apply to contra-causally free decisions. PSR^4 does, but doesn't imply that they are fully determined by other facts.

The weaker principles are strong enough to generate the conclusion that contingent being is caused by a self-existent being. The existence of contingent being seems to require an explanation. Hence, PSR³ as well as PSR² imply that contingent being *bas* an explanation. If our earlier discussion was sound, a self-existent being is the only thing that can provide this explanation.

PSR⁴ is also strong enough to yield the conclusion. If *all* beings are contingent, there is *no* reason for the existence of contingent being in general. Since this violates PSR⁴, a self-existent being must be at least partly responsible for the existence of contingent entities.

But are any of these principles *true?* The question isn't easily answered— partly because philosophers disagree about their nature. Some think the principles are empirical generalizations. Others think that one or more of them are presuppositions of rational inquiry. Still others believe they express necessary truths.

According to the first view, the principle of sufficient reason is an induction from human experience. Impressed with our success in discovering causal explanations, we infer that everything has a cause or explanation.

It isn't easy to determine whether this induction is justified. Science has been extraordinarily successful in discovering causes. On the other hand, some phenomena continue to resist explanation. Human behavior is an example. In addition, much of the universe remains unexplored. (Think of how little we know about the planets in our own solar system.) Our "sample" (the cases in which we have discovered explanations) may simply be too small to justify the sweeping conclusion that *everything* has an explanation. Finally, our sample only includes cases in which one spatio-temporal phenomenon is explained by another. Hence, it provides rather weak support for the claim that contingent reality *as a whole* has an explanation.

Nevertheless, the principle of sufficient reason receives some support from the success of human inquiry, although it should be noted that weaker versions are better supported than stronger ones. For example, there are more cases in which we have discovered *some* reason for contingent facts (necessary conditions, partial causes, and so on) than cases in which we have discovered *sufficient* reasons for them. Hence, PSR⁴ is better confirmed than PSR¹ or PSR³.

Some philosophers believe that the principle of sufficient reason is a presupposition of inquiry. The human mind demands "total intelligibility" (although in practice we may content ourselves with less or fail to realize that total intelligibility is the only thing that would fully satisfy us). The principle of sufficient reason expresses this demand.

The plausibility of this view partly depends upon whether one is employing stronger or weaker versions of the principle. Contemporary science offers explanations that aren't deterministic. For example, theories about subatomic particles allow for random events that lack sufficient reasons (causes that fully determine the phenomena). It seems, then, that reason can be satisfied by accounts that violate PSR¹. If so, PSR¹ doesn't express a demand of reason. On the other hand, reason presumably *would* be dissatisfied with an account which entailed that a contingent fact had *no* explanation (not even a partial one) and thus violated PSR[4].

But should we assume that the demands of reason can be met? Perhaps it is reasonable to trust our mental faculties and endorse their demands in the absence of good reasons for distrusting them. Hence, if some form of the principle of sufficient reason *does* express a demand of the human mind, and there are no good reasons for thinking it false, it may be reasonable to rely on it.

Samuel Clarke and Gottfried Leibniz (1646–1716) thought that the principle of sufficient reason is a necessary truth. Is this plausible?

David Hume (1711–76) thought not. If the principle is necessarily true, its denial entails a logically impossible proposition. Hume pointed out that the denial of the principle of sufficient reason ("Something exists contingently and has no cause") isn't self-contradictory. He concluded that it isn't necessarily true.[23]

This inference is illegitimate. As we saw in Chapter 1, formal contradictions aren't the only kind of logical impossibility. "Something is red and green all over" and "One has no obligation to speak the truth" aren't self-contradictory. Nevertheless, they may be false in all possible worlds.

Other critics claim that they can't see the necessity of the principle. This too is inconclusive. Propositions can be necessary that not everyone sees to be necessary. (Many theists think that "God exists" is a proposition of this kind.) Still, people's intuitions concerning the necessity of the principle conflict, although weaker versions are more likely to seem necessary than stronger ones.[24]

Let us summarize our discussion. The cosmological argument depends upon the principle of sufficient reason. The strongest version of the principle is incompatible with God's freedom. Weaker versions are not and are sufficiently strong to generate the conclusion of the argument.

The principle of sufficient reason has been interpreted as an empirical generalization, a presupposition of rational thought, and a necessary truth. The principle receives some support from the success of human inquiry. It may express a demand of reason, and it strikes some as necessarily true. None of these considerations are conclusive. Nevertheless, they provide some support, and there seem to be no strong reasons for thinking that weaker versions of the principle are false. Some of the weaker versions may therefore be more plausible than their denials.

Conclusion

Modern versions of the cosmological argument attempt to show that contingent being is caused by a self-existent being. They are sound if (1) the existence of contingent being can't be adequately explained by contingent causes and (2) some version of the principle of sufficient reason is true. Both claims are plausible.

As it stands, however, the argument doesn't establish *God's* existence— that the self-existent cause of contingent being is a maximally perfect personal agent. How could one show this?

While the causal activity of a self-existent being may be the only thing that can adequately explain the existence of contingent beings, its *activity* must be contingent. Why is this the case? Suppose that its activity isn't contingent—that the ground of contingent being necessarily exists and (for example) necessarily causes me to exist. Necessary effects of necessary causes are themselves necessary. Hence *I* necessarily exist. But this is absurd. The cause of my existence must therefore act contingently.

In short, if its effect is contingent, the self-existent being's causal act isn't necessitated by its nature or anything else. It thus lacks a sufficient reason. Now one of the more plausible versions of the principle of sufficient reason is PSR^3. PSR^3 implies that a contingent fact that lacks a sufficient reason doesn't require one. Hence, if PSR^3 is true, the self-existent being's causal activity doesn't require a sufficient reason. The most plausible candidates for activities that don't require sufficient reasons are free decisions. Hence, if PSR^3 is true, the self-existent being's causal act is probably a free decision. If it is, the self-existent being is a personal agent.

Is the personal agent God? As we saw earlier in this chapter, some philosophers think that self-existent beings are necessarily unlimited. If they are, the creator is maximally perfect as well as personal.

There are, then, reasons for identifying the self-existent cause of contingent being with God.

THE DESIGN ARGUMENT

Cosmological arguments are based on features that any space-time world would presumably exhibit. Examples are contingent existence or change. Design arguments appeal to things that aren't found in every conceivable space-time world but that are found in ours—beauty, intelligible order, life, consciousness, and so on. Design arguments involve two steps.

The first argues that the world exhibits "apparent design." That is, it seems to contain indications of intelligent planning. The world exhibits apparent design if it is the sort of thing that mind might produce. Thus, William Paley (1743–1805) argued that "every indication of contrivance, every manifestation of design" which exists in a "watch, exists in the works of nature, with the difference on the side of nature of being greater and more . . . [for] the contrivances of nature surpass the contrivances of art in the complexity, subtlety, and curiosity of the mechanism." They are "not less evidently contrivances, not less evidently accommodated to their end or suited to their office than are the most perfect productions of human ingenuity."

The argument's second step attempts to show that a designing intelligence should be postulated to explain the appearance of planning. Paley thought the inference obvious. "There cannot be design without a designer; contrivance without a contriver; order without choice; arrangement without anything capable of arranging; subserviency and relation to a purpose without that which could intend a purpose; means suitable to an end, and executing their office in accomplishing that end, without the end ever having been contemplated or the means accommodated to it. Arrangement, disposition of parts, subserviency of means to an end, relation of instruments to a use imply the presence of intelligence and mind."[25]

David Hume, on the other hand, thought the argument weak; if it established anything, it was only that "the principle which first arranged, and still maintains order in this universe, bears . . . some *remote inconceivable* analogy to the other operations of Nature, and among the rest to the economy of human mind and thought."[26]

We will now discuss the argument's two steps in more detail.

Apparent Design

What is involved in apparent design? Something suggests intelligence if (1) it serves the sorts of ends that human minds typically propose to themselves (health, protection, beauty, benefit or harm to others, and so on) and (2) the results are achieved in a reasonably effective manner.

Both notions are vague. We sometimes act for bizarre reasons. Sometimes we act for no reason at all. Almost anything might be taken as an end by some human mind or other. Nevertheless, some human purposes are more common or more transparent than others. A watch, a gun, and the patterned movements of a dance serve familiar and intelligible ends and thus suggest deliberate purpose. A random arrangement of objects on a desk or a series of erratic bodily movements *might* have been produced deliberately but don't suggest intelligence because their purpose is unclear.

The notion of effectiveness is also imprecise. Effectiveness is sometimes identified with efficiency. An assembly line, a computer, an industrial process, a university administration, or a public health policy can be more or less efficient. Something is inefficient if many of its operations or parts serve no purpose, or its purposes are achieved by wasteful or unnecessarily complicated means.

Efficiency isn't the only sort of effectiveness. Clocks can be more or less efficient but not paintings or poems. Nevertheless, works of art can be ineffective. Suppose that a poem is badly unified. It includes elements that make no contribution to the effect or value of the work as a whole. It also displays features that subvert the poet's intentions. (For example, the poet meant to be solemn but was unintentionally funny.) We conclude that the artist is ineffective—in poor command of his or her material.

Something displays apparent design, then, if it seems to have an intelligible purpose and achieves it in an effective manner. Does the world exhibit apparent design?

Eighteenth- and nineteenth-century versions of the design argument focused on such things as animal organisms, parts of them like the eye, and the motion of the planets. Most critics of the argument admitted that these things display apparent design but insisted that they are best explained by science. For example, critics argued that animal organisms and their parts are more adequately explained by the theory of evolution than by a designer. Partly because of this criticism, modern advocates of the design argument tend to focus on more general features of the universe. F. R. Tennant (1866–1957) is typical of these theists.[27]

Tennant calls our attention to several facts:

1. Although our world provided the right conditions for the appearance of life and consciousness, it might not have. "The fitness of our world to be the home of living beings depends on certain primary conditions, astronomical, thermal, chemical, etc., and on the coincidence of qualities apparently not causally connected with one another, the number of which would doubtless surprise anyone wholly unlearned in the sciences." If any of these apparently unrelated conditions had been absent, life and consciousness would not have emerged.

2. The world possesses a rational structure that can be grasped by human thought. Although nature's mechanisms might have been too complicated or too disorderly to be understood by finite minds, they are not. Human beings are not only capable of acquiring the knowledge they need for survival, they are also able to discover nature's basic laws and hidden processes.

3. The world is "saturated" with beauty. "On the telescopic and on the microscopic scale, from the starry heaven to the siliceous skeleton of the diatom, in her inward parts . . . as well as on the surface, in flowers that 'blush unseen' and gems that the 'unfathomed caves of ocean bear,' Nature is sublime or beautiful. . . . However various be the taste for beauty . . . the more lavishly does she gratify it." This too is significant. The only case in which we are directly acquainted with minds as well as their products is human productive activity. There we find that beauty is almost always the result of deliberate intention. When the intention is absent, the results are "in general . . . aesthetically vile."

4. The world provides a suitable environment for moral growth and activity. "Morality cannot be made without raw material." Virtues can't be developed and exercised unless the world presents real challenges and tasks. But the tasks can't be too formidable. Morality would be pointless or impossible if the world was "indifferent to . . . moral aims, or hostile to . . . ideals." These conditions might not have obtained. The world might have presented few challenges or resisted our best moral efforts. As a matter of fact, it provides real tasks and is "relatively modifiable" by moral ideals.

In short, we can easily conceive of worlds without life, consciousness, intelligible order, beauty, or moral value. Our world, however, is a rational and beautiful whole that contained the conditions needed for the emergence of life, consciousness, rational thought, and moral activity. Tennant concludes that a world with these features is the sort of good a mind might fittingly propose to itself as an end.

But suppose we grant this. Are the means by which this end is achieved "effective"? Kenneth Nelson (1948–) argues that they aren't.[28]

Beauty, intelligible order, life, consciousness, and similar phenomena are the consequences of evolutionary processes that involve variation, competition, and survival of the best adapted. Nature spontaneously produces a variety of chemical aggregates, stellar configurations, organisms, and so on. These compete for survival, and the poorly adapted are eliminated.

Evolutionary processes are "inefficient." There is some similarity between these processes and technological evolution. (Inventors' ideas correspond to variations, the marketplace to competition, and survival in the marketplace to survival of the best adapted.) But natural processes take much longer and provide less evidence of planning. Evolution has many blind alleys and involves much waste. Countless adaptations prove unsuccessful. Variations occur randomly in parts that don't need improvement as well as in parts that do. Indeed, only some variations are even potentially useful. Furthermore, the same mistakes are made over and over (for example, "genetic combinations producing malformed infants"). Even when evolution is "successful," individuals are adapted only to their immediate circumstances and won't survive radical changes in their environment. (Consider dinosaurs, for example.) In short, evolutionary processes aren't the sort of means we would expect a powerful and intelligent agent to employ. The processes by which nature achieves its results may be *compatible* with power and intelligence but they don't suggest it.

How serious is this difficulty? Talk about blind alleys or waste may be misleading. One must ask, "A blind alley or waste from whose point of view?" Is it a waste from the perspective of species that may have temporarily flourished? That the emergence of these organisms led to no *further* result doesn't entail that their existence didn't itself have a certain value.

The important point, however, is that efficiency may be an inappropriate criterion for evaluating nature's mechanisms. If God designed the world, we would expect its parts to effectively serve His purposes. But we shouldn't expect the sort of effectiveness that is desirable in an industrial process or a university administration—namely, efficiency. Efficiency is a value when powers and means are limited, and the designers must husband their resources. God's powers, however, are unlimited; He isn't restricted in His choice of means. Questions of efficiency aren't clearly relevant when resources are inexhaustible. Hence, efficiency is probably an inappropriate criterion for evaluating what may be God's handiwork.[29]

There is a further reason for thinking that efficiency is an inappropriate criterion. Eighteenth- and nineteenth-century versions of the design argument compared the world (or selected parts of it) to a machine. But older versions of the argument compared it to a work of art. Thus, Peter Sterry (d. 1672) called the world "God's poem" since it harmoniously unites "the amplest variety . . . and the most opposed contrarieties."[30] As we saw, works of art aren't appropriately evaluated as efficient or inefficient. If the world is more like a work of art than a machine, efficiency is probably irrelevant. "Inefficient" parts of nature may enhance the splendor of the cosmic drama, contribute to the world's beauty, or be necessary consequences of its intelligible order. Nature's processes may thus be "effective" even if they aren't "efficient."

Our discussion can be summarized as follows. Things that serve intelligible ends in a reasonably effective manner suggest mind and thus exhibit apparent design. The concept of apparent design applies to anything that impresses us as strikingly similar to products of human intelligence—not only tools and machines but also works of art, political systems, and well-ordered lives. The concept is imprecise but advocates and critics of the argument share some understanding of what it involves. They would agree, for example, that the circulatory system or the movement of the heavenly bodies suggests intelligence more readily than the random distribution of rocks on a deserted beach, the heat death of the universe, or the pattern of motes in a sunbeam. They disagree about the concept's application. For example, Nelson denies that it applies to the world as a whole because he thinks that natural processes are inefficient. Tennant, on the other hand, believes that beauty, intelligible order, life, consciousness, rational thought, and moral activity are appropriate ends for an intelligent mind, and that the natural processes that have produced them or made them possible are effective. He thus concludes that the concept of apparent design applies to the world as a whole.

But suppose we grant that the world exhibits apparent design or suggests intelligence. It doesn't follow that a mind caused it. The design may be only apparent and the suggestion misleading. The inference to a designer can't be accepted without further argument. The second step of the design proof will be examined next.

The Inference to a Designer

We can construe the second step of the design argument as an analogical inference, as an inference to the best explanation, or as a probability argument. (These aren't always clearly distinguished in practice.) Each approach has its strengths and weaknesses.

An Analogical Inference

The second step is sometimes formulated as follows:

1. Clocks, poems, computers, dances, and so on, exhibit apparent design and are produced by minds.
2. The world exhibits apparent design. Hence,
3. It too is probably produced by mind.

Inferences of this type are "analogical arguments." They have the following form:

1. x_1, x_2, x_3, etc., has P_1, P_2, P_3, etc., and P_n.
2. x_n has P_1, P_2, P_3, etc. Therefore,
3. x_n probably has P_n. ($P_1, P_2, \ldots P_n$ are variables that take properties as values. The values of $x_1, x_2, \ldots x_n$ are things that have properties.)

We often argue by analogy. For example, suppose I know that many students who attended Glendale High School did poorly on their SAT exams. I am told that Alvin went to Glendale and infer that his scores were also low.

Analogical arguments are strong when (1) few instances of P_1, P_2, P_3, etc., are known to *lack* P_n and (2) there is little or no significant dissimilarity between x_1, x_2, x_3, etc., and x_n. They are weak when these conditions aren't met. For example, the inference to Alvin's poor SAT scores is weak if a number of Glendale graduates are known to have done well on the exam. The inference is also weak if there are significant dissimilarities between Alvin and the students who did poorly. (Thus, the inference loses much of its force if the other students have an impoverished background or a low IQ and Alvin doesn't.)

How strong is the inference to a designer? William Paley argued that there are no cases in which we *know* that apparent design isn't caused by intelligence.[31] This seems right. We don't know that God doesn't exist. Hence, for any instance of apparent design, we don't know that an intelligent mind (namely, God) didn't cause it. The first condition is therefore met.

On the other hand, critics believe there are many dissimilarities between the world and human artifacts. Hume thought that the world is as much like a vegetable or animal as a machine. For example, "it bears a great resemblance to an animal or organized body. . . . A continual circulation of matter in it produces no disorder: a continual waste in every part is incessantly repaired; the closest sympathy is perceived throughout the entire system: and each part or member, in performing its proper offices, operates both to its own preservation and that of the whole."[32] In Hume's opinion, the second condition isn't met since the world isn't much like "a watch or a knitting loom."

Dissimilarities undoubtedly exist. Their significance is less clear. The world isn't much like a steam engine or clock. But steam engines and clocks aren't much like buildings, symphonies, poems, roulette wheels, baseball games, political systems, and well-ordered lives. None of these things are much like the others. Nevertheless, they are all "artifacts," products of intelligent design employing effective means to reasonable ends. The world too exhibits apparent design. Its dissimilarity to a machine may be no more significant than the dissimilarity of machines to poems.

In summary, the analogical version of the design argument is based on a similarity between the world and human artifacts—both exhibit apparent design. In all cases of apparent design where we know whether they have a designer, they *do* have a designer. We hence infer that the world too has a designer. The inference is fairly strong *if* the significance of the dissimilarities between the world and human artifacts isn't much greater than that of the dissimilarities between different kinds of human artifacts.

An Inference to the Best Explanation

The design argument is sometimes construed as an "inference to the best explanation." Suppose I suffer an acute attack of indigestion. Recalling that I ate a plate of cold beef which was left out overnight, that beef often spoils when it isn't refrigerated, and that tainted meat can cause indigestion, I formulate a hypothesis—the beef caused my stomachache. Other hypotheses would also explain the phenomenon (for example, that I am suffering from cancer, or that I am a victim of witchcraft). Nevertheless, if the other hypotheses are less plausible, I am entitled to adopt the "best explanation" and conclude that tainted meat probably caused my indigestion.

We can interpret the design argument in the same way. Apparent design seems to need an explanation. Our experience of human productive activity suggests a hypothesis—the world's apparent design is the product of intelligence. If no other equally good explanatory hypothesis is available, we can legitimately infer that the world probably has a designer.

The strength of these arguments depends on the absence of equally plausible alternative hypotheses. For example, if I exhibit other symptoms of stomach cancer, the hypothesis that my stomach pains are caused by cancer should be taken more seriously. My inference to "Tainted meat caused my indigestion" is weakened because there is a plausible alternative explanation.

Are there plausible alternatives to the designer hypothesis? The two most commonly mentioned are (1) the appearance of design is ultimately due to chance and (2) the appearance of design is caused by processes of inorganic and organic evolution.

According to the "chance hypothesis," the appearance of design is a fortuitous by-product of the interaction of mindless elements and forces. Planets, nebulae, chemical compounds, organisms, and other organized systems are ultimately derived from the behavior of a few simple particles or forces obeying nature's basic laws. These particles, forces, and laws are simply given; that the world contains *these* particles and forces and operates according to *these* laws, rather than others, is a brute fact that has no further explanation. Although the world's basic constituents were the sort needed to produce beauty, life, consciousness, and so on, this was just a lucky chance.

The second hypothesis attributes the appearance of design to evolutionary processes. For example, the emergence of organisms that can think rationally and act morally is explained by biological evolution.

Are these hypotheses as plausible as the designer hypothesis? Do they explain the phenomenon (apparent design) equally well?

The chance hypothesis doesn't really explain apparent design. Rather, it implies that there ultimately *is* no explanation. Such things as life and consciousness may be inevitable given nature's basic particles, laws, and forces, but these particles, laws, and forces aren't themselves inevitable. Why, then, did these laws obtain and these particles and forces occur? According to the chance hypothesis, there *is* no answer. The fact that our world contained the ingredients needed to produce the appearance of design doesn't have an explanation.

While the chance hypothesis is incompatible with the designer hypothesis, the evolutionary hypothesis isn't. The designer may use evolutionary mechanisms to accomplish its purposes. Nor is it clear that the evolutionary hypothesis makes the designer hypothesis superfluous. Beauty and the fact that the world's order is simple enough to be grasped by finite minds don't seem to have a plausible evolutionary explanation. Furthermore, evolutionary processes are *part* of the pattern that most modern versions of the design argument are trying to explain, and one doesn't explain a thing by appealing to part of what needs explaining.[33] Ultimately, then, natural processes, like stellar or biological evolution, either *have* no explanation (and we are back at the chance hypothesis), or they are explained by something that isn't itself part of the pattern of nature—such as a designer.

In short, design arguments are sometimes inferences to the best explanation. Apparent design can be explained by postulating the activity of a powerful and intelligent mind. If alternative explanations are less plausible, one is entitled to conclude that apparent design probably *is* caused by mind.

In modern versions of the design argument, natural processes like stellar or biological evolution and the particles, forces, and laws that are the ultimate constituents of these processes are *part* of the pattern that creates the appearance of design. In these versions, the only alternative to the designer hypothesis may be no explanation at all.

A Probability Argument

We can also interpret the second step as a probability argument. Probability arguments attempt to assess the comparative likelihood of competing hypotheses on the same body of evidence.

We often use probability arguments. Suppose that an apartment has been robbed and we have two suspects—Pound and Eliot. There is a fair amount of circumstantial evidence, *e*, but no eyewitnesses. We must decide between two hypotheses:

P: **Pound committed the theft,** and

E: **Eliot committed the theft.**

Which is more probable on the evidence?

The comparative probability of the two hypotheses is a function of their "prior probabilities" (their probability on the available background evidence). It is also a function of the probability of the evidence if the hypotheses are true (that is, the probability of *e* if *P*, and the probability of *e* if *E*). For example, suppose that (1) the evidence is equally likely on both hypotheses (the probability of *e* on *P* equals the probability of *e* on *E*) but (2) the prior probability of Pound's committing the theft is lower. (Pound has never committed a crime, while Eliot is a convicted thief.) We would conclude that *E* is more probable than *P*. Suppose, on the other hand, that (1) the prior probabilities of the two hypotheses are equal (both suspects have long criminal records) but (2) the evidence is more likely on *P* than on *E*. (Both Pound and Eliot were observed near the scene of the crime and both were carrying burglars' tools, but the stolen goods were found in Pound's car.) We would conclude that *P* is more probable than *E*.

The important point, however, is that a hypothesis with a lower prior probability can be more probable than a hypothesis with a higher prior probability *if* the evidence is much more probable on the first hypothesis than the second. For example, suppose that Pound is a solid citizen who has never been known to act criminally, while Eliot is a convicted thief. The prior probability of *P* is much lower than the prior probability of *E*. But now suppose that only one questionable witness places Eliot near the scene of the crime, while several reliable witnesses observed Pound enter the apartment building with what looked like burglars' tools, and that the stolen goods were found locked in the trunk of his car. The evidence is thus much more probable on *P* than on *E*. We would undoubtedly conclude that in spite of Pound's previously untarnished record, *P* is more probable than *E*.

The relevance of the example is this. We are confronted with apparent design and must choose between two hypotheses:

D: **An intelligent and powerful mind is the cause of apparent design (the "designer hypothesis"),** and

N: **No supernatural reality underlies natural processes (the "naturalistic hypothesis").**[34]

Which is more probable on the design evidence (that is, apparent design)?

The comparative probability of the two hypotheses is a function of their prior probabilities and the probability of the evidence on the hypotheses (that is, the probability of apparent design if there is a designer and the probability of apparent design if supernaturalism is false). The prior probability of *D* may be lower than the prior probability of *N*. Nevertheless, if the probability of apparent design on the designer hypothesis is higher than its probability on the naturalistic hypothesis, *D* may be more probable than *N*.

The important questions, then, are these: (1) How low *is D's* prior probability? (2) Is the probability of apparent design on the designer hypothesis sufficiently high when compared with its probability on the naturalistic hypothesis to offset the designer hypothesis's lower prior probability?

While the prior probability of the designer hypothesis may be lower than the prior probability of the naturalistic hypothesis, it isn't negligible. Religious experience, the fact that God's existence seems logically possible and that His possibility entails His existence, the occurrence of alleged revelations, and other things of this kind give theism a certain probability apart from any support it may receive from the existence of apparent design. Even if the prior probability of *D* is less than one in two, it isn't close to zero.

The probability of apparent design on the designer hypothesis is 1. (*D* entails "Apparent design exists." Hence, if *D* is true, the occurrence of apparent design is certain.) Its probability on the naturalistic hypothesis intuitively seems quite low, although there is no way of proving that this intuition is sound.

Theists sometimes argue that the occurrence of apparent design is analogous to the occurrence of a set or run of improbable events. Suppose I throw a die and a six turns up. Although the probability of a six turning up is only one in six, no explanation is called for. But the situation is different if there are fifty of us, we are each given a different die, and we each throw a six. It is also different if I continue to throw my own die and get a six every time. Sets of improbable occurrences and runs of improbable occurrences need an explanation.

A. C. Ewing (1899–1973) thinks that the occurrence of apparent design is analogous to a *run* of improbable occurrenccs.[35] The occurrence of some goodness, order, or beauty may not require an explanation. However, the pervasiveness of these things and their continued occurrence constitute a run. This run is as improbable as my continuing to throw sixes and requires an explanation. Tennant seems to think that the occurrence of apparent design is analogous to a *set* of improbable occurrences. For example, he calls our attention to the countless things that must occur for life and consciousness to be possible. There hasn't been just *one* lucky chance but countless lucky chances. This set is as improbable as all fifty of us throwing a six, and an explanation is called for.

Neither analogy is entirely apt. For example, occurrences of goodness, order, or beauty aren't causally independent of one another in the way that successive throws of a die are. Arguments like Ewing's and Tennant's should be treated with caution. Ultimately, one must appeal to one's general impression of the comparative likelihood of apparent design on the two hypotheses.

In summary, the third version of the design argument asks us to compare the probability of the designer hypothesis with the probability of its rivals. The prior probability of the designer hypothesis may be lower than the prior probability of its most plausible alternatives. Nevertheless, if the probability of apparent design on the designer hypothesis is high and its probability on the alternatives is low, the designer hypothesis may still be the most probable on the evidence.

Conclusion

The design argument has two steps. One must show that the world exhibits apparent design—that it really is analogous to human artifacts. One must then show that the existence of apparent design justifies an inference to a designer. There are three ways of doing this. One can appeal to the fact that human artifacts have designers and argue by analogy. One can try to show that the designer hypothesis provides the best explanation of apparent design. Finally, one can argue that the designer hypothesis is more probable on the design evidence than its rivals.

Each version of the design argument presents similar problems. Our assessment of design arguments depends on (1) the strength of our impression that the world exhibits apparent design. (Does it really seem like a machine or work of art?) It also depends on (2) how striking the differences between the world and human artifacts seem to us, (3) our sense of the comparative plausibility of alternative explanations, and (4) our intuitive estimate of the prior probabilities of the designer hypothesis and its rivals, and of the probability of the design evidence upon these hypotheses.

Thus, our estimate of the strength of the design argument ultimately rests on our general impressions and intuitions. Rational and informed men and women may therefore reach different verdicts. The theist's judgments ("The world exhibits apparent design," "The probability of apparent design on the naturalistic hypothesis is low," and so on) are reasonable. They may be more reasonable than the conflicting assessments of his or her critics. Nevertheless, the latter's judgments can't be dismissed as irrational or perverse.

Even if the design argument is successful, it shows only that the world is rooted in mind and reflects its purposes. It doesn't show that this mind is omnipotent, omniscient, or perfectly good. The evidence may not even show that there is only one divine mind rather than several cooperating designers. Hence, the design argument doesn't establish God's existence.

Does it *confirm* theism? We should distinguish two alternative conclusions—(1) the design evidence points to power, intelligence, and goodness but *leaves open* whether these attributes are limited and (2) the design evidence points to *limited* power, intelligence, and goodness. If the argument supports the first conclusion, theism is confirmed—for God *is* an intelligent, powerful, and good mind although He is also much more than that. If the argument leads to the second conclusion, it doesn't confirm God's existence. Indeed, it disconfirms it. If a *limited* entity is the source of the world's order, an omniscient, omnipotent, and perfectly good being is not.

Which conclusion is better supported? The evidence doesn't point to limited *power and wisdom.* Infinite power and wisdom aren't *needed* to explain apparent design but seem perfectly consistent with it. On the other hand, philosophers like David Hume and John Stuart Mill (1806–73) think the pattern of events *does* point to limited goodness.[36] If they are right, the evidence supports the second conclusion and God's existence is disconfirmed.

Are they right? Are evil and suffering inconsistent with the existence of an *infinitely good,* powerful, and wise being? We will discuss this important issue in Chapter 3.

APPENDIX: MIRACLES

Design arguments and arguments from miracles have a similar structure. An argument from design has two steps. One first establishes the existence of apparent design and then shows that mind is its cause. An argument from miracles also has two steps. One first argues that some religiously significant event violates a law of nature and then argues that its cause is a supernatural agent.

What makes events religiously significant? Benedict XIV (1675–1758) thought that the point of miracles is to confirm the faith or demonstrate someone's sanctity. More broadly, religiously significant events are those that "contribute significantly towards a holy divine purpose for the world." They can do this by bringing about good or by being a "contribution to or foretaste of the ultimate destiny of the world."[37] Thus, an apparently inexplicable healing is religiously significant because its immediate effects are good and because it foreshadows the Kingdom of God, where pain and disease are unknown.

But miracles in the traditional sense are not only religiously significant. They also violate natural laws.

Some critics think that the notion of a violation of natural laws is incoherent. "An event e violates a law of nature L" entails "L is true, L implies e won't occur, and e occurs." Since this is logically impossible, violations of natural laws are logically impossible. The critic concludes that there can't be counterinstances to natural laws. A counterinstance to a generalization shows that it isn't a true generalization and hence *isn't* a law of nature.

Richard Swinburne (1934–) thinks this is mistaken. Laws of nature can have "nonrepeatable counterinstances."[38]

According to Swinburne, an event like Jesus's resurrection or the parting of the Red Sea (as described in Exodus) is a violation of a natural law L provided that five conditions are satisfied.

1. There is very good evidence for L.

2. L predicts that the event won't occur.

3. The event occurs but is a "nonrepeatable counterinstance to L." That is, similar events won't occur in similar circumstances. Since it is nonrepeatable, the event's occurrence won't affect our assessment of the likelihood of other events of that type. Thus, Christians are no more inclined to believe that other people will rise from the dead after three days than are non-Christians.

4. No plausible modification of L satisfactorily accounts for the event's occurrence. For example, suppose we were to modify "Dead people don't rise from the grave" by adding the clause "except in circumstances empirically similar to those surrounding Jesus's death." Our modified law would be false. Other people in the same circumstances stay dead.

5. L predicts accurately in all other instances.

Swinburne maintains that the conjunction of 1 through 5 is consistent. Since "e violates a law of nature L" is equivalent to "e satisfies conditions 1 through 5," violations of natural laws are logically possible.

The first step in an argument from miracles, then, is to show that some event is religiously significant and violates a law of nature (satisfies Swinburne's five conditions). The second step is to show that the only plausible explanation of the event is the activity of a supernatural agent.

As in the case of the design argument, the second step of the argument from miracles can be formulated as an analogical inference, as an inference to the best explanation, or as a probability argument.

For example, one can argue that religiously significant violations of natural laws are analogous to the sorts of things an intelligent human agent might do (cure a disease, for example, or attest to the truth of a doctrine). One then infers that their cause is also an intelligent agent.

Alternatively, one can argue that divine activity provides the best explanation for miraculous events. Since natural laws are violated, natural explanations aren't available. Hence, we must either explain the event by postulating the activity of a supernatural agent or attribute it to chance. The latter, however, is implausible in the case of many traditional miracles—Jesus's resurrection, for example, or the parting of the Red Sea.

One can also interpret the second step probabilistically. The rival hypotheses would include

D* **A supernatural agent causes religiously significant violations of natural laws (the "supernaturalistic hypothesis"),** and

N* **Every event—including any violation of natural laws—either is produced by natural causes or has no cause (the "naturalistic hypothesis").**

While the prior probability of the supernaturalistic hypothesis may be lower than the prior probability of the naturalistic hypothesis, the probability of a religiously significant violation of natural laws is much higher on the first hypothesis. Hence, the supernaturalistic hypothesis is more probable than the naturalistic hypothesis on the evidence provided by religiously significant violations of natural laws.

The argument from miracles differs from the argument from design in one important respect. The second step of the design argument is more controversial than the first. Many critics of the argument concede that the world exhibits apparent design although they deny that this justifies postulating a designer. By contrast, the first step of the argument from miracles is more controversial than the second. Critics may concede that *if* religiously significant violations of natural laws occur, they are best explained by the activity of supernatural agents. The alternatives are to admit that there isn't any explanation or to insist that there is a natural explanation although we have no idea of what it would be like. Neither alternative is plausible. (Recall that if an event violates a law of nature L, we have no idea of how to modify L so that it satisfactorily accounts for the event.) What critics usually deny is that we have good reasons for thinking that religiously significant violations of natural law *occur*.

David Hume is typical. Few of us have witnessed a miracle. Our evidence for their occurrence is human testimony, and testimony isn't always reliable. In evaluating it, we must consider the inherent probability of the reported occurrence. Generally speaking, the more improbable an event, the more reason to distrust reports of its occurrence.[39] Many traditional miracles are very improbable. For example, the resurrection of a dead man runs counter to the accumulated experience of humankind. We must therefore weigh the event's improbability against the improbability of the witnesses being mistaken or lying. Their testimony should be accepted only if the improbability of the latter is greater than the improbability of the former.

No testimony is sufficient to establish a miracle, unless the testimony be of such a kind, that its falsehood would be more miraculous, than the fact, which it endeavors to establish. . . . When anyone tells me, that he saw a dead man restored to life, I immediately consider with myself, whether it be more probable, that this person should either deceive or be deceived, or that the fact, which he relates, should really have happened. I weigh the one miracle against the other; and according to the superiority, which I discover, I pronounce my decision, and always reject the greater miracle. If the falsehood of his testimony would be more miraculous, than the miraculous event which he relates; then, and not till then, can he pretend to command my belief or opinion."[40]

Hume thought that the falsehood of the witnesses' testimony is invariably less "miraculous." In his opinion, the improbability of violations of natural laws always outweighs the probability that reports of their occurrence are trustworthy.

But Hume implicitly assumed that theism is false. If traditional theism is true, miracles aren't unlikely. Whether violations of natural laws are inconsistent with the texture of reality depends upon its nature. If the story of reality is only a story of "atoms, and time and space and economics and politics" (that is, if naturalism is true), miracles are out of place. Their occurrence would be totally anomalous, unconnected with the rest of reality, and inconsistent with our knowledge of it. If, however, the story of reality is a story of death and rebirth, salvation and damnation, miracles probably aren't out of place. Events like Jesus's resurrection or the parting of the Red Sea wouldn't "threaten the structure of the world but reveal it."[41]

In short, one's assessment of the inherent probability of miracles should be guided by one's convictions about the nature of reality. If naturalism is true, the inherent probability of miracles is very low. Miracle reports probably aren't credible enough to offset this low probability. If theism is true, the inherent probability of miracles is higher. In some cases, testimony may be sufficiently credible to justify believing in their occurrence.

In summary, arguments from miracles have the same structure as arguments from design. In each case, one first establishes the existence of an anomalous fact (apparent design or religiously significant violations of natural laws) and then tries to show that it should be explained by the activity of an intelligent agent.

The second step of design arguments is more controversial than the first. In an argument from miracles, however, the major problem is the first step. One's assessment of its strength depends upon one's general picture of reality. If theism is true, some miracle stories may be acceptable. If one doesn't have independent reasons for believing theism, reports of alleged miracles should probably be discounted. The case for the occurrence of religiously significant violations of natural laws thus *depends* on the truth of theism. Therefore, one can't appeal to miraculous occurrences to *establish* theism. Nevertheless, miracle reports by apparently trustworthy witnesses may *confirm* it, since they are the sort of thing one might expect if theism were true.

Notes

1. Immanuel Kant, *Critique of Pure Reason,* trans. Norman Kemp Smith (London: Macmillan, 1956), 507.

2. Charles Hartshorne, *Anselm's Discovery* (LaSalle, Ill.: Open Court, 1965), 3.

3. Nor is the epistemic possibility of "God exists" conclusive. A proposition is epistemically possible if we don't know that it is false. Some epistemically possible propositions, however, are logically impossible. For example, some mathematical and logical propositions are such that no one knows whether they are true. Both they and their denials are thus epistemically possible. Suppose p is one of these propositions. If p is true, it is necessarily true and so not-p is logically impossible. If p is false, however, it is necessarily false and hence logically impossible. Thus, while both p and not-p are epistemically possible, either p or not-p is logically impossible. Hence, at least one epistemically possible proposition is logically impossible.

4. The point is not merely that the impossibility of "God exists" isn't obvious to us but that its possibility *is* (or seems) obvious to us. The impossibility of some complex mathematical or logical formula may not be obvious to us, but its possibility isn't obvious to us either. By contrast, the logical possibility of propositions like "Unicorns exist" appears obvious on their face. "God exists" seems more like the latter than the former. (Cf. Clement Dore, *Theism,* Dordrecht: D. Reidel, 1984, 72–74.)

5. Henry More, *Antidote Against Atheism,* vol. 1 of *A Collection of Several Philosophical Writings* (New York: Garland, 1978), appendix, chapter V.

6. For an argument of this type, see Richard Swinburne, *The Existence of God* (Oxford: Oxford University Press, 1979), 97f. and James Ross, *Philosophical Theology* (Indianapolis: Bobbs-Merrill, 1969), 228–34.

7. For an argument of this type, see George H. Joyce, *Principles of Natural Theology* (London: Longmans, Green, 1923), 285.

8. Henry More may have been the first to see this. See *Antidote Against Atheism,* book I, chapter VII.

9. Dore, *Theism,* 169. Unlike the idea of (for example) a perfect island, the idea of a maximally perfect being isn't artificially constructed by arbitrarily conjoining unconnected ideas (such as the idea of necessary existence and the idea of an island possessing every feature that could be desired in an island).

10. A pragmatic argument is also possible. (See the discussion of William James in Chapter 6.) "Either (1) God is possible or (2) God isn't possible" is a forced option. (The alternatives are exhaustive.) The option is also momentous. If the ontological argument is valid, believing the first alternative commits me to theism and the way of life it entails. The second alternative, on the other hand, forecloses a way of life that countless thousands have found deeply meaningful. Finally, the option is live; I have some tendency to believe each of the alternatives. (I have a strong tendency to believe that God's existence is possible, but I also have some tendency to believe that God doesn't exist. Now if the ontological argument is valid, God's nonexistence entails His impossibility. Once I recognize this, I acquire some tendency to believe that His existence isn't possible.) Suppose, then, that the issue is intellectually undecidable. My passional nature, which demands hope and meaning, should lead me to believe (1) rather than (2). Note that this argument won't support belief in the possibility of near gods, perfect devils, and so on. For once I realize that the possibility of these entities entails their existence, I have no tendency to believe in their possibility; hypotheses to the effect that these beings are possible are no longer live for me.

11. More accurately, we have a reason for accepting the argument's conclusion *if* our confidence in its premises isn't based on our belief in the conclusion. If our only reason for thinking God is possible is that He exists, then we can't use the argument to *establish* His existence without begging the question.

12. Though doing so has a cost. Rejecting the argument's conclusion commits one to rejecting one or more of its premises—premises that, when considered apart form the conclusion, have a fair amount of independent plausibility.

13. Scientific evidence that the universe had a beginning has sparked renewed interest in this version of the cosmological argument. For an excellent history of this version, and an interesting defense of its central contentions, see William Craig, *The Kalam Cosmological Argument* (New York: Barnes and Noble, 1979).

14. Thomas Aquinas, *The Summa Theologica*, in *Introduction to Saint Thomas Aquinas*, ed. and trans. Anton C. Pegis (New York: The Modern Library, 1948), part I, question 2, article 3, pp. 25–26.

15. For excellent discussions of this sort of cosmological argument, see William Craig, *The Cosmological Argument from Plato to Leibniz* (New York: Barnes and Noble, 1980), Anthony Kenny, *The Five Ways* (New York: Schocken Books, 1969), and Patterson Brown, "Infinite Causal Regression," *The Philosophical Review* LXXV (1966): 510–25.

16. Samuel Clarke, *A Demonstration of the Being and Attributes of God* (London: Printed by W. Botham for James Knapton, 1705), 25–27. Reprinted by Friedrich Frommann Verlag, Stuttgart, 1964.

17. Hick makes this distinction in "God as Necessary Being," *The Journal of Philosophy* LVII (1960): 725–34. For its application to the cosmological argument, see Hick's *Philosophy of Religion* (Englewood Cliffs, N.J.: Prentice-Hall, 1963), 20–23.

18. Might not the first member's existence be caused by a dependently necessary being? It might, but (as we saw in the section on the ontological argument) dependently necessary beings ultimately depend for their existence on self-existent beings.

19. Paul Edwards, "The Cosmological Argument," in *Philosophy of Religion: Selected Readings,* ed. William Rowe and William Wainwright (New York: Harcourt Brace Jovanovich, 1973), 143.

20. Cf. William Rowe, *The Cosmological Argument* (Princeton, N.J.: Princeton University Press, 1976), chapter III.

21. For a fuller discussion of contra-causal freedom, see the section on the free will defense in Chapter 3.

22. Charles Hartshorne, *Anselm's Discovery*, 70–71.

23. David Hume, *Dialogues Concerning Natural Religion* (Indianapolis: Bobbs-Merrill, 1970), part IX.

24. Many undoubtedly don't see the necessity of (for example) PSR[4]. However, it isn't clear that it intuitively seems to them that PSR[4] *isn't* necessary. They may have no clear intuitions either way. A failure to see PSR[4]'s necessity doesn't carry much weight. A claim to intuit its non-necessity would carry more weight though it, too, would be inconclusive.

25. William Paley, *Natural Theology: Selections* (Indianapolis: Bobbs-Merrill, c1963), 13, 8–9

26. David Hume, *Dialogues*, 218. (My emphasis.)

27. F. R. Tennant, *Philosophical Theology*, vol. II (Cambridge: Cambridge University Press, 1930), chapter IV. The quotations in the next few paragraphs are from this chapter.

28. Kenneth Nelson, "Evolution and the Argument from Design," *Religious Studies* 14 (1978): 423–42.

29. Cf. Thomas V. Morris, "The God of Abraham, Isaac, and Anselm," *Faith and Philosophy* 1 (1984): 179.

30. Quoted in Frederick J. Powicke, *The Cambridge Platonists: A Study* (Westport, Conn.: Greenwood Press, 1970), 185–86.

31. William Paley, *Natural Theology*, 37.

32. David Hume, *Dialogues*, 170f.

33. More accurately: Evolutionary processes are *constituents* of a pattern that exhibits beauty, order, and intelligibility, and *causes* of the emergence of life, consciousness, and moral agency. Evolutionary processes don't explain why there is a world whose patterns exhibit those properties, and whose mechanisms lead to those effects, rather than a world that doesn't display those properties or contain mechanisms leading to those effects.

34. This is oversimplified since there are other hypotheses to consider (for example, that there are several designers). Nevertheless, the naturalistic hypothesis is the designer hypothesis's most important rival.

35. A. C. Ewing, "Two 'Proofs' of God's Existence," *Religious Studies* 1 (1965): 29–45.

36. John Stuart Mill, *Theism* (New York: Liberal Arts Press, c1957), Part II: "Attributes."

37. Richard Swinburne, *The Concept of Miracle* (New York: St. Martin's Press, 1970), 8.

38. Ibid., chapter 3.

39. Or, more accurately, the more improbable an event *of that kind*, the more reason to distrust reports of its occurrence. It is very improbable that 26,507 is the winning lottery number. But we don't (and shouldn't) mistrust newspaper reports that that *was* the winning number since the occurrence of events of that kind isn't improbable. (It was virtually certain that some ticket would win.)

40. David Hume, *An Inquiry Concerning Human Understanding* (Indianapolis: Hackett, 1977), 77. Hume's arguments are criticized by C. S. Lewis, *Miracles* (New York: Macmillan, 1947) and Swinburne, *Concept of Miracle.*

41. Lewis, *Miracles*, 102. The second quotation is from J. P. M. Sweet, "The Theory of Miracles in the Wisdom of Solomon," in *Miracles*, ed. C. F. D. Moule (London: A. R. Mowbray, 1965), 121.

For Further Reading

For two important versions of the ontological argument see Anselm, *Proslogion* ii–iv and *On Behalf of the Fool* by Guanilo with Anselm's *Reply* (in *Basic Writings*, trans. S. N. Deane [La Salle, Ill.: Open Court, 1962]), and Rene Descartes, *Meditations* V *(Discourse on Method and Meditations on First Philosophy*, trans. Donald A. Cress [Indianapolis: Hackett, c1980]). Immanuel Kant's famous objection to the argument (*Critique of Pure Reason*, trans. Norman Kemp Smith [London: Macmillan, 1956], 500–506) is criticized by Alvin Plantinga in "Kant's Objections to the Ontological Argument," *The Journal of Philosophy* 63 (1966): 537–46. For an important recent defense of the ontological argument see Alvin Plantinga, *God, Freedom, and Evil* (New York: Harper and Row, 1974), 85–112.

For further discussion of the cosmological argument, see William L. Craig, *The Cosmological Argument from Plato to Leibniz* (New York: Barnes and Noble, 1980). Craig's *The Kalam Cosmological Argument* (New York: Barnes and Noble, 1980) defends the claim that the world has a beginning and so must have a cause. Anthony Kenny, *The Five Ways* (New York: Schocken Books, 1969) discusses Aquinas's cosmological arguments. The best treatment of the modern cosmological argument is William Rowe, *The Cosmological Argument* (Princeton, N.J.: Princeton University Press, 1976). Standard criticisms of the cosmological argument are found in David Hume, *Dialogues Concerning Natural Religion* (Indianapolis: Bobbs-Merrill, 1970), part IX, and Paul Edwards, "The Cosmological Argument," in *The Cosmological Arguments*, ed. W. R. Burrill (Garden City, N.Y.: Doubleday, Anchor Books, 1967).

The best traditional versions of the design argument are William Paley, *Natural Theology: Selections* (Indianapolis: Bobbs-Merrill, c1963) and F. R. Tennant, *Philosophical Theology*, vol. 2 (Cambridge: Cambridge University Press, 1930). The most influential critique of the argument is David Hume, *Dialogues Concerning Natural Religion*. For an excellent discussion of Hume's arguments, consult the editor's comments in Nelson Pike's edition of *Dialogues* (Indianapolis: Bobbs-Merrill, 1970). Peter Van Inwagen, *Metaphysics* (Boulder, Colo.: Westview Press, 1993), chapters 7 and 8, is a good recent critique of design arguments.

Moral arguments attempt to infer God's existence from things like conscience and the objectivity of moral value. Interesting versions of this argument are found in Immanuel Kant, *Critique of Practical Reason*, trans. Lewis W. Beck (New York: Liberal Arts Press, 1956), part II, chapter 2; A. E. Taylor, *The Faith of a Moralist* (London: Macmillan, 1930); H. P. Owen, *The Moral Argument for Christian Theism* (London: George Allen and Unwin, 1965); and George Mavrodes, "Religion and the Queerness of Morality," in *Rationality, Religious Belief, and Moral Commitment*, ed. Robert Audi and William J. Wainwright

(Ithaca, N.Y.: Cornell University Press, 1986). The moral argument is criticized by William G. Maclagen, *The Theological Frontier of Ethics* (London: George Allen and Unwin, 1961), chapters III and VI, and by J. L. Mackie, *The Miracle of Theism* (Oxford: Clarendon Press, 1982), chapter 6.

Richard Swinburne, *The Existence of God* (Oxford: Clarendon Press, 1979) develops an important probability proof for God's existence that combines features of several traditional arguments. For a highly critical discussion of Swinburne's argument, see J. L. Mackie, *The Miracle of Theism*, 95–101. William L. Craig and Quentin Smith, *Theism, Atheism, and Big Bang Cosmology* (New York: Oxford University Press, 1993) debate the theistic implications of recent scientific cosmology. A less technical treatment of scientific and other evidence for God's existence is found in R. Douglas Geivett, *Evil and the Evidence for God* (Philadelphia: Temple University Press, 1993), chapters 6 and 7.

The most effective attack on the doctrine of miracles is still David Hume, "Of Miracles," section X of *An Inquiry Concerning Human Understanding* (New York: Hackett, 1977). The best recent defenses of the doctrine are C. S. Lewis, *Miracles* (New York: Macmillan, 1947) and Richard Swinburne, *The Concept of Miracle* (New York: St. Martin's Press, 1970).

CHAPTER 3

The Problem of Evil

THE PRINCIPAL DIFFICULTY confronting the theist is the existence of natural and moral evil. Moral evils are the bad actions of moral agents and the consequences of those actions. Natural evils are caused by other factors. Genocide and its consequences are an example of the first. Cancer is an example of the second. Both types of evil occur, and occur in great quantity.

Is their occurrence consistent with the existence of an infinitely powerful, wise, and good God? David Hume thought not. If God is omnipotent and omniscient, how can we

> assert the moral attributes of the Deity, his justice, benevolence, mercy, and rectitude, to be of the same nature with these virtues in human creatures? His power we allow infinite: whatever he wills is executed: but neither man nor any other animal is happy: therefore he does not will their happiness. His wisdom is infinite: he is never mistaken in choosing the means to any end: but the course of nature tends not to human or animal felicity: therefore it is not established for that purpose. Through the whole compass of human knowledge, there are no inferences more certain and infallible than these. In what respects, then, do his benevolence and mercy resemble the benevolence and mercy of men?
>
> Epicurus's old questions are yet unanswered. Is he willing to prevent evil, but not able? then is he impotent. Is he able, but not willing? then is he malevolent. Is he both able and willing? whence then is evil?[1]

In short, the existence of God and the existence of evil appear incompatible. Since evil clearly exists, belief in God's existence seems irrational. This is a serious problem and, unlike other difficulties, troubles ordinary as well as sophisticated theists. While puzzles about omnipotence or omniscience seldom disturb a believer's faith, an experience of the world's evils often does so.

The seriousness of the problem is indicated by the fact that some theists have modified their position in the face of it. For example, theists have occasionally contended that human standards of moral right and wrong don't apply to God and that, therefore, He shouldn't be regarded as morally good or as morally evil. Henry Mansel (1820–71), for instance, argued that

> It is a fact, which experience forces upon us . . . that the representation of God after the model of the highest human morality which we are capable of conceiv-

70

ing is not sufficient to account for all the phenomena exhibited by the course of his natural Providence. The infliction of physical suffering, the permission of moral evil, the adversity of the good, the prosperity of the wicked, . . . are facts which no doubt are reconcilable, we know not how, with the infinite goodness of God, but which certainly are not to be explained on the supposition that its sole and sufficient type is to be found in the finite goodness of man.[2]

If Mansel is right, the problem is solved. For if God *isn't* morally good, evil doesn't count against His existence.

But this resolution of the problem is unsatisfactory for two reasons. In the first place, a belief in God's moral goodness is deeply embedded in the major theistic traditions. In the second place, the resolution appears to be incompatible with the nature of theism. Moral standards don't apply to everything. They don't apply to stones, or to the Mona Lisa, or to a transcendent state like Nirvāna. The Mona Lisa, for example, is neither morally good nor morally bad though it may be excellent in other respects. But stones, pictures, and Nirvāna aren't persons. Persons are moral agents, and moral agents are subject to moral appraisal. Since theists believe that the underlying principle of reality is personal, they are committed to the claim that God is subject to moral standards.

While few theists are willing to abandon the claim that God is morally good, some are prepared to qualify the doctrines of omnipotence and omniscience. For example, Peter Bertocci (1910–89) thinks that "out of respect for what seem the facts of human experience, it seems necessary to modify our conceptions of God. If we deny God's goodness, we are in fact denying that the cosmic Mind is God, for goodness is supreme in qualifying a being as God. If we limit God's reason and knowledge, we cannot account for the order of nature and man as we know it. The most reasonable suggestion is to limit God's power."[3]

Is limited power or knowledge compatible with the appropriateness of theistic attitudes and practices? The answer to this question isn't entirely clear but appears to depend on two considerations—first, whether the limitations on God's knowledge and power are necessary or contingent and, second, the nature and extent of the limitations.

Theistic worship or adoration involves total devotion and unconditional commitment. These attitudes are *clearly* appropriate only when directed toward a maximally perfect being. If the limitations on power and knowledge are contingent, however, it is possible for a being to be free from them. But if a being can be free from them, then a God who is subject to these limitations is surpassed by a possible being whose power and knowledge are unlimited. He isn't therefore maximally perfect. If, on the other hand, the limitations are necessary, any possible being is subject to them. If any possible being is subject to them, the fact that God is limited in those ways doesn't imply that a being can be greater than God. One might argue, for example, that it is logically impossible to know future contingents or to determine how moral agents will freely behave if they are created. If this is true, then even though God's knowledge of and control over the future are limited, these powers couldn't be greater than they are.

The nature and extent of these limitations are also important. If a being's power or knowledge is severely limited, one can't appropriately worship or adore it even if its limitations are necessary. The belief that God is weak or impotent or stupid, for example, is clearly incompatible with the legitimacy of worship, devotion, and commitment. It is less clear that God's knowledge and power must be unlimited if theistic attitudes are to be appropriate. At precisely what point limitations in power and knowledge would make these attitudes unjustified is uncertain. Nevertheless, God's power and knowledge can't be qualified beyond a certain point without abandoning theism.

If that is the case, then the problem of evil can't be easily resolved by limiting God's power or knowledge. Evil not only exists, but also exists in enormous quantities. The theist who wishes to respond to the problem of evil by limiting God's power or knowledge is thus faced with a dilemma. If theists severely limit God's power or knowledge, they make God an inappropriate object of theistic attitudes and practices. If they do not, they must reconcile the existence of a good being whose power and knowledge vastly surpass those of any other creature with the enormous amount of evil that exists. Limiting God's power and knowledge may mitigate the problem of evil but doesn't resolve it.

Our discussion can be summarized as follows. The problem of evil is created by the existence of evil, the belief that God is morally good, and the belief that God's power and knowledge vastly surpass that of any other being. One can't resolve the problem by abandoning one of these beliefs without abandoning theism. If God is not morally good, then either God isn't a person or He is a morally imperfect person who is unworthy of worship. If God's power and knowledge aren't vastly superior to that of any other being, one can't plausibly regard God as a perfect being, and total devotion and unconditional commitment are inappropriate.

The remainder of the chapter will examine ways in which theists attempt to resolve the problem while retaining their belief in the existence of a God with unlimited power, knowledge, and goodness. The first section discusses the compatibility of God's existence and the existence of evil. The second explores the possibility that evil is a necessary condition of certain great goods. The third examines the claim that evil isn't attributable to God but is a consequence of human freedom. The fourth considers the contention that God can't be blamed for creating a world that is less perfect than other worlds He might have created. The fifth looks at the problem of "gratuitous evil"—horrendous evils that are apparently pointless.

ARE GOD AND EVIL COMPATIBLE?

The claim that one state of affairs is incompatible with another is ambiguous. It may mean that the states of affairs are logically incompatible (that is, that it is logically impossible that both of them obtain). Or it may mean that the existence of one would constitute overwhelming evidence for the nonexistence of the other. John's being a bachelor and John's being married are incompatible in the first sense. John's moral innocence and his (apparent) mistreatment of his family and friends are incompatible in the second sense. (But they are not incompatible in the first. It is logically possible that his apparent mistreatment is *only* apparent; that his unorthodox conduct is really intended for their good.) We will first examine the contention that God and evil are logically incompatible and then discuss the claim that the existence of evil constitutes overwhelming evidence for the nonexistence of God.

Critics of theism have often claimed that the existence of God and the existence of evil are incompatible in the first sense.[4] They appear to be mistaken.

Of course even these critics would concede that the propositions

1. God (an omnipotent, omniscient, and morally perfect being) exists, and

2. Evil exists

are not obviously incompatible in the way in which "John is a bachelor" and "John is married" or "Napoleon was from Corsica" and "Napoleon was not from Corsica" are obviously incompatible. Nevertheless, propositions whose logical inconsistency isn't obvious can sometimes be shown to be logically incompatible. The most effective way of doing this is by deducing a logically impossible statement from the conjunction of these propositions and certain necessary truths.[5]

Are there any necessary truths that when conjoined with "God exists" and "Evil exists" entail a logically impossible statement? It isn't clear that there are. The following statement seems to be necessarily true:

3. If a being is good and is both cognizant of an evil and able to eliminate or prevent it, then the being will eliminate or prevent it unless he or she has a morally sufficient reason for not doing so.

But 1, 2, and 3 don't entail a logically impossible proposition. The conjunction of 1 and 3 does logically imply that God has a morally sufficient reason for not eliminating or preventing any evils that exist. The latter, however, is compatible with 2—namely, that evil exists. Perhaps God does have a morally sufficient reason for permitting existing evils. Theists would be inconsistent only if they were to hold that

4. Evils exist that God has no morally sufficient reason for permitting,

and theists believe nothing of the kind.

This result can be generalized. The only necessary truths that seem at all likely to yield a logically impossible statement when conjoined with 1 and 2 are propositions like 3 (that is, necessary truths about what good beings would do). Propositions of this kind may entail that a morally perfect, omnipotent, and omniscient being wouldn't permit evils of a certain sort (for example, evils that it has no morally sufficient reason for permitting), but they do not logically imply that there will be no evil at all. If they don't, they can't be used to show that the conjunction of "God exists" and "Evil exists" is logically impossible.

The importance of this result shouldn't be exaggerated. Even if "God exists" and "Evil exists" are logically compatible, they may not be compatible in the second sense. That is, the existence of evil may constitute overwhelming evidence for believing that God doesn't exist. Even if the logical problem of evil is resolved, the evidential problem of evil is not.

Why should one suppose that the existence of evil provides good reasons for believing that God doesn't exist? The resolution of the logical problem of evil suggests the answer. "God exists" and "Evil exists" are logically compatible because the existence of God doesn't necessitate the nonexistence of evil but only the nonexistence of evils of certain sorts, presumably evils that God has no morally sufficient reason for permitting. But if it does necessitate the latter, and if some existing evils are of that kind, then God doesn't exist. The evidential problem of evil is created by the fact that there *do* appear to be evils of that kind.

The critic argues that the theists' inability to provide morally sufficient reasons for God's permission of evil is a good reason for thinking that some existing evils are such that God has no morally sufficient reason for permitting them. If the critic's attack is to be persuasive, he or she must therefore do two things. The critic must give reasons for thinking that if God existed and had morally sufficient reasons for permitting evil, the theist would know them. The critic must also show that the reasons that theists offer are insufficient to justify the permission of evil. Theists, on the other hand, must either provide some indication of what God's reasons would be like or show why the demand that they provide them is unreasonable.

Whether God's reasons for permitting evil would be accessible to us will be examined in the final section of this chapter. We shall see that even if God exists and has morally sufficient reasons for permitting an evil, the theist may not know them. It may therefore be unfair to demand that the theist provide such reasons. But the force of this point shouldn't be exaggerated. We are aware of the existence of countless goods and evils, and we have *some* understanding of goods and evils in general and of the connections between them. We *know*, for example, the horror of human cruelty and the evil of suffering, and it is as clear as such a thing could be that in some cases a creature's suffering isn't a necessary condition of any good it will enjoy in this life. Although it may be unfair for the critic to demand that the theist provide a complete or full account of God's reasons for permitting evils, it isn't unreasonable to ask the theist to provide some account of what God's reasons might be like.

We have argued that critics haven't shown that the existence of evil is logically incompatible with God's existence. Nevertheless, the existence of evil is a good reason for believing in God's nonexistence provided that (1) if God did exist we would know why He permits evil and (2) we do not know why He does so. While our knowledge of God's plan would probably be imperfect, it isn't clear that His purposes would be totally opaque to us. Theists should therefore be able to provide us with some idea of what God's reasons for permitting evils might be like. The next section examines some attempts to do this.

THE GREATER GOODS DEFENSE

Among the more popular accounts of God's reasons for permitting evil are versions of the "greater goods defense." For example, Jonathan Edwards (1703–58) claims that when God permits sin, "it is for the sake of the good of which it will be an occasion . . . he does restrain it when the good is not in view." God may "suffer that which is unharmonious in itself," but He does so "for the promotion of the harmony" of the whole.[6]

Greater goods defenses attempt to show that God's creation or permission of evil is necessary to secure some great good. This defense attempts to show (roughly) that (1) evil or its permission is logically necessary to some good, that (2) this good outweighs the evil, and that (3) there are no alternative goods not involving those evils that would have been better. The first condition reflects the assumption that God is only subject to logical constraints and is therefore unable to bring about a good without bringing about or permitting an evil only when the evil or its permission is a logically necessary condition of the good. The second and third conditions are designed to ensure that the state of affairs that includes both the good and the evil will be better than any other state of affairs that God might have produced in its place. Suppose that these conditions are met by human suffering. We then have an answer to the question "Why does God permit human suffering?" By permitting it, God brings about more good than if He were to do something else.

Are utilitarian calculations of this sort somehow unfitting? Jonathan Edwards argued that even though "Permit evil that good may come" is an inappropriate maxim for human beings, it *is* appropriate for God. Human beings are deficient in wisdom and goodness. They are liable to misjudge the consequences of their actions and to use the maxim as an excuse for acting in their own self-interest. It is therefore undesirable for human beings to act upon it. This isn't true of God. God's wisdom is infinite and His goodness is perfect. It would therefore be better for God to act on this maxim than on any other.[7]

In the remainder of this section we will examine two types of good that have been thought to entail evil or its permission and to be sufficiently valuable to be worth having at that price—moral good and the world's order and constancy.

Moral Good, Natural Order, and the Necessity of Evil

If the greater goods defense is to be plausible, the theist must show that the goods in question really do entail evils or their permission. The following two subsections argue that whether the goods in question do so depends upon how they are specified.

Moral Good and the Necessity of Evil

Theists sometimes contend that moral goods like courage, compassion, fortitude, forgiveness, and forbearance logically presuppose the existence of evil. For example, Origen (c. 185–255) argued that "virtue, if unopposed, would not shine out nor become more glorious by probation. Virtue is not virtue if it be untested and unexamined." Without evil, "there would be no crown of victory in store for him who rightly struggled."[8] Some moral goods are *responses* to evils and hence couldn't exist without them.

In order to simplify our discussion, we will concentrate on the contention that compassion necessitates evil. The truth of this claim depends upon whether one is speaking of the virtue of compassion, of compassionate responses in general, or of the compassionate responses of people who are fully informed of the relevant facts. The claim that compassion entails evil is clearly true only when compassion is used in the third sense. Why is this the case?

The *virtue* of compassion must be distinguished from the morally good responses to misfortune and suffering that express it. The latter are actions, feelings, or emotions. The former is a disposition or habit. Even if compassionate responses to suffering or misfortune entail the existence of evils to which they are responses, the virtue of compassion does not. A habit or disposition is simply a *readiness* to respond in a certain way *if* and when the appropriate occasions arise. Without suffering and misfortune, there would be no situations in which it would be appropriate for a person to respond compassionately. Nevertheless, it might be true that he or she *would* have responded compassionately if the world *had* contained those evils. Since a person could possess a compassionate disposition even if the world was devoid of suffering and misfortune, the virtue of compassion doesn't entail the evils in question.[9]

Nor do compassionate responses entail the existence of evil. One can compassionately respond to what one *mistakenly* believes to be another's misfortune. Suppose that having been falsely told that a friend's child was killed in an accident, I attempt to console him. My response is genuinely compassionate, but its object is an apparent evil, not a real one.[10]

Theists are on firmer ground if they specify the moral good as the compassionate responses of men and women who are fully informed of the nature of the situations in which they find themselves. This good entails suffering or misfortune. It is necessarily true that if a person responds compassionately to another creature, he or she believes that it is in distress. It is also necessarily true that if the belief is correct, then the creature *is* in distress. It follows that it is necessarily true that if a person responds compassionately to another creature and is fully informed of its situation, then the creature is in distress.

Thus, compassionate responses by persons who are fully informed of the relevant facts logically require evil. The same may be true of courageous responses, acts of forgiveness, and displays of fortitude. There are other types of virtuous responses by persons who are fully informed of the relevant facts that do not entail the existence of evil. For example, speaking the truth, keeping a promise, or a courteous response are not normally responses to existing evils. It isn't true, then, that there could be no intelligent and informed virtuous responses without evil. Nevertheless, if there was no evil, the world couldn't contain virtuous responses *of a certain type*—namely, intelligent and informed responses that consist of alleviating, resisting, and overcoming evil.

A world without evil might not be a world without virtue but it would be a world without enlightened and informed acts of forgiveness, compassion, courage, fortitude, and so on.

Some theists claim that moral growth and development also require the existence of evil. For example, John Keats (1795–1821) thought this world might be "a vale of soul-making."

> How are souls to be made? . . . How, but by the medium of a world like this? . . . I can scarcely express what I but dimly perceive . . . [but] I will put it in the most homely form possible—I will call the world a school instituted for the purpose of teaching little children to read—I will call the human heart the horn book used in that school—and I will call the child able to read, the soul made from that school and its horn book. Do you not see how necessary a world of pains and troubles is to school an intelligence and make it a soul? A place where the heart must feel and suffer in a thousand diverse ways![11]

"Moral growth and development entail evil" is also ambiguous. The theist may be referring to the moral growth and development of individuals or to the moral growth and development of the human race. The ambiguity is important because two different goods appear to be at stake. In the first case, what the theist has in mind is a process through which individuals grow in righteousness or sanctity by struggling with their own weaknesses and difficulties and by learning how to deal with the evil around them. For example, a timid person may acquire courage by coming to terms with his or her fears and resolutely facing dangers. This sort of development can't plausibly be ascribed to the human race. We are neither more righteous nor more holy than men and women of the past. The most that could be claimed is that, as humanity matures, its conscience becomes more sensitive, its loyalties less narrow, its moral vision more comprehensive. Even this is uncertain. We are more sensitive than our forebears to evils like slavery and torture but may be less sensitive to sexual irresponsibility and disloyalty. In any case, the good that is involved in the moral development of the human race (moral knowledge or insight) is different from the good that is involved in the moral development of individuals (righteousness or sanctity).

Do these goods necessitate evils? They clearly do, *if* the goods are specified in a certain way—if righteousness or sanctity is specified as a righteousness or sanctity acquired by successfully struggling with evil, or if moral knowledge is specified as a moral knowledge partly acquired through our experience of evil. But other types of righteousness or sanctity and other types of moral knowledge don't logically require the existence of evil. God, for example, would have been perfectly good and wise even if no evil had existed. Furthermore, God could have created beings who were good by nature and therefore didn't need to acquire their goodness by struggling with evil. He could also have endowed the human race from its beginning with perfect moral insight.

Our discussion suggests the following conclusion. Some moral goods entail evils and others do not. Those that do are moral goods that involve an intelligent and informed response to real evils—goods like intelligent and informed acts of compassion or forgiveness, a moral character gained by successfully struggling with temptation, weakness, and suffering, and moral insight acquired as a result of humanity's reflection on its experience of good and evil.

Natural Order and the Necessity of Evil

Some theists think that natural evil is a necessary consequence of the interaction of minds and bodies in a world governed by natural laws. They believe natural order and regularity is good, however, because it is logically necessary for human life and moral activity. For example, C. S. Lewis (1898–1963) maintains that a common material world, governed by laws, is necessary for human society and human freedom.

> Society . . . implies a common field or "world" in which its members meet. . . . But if matter is to serve as a neutral field it must have a fixed nature of its own. . . . Again, if matter has a fixed nature and obeys constant laws, not all states of matter will be equally agreeable to the wishes of a given soul, nor all equally beneficial for that particular aggregate of matter which he calls his body. If fire comforts that body at a certain distance, it will destroy it when the distance is reduced. . . . And this is very far from being an evil. . . . [although] it certainly leaves the way open to a great evil. . . . The permanent nature of wood which enables us to use it as a beam also enables us to use it for hitting our neighbor on the head. . . . We can, perhaps, conceive of a world in which God corrected the results of this abuse of free will by His creatures at every moment: so that a wooden beam became soft as grass when it was used as a weapon. . . . But such a world would be one in which wrong actions were impossible, and in which, therefore, freedom of the will would be void. . . . Fixed laws, consequences unfolding by causal necessity, the whole natural order, are at once the limits within which [our] common life is confined and also the sole condition under which any such life is possible. Try to exclude the possibility of suffering which the order of nature and the existence of free wills involve, and you find that you have excluded life itself.[12]

Arguments of this kind have a certain intuitive plausibility but need to be spelled out more clearly.

Moral activity is a form of rational activity. Rational activity involves foresight and deliberation. Foresight and deliberation are possible, however, only if one has some expectations regarding the future. If one had no idea what the future would be like, one couldn't foresee the likely consequences of alternative courses of action, and deliberation would be impossible. Nor could a person intend to do one thing by doing another. One could not, for example, intend to shoot someone if one had no idea of what would happen if one were to pull the trigger. ("A intends to bring about x by bringing about y" entails "A believes that there is some likelihood that bringing about y will result in x." I can't intend to make rain fall by eating butter, since I do not believe that there is any connection between the two.) Foresight, deliberation, and certain sorts of intention thus seem to presuppose the existence of some expectations regarding the future. Foresight, deliberation, and the formation of these intentions can thus be *rational* only if the expectations on which they are based are rational.

Are rational expectations about the future possible only if nature is lawful? There are two possible types of rational expectations. Rational expectations may be based upon our experience of nature's normal operations or they may be acquired in nonstandard ways (by clairvoyance, for example, or by a divine revelation). Natural order and regularity aren't necessary for the second kind of rational expectation. Even if nature's operations were irregular, God could miraculously endow us with knowledge of the future.

Rational expectations of the first type, however, are possible only if nature behaves in lawlike and regular ways. For example, experience shows us that poor health is often associated with an inadequate diet and too little exercise. We therefore conclude that we will probably injure our health if we fail to exercise and do not eat properly. Our reasoning is legitimate since it is reasonable to believe that because these things have been correlated in the past, they will continue to be correlated in the future. This belief presupposes that nature behaves lawfully.

Natural order and regularity may thus be necessary if creatures are to form rational expectations *autonomously* (that is, on the basis of their *own* investigations of nature and their own inferences). Autonomous rational activity and thus autonomous *moral* activity may entail the existence of a lawful natural order.

But why suppose that such an order must include natural evil? There are two possibilities to consider. The first is a natural order in which the occurrence of natural evil is empirically impossible. (Roughly, an event is empirically impossible at time t if its occurrence at t is incompatible with natural laws and the history of the universe up to t.) The second is a natural order in which natural evil is empirically possible but never occurs.

If natural evil were empirically impossible, then people couldn't harm themselves or others. Intelligent and reasonably well-informed beings could not even intend to do so. One can intend to harm someone only if one thinks it is (empirically and not merely logically) possible to do so. Beings who were aware of the kind of world in which they lived would know that this wasn't possible. Since most significant forms of moral evil include an intention to cause harm, these beings could not engage in them. The fact that they never harm anyone or even try to do so wouldn't be a consequence of their freely refraining from harm, but of their inability to cause it.

Must natural evil be actual as well as empirically possible? Even if evil were empirically possible, autonomous rational agents might be unable to intend harm if none of them had experienced real evils. Richard Swinburne has argued that an intention to cause harm presupposes the knowledge that certain sorts of behavior will cause harm and an appreciation of what pain, mental anguish, and other kinds of harm are like.[13] Initially (that is, before anyone has actually formed an intention to cause harm), there is only one way in which this knowledge and understanding could be nonmiraculously acquired—by drawing inferences from one's experience of people being struck by heavy objects, burned by fire, and other natural evils.[14] If Swinburne is right, autonomous rational beings can intend to cause harm only if some natural evils actually occur.

The argument can be summarized as follows:

1. If creatures couldn't depend upon nature's regularity, they wouldn't be able to form rational expectations on the basis of their own experiences and powers of reasoning. Autonomous rational activity thus seems to presuppose the existence of a lawful natural order.

2. Certain kinds of significant moral choices presuppose the empirical possibility of natural evil. If the occurrence of natural evils was incompatible with the nature of the universe, one could not cause harm. A rational and informed being couldn't even intend to do so.

3. If autonomous and informed beings are to be capable of intending harm, then the actual occurrence of some natural evil may also be necessary. An intention to cause harm presupposes a belief that one's action will cause harm and some understanding of what harm involves. Perhaps the only nonmiraculous way in which these things can be acquired is through people's experience of natural evil.

Another consideration is also relevant. Natural laws and natural kinds may be essentially connected. "Water" that wasn't composed of H_2O, didn't freeze at zero degrees centigrade, and so on, wouldn't *be* water.[15] A system of natural laws which precluded natural evil would be very different from that which obtains. So the kinds of things that exist in a world governed by those laws would also be different. It isn't easy to see how a world in which evil was empirically impossible could contain tigers, for example, or human beings. Yet a world without things of that kind wouldn't be obviously better than our own.

If these points are correct, then the occurrence of natural evils may be entailed by a good—namely, the existence of autonomous moral agents who have some understanding of the nature of the world in which they live and are free to make significant moral decisions.

Conclusion

This section has examined several goods that are sometimes thought to logically require evil. We have seen that whether the implications hold depends on precisely how the goods are specified. Once the nature of the relevant goods has been clarified, it becomes clear that some alleged entailments don't hold. For example, many of the virtuous activities associated with love or friendship would be possible even if there was no evil. Moral knowledge and insight could be acquired miraculously and not through humanity's experience of good and evil. Nevertheless, some goods entail evil. Among these are virtuous responses to real evils, certain kinds of autonomous moral activity, and the existence of familiar natural kinds. The value of these goods will be examined in the next section.

The Value of the Goods

Suppose one concedes that some goods entail evils. One may still wonder whether the value of these goods is great enough to justify their permission. A person's answer to this question will be determined by the standards he or she uses to evaluate goods.

Critics often assume that the only appropriate standard for evaluating the quality of human existence is happiness and that happiness should be understood as a balance of pleasure over pain. A world without suffering, misery, or wickedness—and therefore without compassion, fortitude, or forgiveness—would contain less pain and more pleasure than our own. A world inhabited by creatures who didn't have to acquire moral knowledge and rectitude by struggling with evil, but were naturally endowed with them, might be happier than ours.

But would these worlds be better? A compassionate or forgiving response might be valuable for its own sake and not simply because it tends to reduce suffering and misfortune. If that were true, then a world containing compassionate or forgiving responses might be better than a world without them even if the first world contains no more happiness than the second.

Certain sorts of character might also be valuable apart from any tendency they have to produce happiness. The goodness of a Socrates or an Augustine is qualitatively different from that of a creature which possesses its goodness as a natural endowment. The former is acquired through a victorious struggle with weakness, temptation, and evil while the latter isn't. This struggle leaves its mark on the character that is formed by it and gives it a distinctive tone or flavor. This doesn't imply that a Socrates or an Augustine is holier or more righteous than a being who is innately good or even that the goodness of a Socrates or an Augustine is better. (God is innately good, and His goodness is greater than that of any creature.) But it does imply that their goodness is qualitatively different, and goodness of this sort may be worth having. The quality of a Chablis is different from the quality of a Burgundy, but both are good wines. Even if Burgundy is better than Chablis, the world may be better for having both.

Some of the defenses we have considered place a high value on freedom and autonomy. Many theists believe that evil is worth tolerating if it is the price of significant moral freedom. They also think that it is important for us to acquire our understanding of the world and our duties by using our own powers even if this involves experiencing real evils.

Other theists are struck by the natural world's beauty and splendor. They wonder whether a world without carnivorous beasts, for instance, or physically vulnerable creatures like us, would be better than our own.

While these evaluations can be challenged, it isn't clear that they are unreasonable or morally insensitive. The important point is that the principal issue between theists and their critics may be the issue of standards. The theist can specify goods that entail the existence or permission of evil. But in appealing to these goods, he or she invokes certain standards. For example, when theists argue that compassionate responses by persons who are informed of the relevant facts justify God's permission of the evils these responses entail, they are assuming that knowledge is better than delusion. They are also assuming that a world in which beings who understand their situation compassionately respond to real evils is better, other things being equal, than a world in which deluded creatures compassionately respond to unreal evils. By contrast, critics often assume that the only legitimate reason for permitting suffering is to maximize pleasure and minimize pain.

It is thus important for theists and critics to state their standards clearly. When they do, they will often find that they are invoking different standards and that the argument should be joined at this point.

THE FREE WILL DEFENSE

Most versions of the greater goods defense presuppose that God is limited only by logical facts and values.[16] One of the oldest and most popular explanations of evil, however, implicitly presupposes that God is limited by a certain sort of contingent fact—facts about the behavior of free creatures.

God wishes to enter into loving relations with His creatures. But genuine love is an expression of the free commitment of both parties. Love between God and His creatures is therefore possible only if creatures are free—that is, if they are able to reject His love as well as respond to it. Freedom is a great good. Without it we couldn't share in God's goodness by freely loving Him. Nevertheless, the creation of free creatures involved the risk that persons would misuse their freedom and reject the good, and this is what happened. Gregory of Nyssa (355–c. 394) expresses it this way.

> He who made man for participation in his own unique good and equipped his nature with the capacity for all kinds of excellence . . . would never have deprived him of that noblest and most precious of goods; I mean the gift of freedom and self-determination. For if necessity in any way ruled the life of man, the "image" [of God] would have been falsified in that particular. . . . How could a nature which was subjugated and enslaved to any kind of necessity be called an "image" of the nature of the [divine] King? . . . How is it then, you will ask, that he who had been honoured with the whole range of excellent endowments has exchanged those good things for worse? . . . It is not God who is responsible for the present evils, since he has constituted your nature so as to be uncontrolled and free. The responsibility is with the perverse will which has chosen the worse rather than the better.[17]

The free will defense thus explains moral evil by appealing to the limitations imposed upon God by human freedom. Alvin Plantinga (1932–) has provided the most careful explanation of the nature of these limitations.[18] Although his discussion is technical, it is important and has had a major impact on contemporary philosophy of religion.

A person's essence is the set of all those properties and only those properties that the person must have to be the person he or she is. A person's essence thus includes all and only those properties which that person has in every possible world in which the person's essence is instantiated (that is, in every possible world in which that person exists).[19] Socrates' essence, for example, includes the properties of being identical with Socrates and being human but doesn't include the properties of being snub-nosed or being a philosopher. (Socrates might not have been a philosopher, and his nose might have been aquiline.)

If persons are genuinely free, then their essences won't include properties with respect to which they are free (that is, properties such that whether or not they have them depends upon the choices they freely make). Suppose, for example, that Socrates was free with respect to the property "refusing to escape from prison." Socrates chose not to escape but to accept death. He therefore has this property. But if Socrates was free, he might have chosen to flee, and in that case he wouldn't have had it. Since there are possible worlds in which Socrates doesn't have the property "refusing to escape from prison," it isn't included in his essence.

Furthermore, if Socrates was genuinely free with respect to the property "refusing to escape from prison," his refusal wasn't necessitated by natural causes, by his own character and past choices, or by God's causal activity. There are thus not only possible worlds in which Socrates chooses to escape, but also possible worlds in which the past is relevantly similar to the past in our own world up to the moment at which Socrates makes his decision and in which Socrates chooses to escape. That is, there are possible worlds in which the natural laws are the same as those in our world, God's actions up to the moment at which Socrates made his decision are the same, the past history of the instantiation of Socrates' essence is the same, and so on, but in which Socrates decides to escape.

Consider, then, the following subjunctive conditional.

1. If Socrates' essence were instantiated, the instantiation of that essence (namely, Socrates) would refuse to escape from prison.

Statement 1 is in fact true. But notice two things. First, it is only contingently true. If Socrates was free with respect to refusing to escape from prison, there are possible worlds in which he chooses to escape. And, of course, in those worlds 1 is false. But also notice that while God can and does determine the world's constituents and the laws that govern their behavior (that the world contains hydrogen atoms, that Socrates' essence is instantiated, that $e = mc^2$, and so on), He cannot determine that 1 is true. Why is this the case?

By hypothesis, Socrates is free with respect to refusing to escape. Whether or not he has this property is up to him. Now God has created Socrates. He has thus determined that

    2. Socrates' essence is instantiated

is true. Suppose, then, that He had determined that 1 is true. Statements 1 and 2 entail

    3. Socrates refuses to escape from prison.

If God determines that 1 and 2 are true, and if 1 and 2 entails 3, then God determines that 3 is true. He thus determines that Socrates refuses to escape.[20] But if that is the case, then Socrates' refusal to escape wasn't a free action, and so Socrates wasn't really free with respect to it.

This result can be generalized. Where the essences in question are the essences of possible free persons, each essence is associated with a set of subjunctive conditionals describing how the instantiation of that essence would freely behave if the essence were instantiated.[21] While these conditionals are only contingently true, holding in our world but not in some others, their truth is a reflection of the freedom of the persons who have those essences. Given that these persons are free, the conditionals cannot be *made* true by natural causes, by their own past, *or by God*. God's choices are therefore constrained not only by logical facts and value facts but also by a complex set of contingent facts—those expressed in the subjunctive conditionals describing how free persons would freely behave that happen to be true in our world.

Now suppose that Socrates was free with respect to a morally wrong action A and that the set of conditionals associated with Socrates' essence includes

    4. If Socrates' essence were instantiated, the instantiation of that essence (namely, Socrates) would do A.

If it does, then even though there are logically possible worlds in which Socrates never acts badly, God can't instantiate any of those worlds. To do so, He would have to instantiate Socrates' essence. However, if God were to instantiate Socrates' essence, then, given the truth of 4 (over which He has no control), the instantiation of Socrates' essence would act badly on at least one occasion. But in that case God would *not* have succeeded in instantiating one of the worlds in which Socrates never acts badly. Worlds of that type are logically possible but they are not, as a matter of contingent fact, creatable.

Suppose finally that this taint or flaw isn't peculiar to Socrates but affects the essence of every possible free person, or (less strongly) suppose that it affects most essences of free persons in the set of essences that, because of its overall value, is best worth creating. Under these conditions, God seems to have a morally sufficient reason for creating a world containing moral evil. If the flaw affects every essence, then the permission of moral evil is a necessary condition of the existence of free persons. If the flaw affects most essences in the set best worth creating, then the permission of evil is a necessary condition of the greatest creatable good. While the necessities in question are only contingent, they aren't contingencies over which God has any control. He cannot, then, be blamed for submitting to them.

The free will defense can be summarized as follows. If a person's sinful action is genuinely free, then the fact that the person would act sinfully in those circumstances isn't necessitated by the person's essence, by his or her character and past decisions, by natural causes, or by God. The fact that the person would act in that way in those circumstances just *is* true. It isn't *made* true by any other fact and thus isn't made true by some fact about God. Contingent facts of this kind are simply given and, together with logical facts and value facts, provide the framework within which God must make His creative decisions. If the set of facts with which God is confronted includes the fact that a person would act badly if he or she were created or placed in a particular set of circumstances, then God can't create that person or place the person in those circumstances and prevent the person from sinning. Even though there are many possible worlds in which the contingent facts about what that person would freely do are different, God must accommodate Himself to the facts that obtain. Nevertheless, there may be morally sufficient reasons for creating that person or placing the person in those circumstances. If doing so would result in more overall good, then God would be justified in His action even though He foresees that the person will act sinfully.

The free will defense is exposed to two important objections. The first is that it mistakenly assumes that God's determination of human behavior is incompatible with its freedom. The second is that the free will defense is incompatible with God's sovereignty and omnipotence. We will now discuss these objections.

Is Determinism Compatible with Freedom?

The free will defense presupposes that free choices can't have causally sufficient conditions and that God cannot, therefore, determine that creatures freely choose to act rightly. This is a controversial assumption. Determinists contend that none of our choices are "contra-causally free." All of them have sufficient causal conditions. It is therefore causally impossible for any other choices to have been made in the circumstances in which they were made. Many determinists, however, are "compatibilists." Compatibilists believe that causal determinism is consistent with human freedom. If they are right, God could ensure that His creatures always act well without destroying their freedom.

Although compatibilists and incompatibilists agree that an action is free only if the agent who performed the action could have refrained from doing so, they interpret this condition in different ways. The compatibilist thinks that for this condition to be met it need only be true that *if* the agent had chosen to refrain from performing the action, he or she would have done so. Suppose, for example, that someone deliberately fails to rescue a drowning child. His failure to rescue her is free provided that if he had chosen to rescue her, he would have done so. And this conditional is true if he knew how to swim, was not too far from her, and so on. The fact that his decision not to rescue the child was causally determined is irrelevant; for even though his decision was causally necessary, it is nonetheless true that if he *had* chosen to rescue her, he would have done so. It is thus true that he *could* have rescued her. His failure to do so was therefore free.

The incompatibilist, on the other hand, argues that unless the agent's choice was contra-causally free (that is, unless the agent's choice was underdetermined by its causal antecedents), there was no *genuine* alternative to the agent's action. The agent could not *really* have refrained from acting as he did. Hence, his action wasn't free.

Compatibilists, in short, argue that it is the *nature* or *character* of its causes that determine whether an act is free. Such things as duress, lack of opportunity or ability, psychological disorders, and so on, are incompatible with an agent's freedom. But other causes (a normal genetic makeup, for example, or a good home environment) are not. Incompatibilists, on the other hand, maintain that the issue is not so much the nature of the causes as whether those causes determine the choices that an agent makes. The intuition behind their claim is that if an agent's choices aren't contra-causally free but are ultimately necessitated by factors over which it has no control (the past history of the universe, for example, or God's eternal decrees), then the agent's choices are not within its control. The agent thus isn't responsible for them.

The free will defense presupposes the truth of incompatibilism. While the defense has played an important role in the history of theism, it should be noted that many theists have been determinists. Orthodox Muslims, many Lutherans and Calvinists, and some Thomists have been theological determinists. They believed that God's eternal decrees are a causally sufficient condition of everything that takes place, including human actions. While they didn't deny that human beings are responsible for their actions, they reconciled responsibility with determinism by adopting compatibilism. Although this position protects God's sovereignty, it makes the problem of evil more intractable. If God determines everything, He determines every act of treachery, cruelty, or injustice. It is difficult to see how this can be reconciled with His goodness.

Theological determinism isn't essential to classical theism. Nevertheless, there *are* doctrines essential to classical theism that create problems for theological incompatibilists. Classical theists believe that God is essentially good and therefore cannot act badly. They also believe that God is a free moral agent. If God's actions are free even though He cannot act badly, then some sorts of necessitation are compatible with freedom.

The fact that God necessarily acts well also suggests that the free will defense overestimates the value of contra-causal freedom. Although God cannot act badly, His agency is immeasurably greater or more perfect than any other kind of agency. If God had constructed us in such a way that we could not act badly, we would not be contra-causally free. Nevertheless, our agency would be more like His and thus much better than it is.[22]

Theological incompatibilists must therefore address two questions. Is the belief that God is an essentially good free agent inconsistent with incompatibilism? Does the theological incompatibilist overestimate the value of contra-causal freedom?

Jonathan Edwards provides three criteria for free moral agency. A moral agent must be a rational being who perceives "the difference between moral good and evil." The agent must have "a capacity of choice . . . and a power of acting according to his choice." The agent must also be capable "of being influenced in his actions by moral inducements or motives."[23] God clearly satisfies the first and third conditions. His moral knowledge is perfect and His behavior is guided by moral considerations. It is because God, who is by nature good, sees that it would be morally wrong or unfitting to do certain things that He does not, indeed cannot, do them. But does He satisfy the second condition? That is, does God have "a capacity of choice and a power of acting according to his choice"? Compatibilists like Edwards believe that this condition is met because God's actions are expressions of His inclinations. An incompatibilist who thinks that freedom is incompatible with *any* kind of necessitation believes that more is required—that if God genuinely has a capacity for choice, it must be possible for Him to have made other choices. Can this condition be met if God is essentially good?

The condition could be met with respect to some choices. It would be met if the alternatives between which God chooses included two or more such that while God has a morally sufficient reason for choosing one of them, he does not have morally sufficient reason for choosing one rather than another. Suppose, for example, that two creatable worlds are equal in value but superior to all other creatable worlds, and that God chooses to create the first. God's choice of the first is an expression of His wisdom and goodness, but these properties don't determine His choice. (The creation of the second world would have been equally compatible with His perfections.) Incompatibilists who believe that freedom is incompatible with any kind of necessitation can thus consistently maintain that an essentially good God is free in certain respects. They cannot, however, consistently maintain that God freely chooses to *act well*. God's nature may not necessitate His choosing one good rather than another but it does necessitate His choosing the good.

Suppose, though, that the necessity of God's actions was compatible with His freedom with respect to those actions. An unrestricted incompatibilism (which asserts that freedom is incompatible with *any* kind of necessitation) would then be false. It doesn't follow that the necessity of *human* actions is compatible with their freedom. The sorts of necessity involved in the two cases are significantly different.

Classical theists believe that the sources of God's actions lie in His own nature. God is genuinely independent, neither determined nor causally affected by other powers. His activity is therefore fully autonomous. If, on the other hand, the choices of human agents are causally necessary consequences of conditions that ultimately extend beyond their control, human agents aren't genuinely independent and their activities are not autonomous. The two sorts of necessity are thus significantly different. Consequently, even if the first sort of necessity is compatible with a capacity for free moral choice, we cannot infer that the second sort of necessity is compatible with a capacity for free moral choice. Classical theism may entail that freedom is compatible with some sorts of necessitation. It doesn't entail that *causal* necessitation is compatible with *human* freedom.

The distinction between these two sorts of necessitation also has a bearing on our second question. Suppose that God could have constructed human beings in such a way that they could choose between goods but not between good and evil. Does this imply that human agency would be more like God's agency (and thus better than it is)?

An important feature of God's righteous activity is its autonomy. Freedom from causal necessitation may be necessary if human righteousness is to resemble God's righteousness in this respect. Suppose that God did construct human beings in such a way that it was impossible for them to choose evil. While the immediate cause of a person's righteous actions would lie within his or her own nature, its ultimate cause (God's decrees) would not. But in that case, the agent would not be genuinely independent and its actions would not be genuinely autonomous. In short, if God were to determine that rational creatures always act rightly, then, while the agency of those creatures would resemble God's agency more closely in one respect, it would resemble it less closely in another.

Our results can be summarized as follows:

1. The free will defense assumes that the casual determination of human behavior is incompatible with its freedom. This thesis is controversial and seems to conflict with the doctrine that God is a free moral agent who cannot act badly.

2. The claim that freedom is incompatible with *any* kind of necessitation *is* inconsistent with the claim that God is essentially good and freely chooses to act well. It is not inconsistent with the claim that God is essentially good and freely chooses between various goods.

3. *Human* freedom might be incompatible with *causal* necessitation even if the freedom of God's acts is consistent with the fact that they are necessitated by His goodness and wisdom. This restricted claim is sufficient for the purposes of the free will defense.

4. The doctrine of God's essential goodness doesn't cast serious doubt on the value of the sort of freedom ascribed to human agents by the free will defense. The necessity that is imposed upon God's actions by His essential goodness is different in kind from the necessity that would be imposed upon human choices by natural causes or God's decrees. The perfection of God's agency doesn't imply that freedom from causal necessitation has little value. Indeed, it suggests that it has great value. Contra-causal freedom may be necessary if human activity is to mirror God's own autonomous activity.

Is God's Power Limited?

Some critics claim that the free will defense limits God's power and impairs His sovereignty. The subjunctive conditionals that describe how persons would freely behave if they were created or placed in certain circumstances impose constraints upon God's activity. These constraints may severely restrict His choices. Suppose, for example, that the set of contingently true conditionals is such that there is no person whom God could create who would invariably choose to do the right thing if he or she were created. If that were the case, then, even though God might wish to create a world in which rational beings always freely choose to do the right thing, He couldn't do so. Given this set of conditionals, no being could have created a better world. Nevertheless, if a different set of conditionals had obtained, God's desire for the good would have been realized more fully.

Furthermore, as Jonathan Edwards pointed out, if the constraints implied by the free will defense obtain, then God appears to be subject to a kind of "fate" or "necessity" (namely, the character of human decisions) over which He has no control and to which He must submit. But if that is the case, God isn't fully in charge of things. History is the product of innumerable decisions, only some of which are God's. Sovereignty and power are shared among many agents and, hence, God's own sovereignty and power are limited. This seems objectionable for two reasons. It appears to be incompatible with traditional understandings of God's omnipotence and sovereignty. It may also undermine the traditional theist's confidence in God's ultimate triumph over evil.

Freedom and God's Power and Sovereignty

The concepts of divine omnipotence and divine sovereignty are "open textured." While there is rough agreement concerning what is and is not included within the scope of God's power and sovereignty, the agreement is by no means complete. No definition of these concepts is universally accepted. Given the open texture of the relevant concepts, it isn't enough to show that the constraints imposed by human freedom are incompatible with omnipotence and sovereignty as defined by some philosophers or theologians, for their definitions can be challenged. For example, the constraints are clearly incompatible with divine omnipotence if an omnipotent being is defined as one that can bring about any logically possible state of affairs. (It is logically possible that Socrates freely chooses to escape from prison, but God cannot bring about this state of affairs.) What is less clear is that the traditional notion of God's omnipotence should be articulated in these terms. The idea that God's options are somehow limited by human freedom is as ancient as the notion that He is sovereign and all-powerful. There is therefore a presumption that God's power and sovereignty have normally been understood in such a way as to accommodate human freedom. That is, there is a presumption that the sort of constraint imposed by human freedom has been built into the theist's conceptions of divine power and sovereignty from the beginning. If that is the case, then a consideration of the constraints imposed by human freedom will simply lead to a fuller understanding of traditional concepts rather than their modification.

Freedom and God's Triumph

The second objection is that unless God is fully in control of events, we have no guarantee that good will ultimately triumph over evil. We can perhaps be assured that God would not have created the world if He hadn't foreseen that the good it contains would, on balance, outweigh its evil. But that is compatible with the possibility that the same ambiguous mixture of joy and sorrow, wickedness and righteousness, that has characterized history to the present will continue to do so until the end of time.

Two responses can be made to this objection. William James argued that the limitation we are discussing is compatible with a *virtual* assurance that God will succeed in bringing world history to a splendid conclusion.[24] The objection underestimates the extent of God's power and the importance of His decisions. God may be compared with a chess master who is playing against a novice. The chess master can't control the moves of his opponent. Furthermore, it is abstractly possible that the novice will defeat him. (Perhaps by sheer luck the novice will make some extraordinarily good moves.) Nevertheless, given the chess master's experience and skill, we are morally certain that the novice will lose. Similarly, the limitations imposed by human freedom preclude any absolute guarantee of God's ultimate triumph over evil. (Perhaps most creatures will ultimately refuse God's grace.) But given God's power and wisdom and the limitations of creatures, they don't preclude a rational confidence in God's ultimate victory.

The second response concedes that reason can't establish the claim that good will triumph over evil. According to this view, philosophy can only provide reasons for thinking that God has a morally sufficient reason for permitting evil. This statement entails that the world which God has created is a good one. The belief in God's ultimate victory, however, is based on revelation, not philosophical argumentation. It is therefore unfair for the critic to demand anything more than grounds for thinking that the theist's confidence in God's victory is compatible with his or her other religious beliefs and with our general knowledge of the nature of reality.

Conclusions

1. The free will defense entails that God is subject to the nonlogical constraints imposed by human freedom. Thus, God can't do certain things that it is logically possible for Him to do. The defense also implies that if God does choose to create free beings, then the history of the world will be partly determined by those beings. God's control of the course of events will therefore be incomplete. The free will defense

is consequently incompatible with some traditional understandings of God's power and sovereignty—that of orthodox Islam, of some types of theistic Hinduism (Dvaita Vedānta), and of Christian theologians like Augustine, Aquinas, Luther, and Calvin.

2. The defense is compatible with the belief that there is no significant proportion between the power of a being who can call worlds into being and our own power, or between God's ability to control events and ours. It is therefore compatible with a rational confidence in God's triumph over evil. The free will defense is accordingly consistent with traditional Judaism, other forms of theistic Hinduism such as Viśiṣṭādvaita Vedānta, and those strands in Christianity that believe that our response to God's grace isn't determined by God.

3. There is, then, a tension between the free will defense and *certain forms* of theism. But the defense isn't incompatible with classical theism as such.

MUST GOD CHOOSE THE BEST?

Critics of theism argue that an omnipotent and omniscient being couldn't have a morally sufficient reason for permitting evil. Theists deny this and often try to provide some account of what God's reasons might be like. As we have seen, these accounts typically attempt to show that the world which God has created is somehow better than it would be if it didn't contain evil. The critic usually responds by trying to show that God could have created a better world. Both parties to the dispute tend to assume that God must act for the best. An omnipotent and omniscient being is at fault if He creates a world which is less good than some other world that He might have created.

The assumption that God has an obligation to act for the best often rests on the further assumption that there is a best possible world. The latter may be denied. Thomas Aquinas, for example, thought that any possible created order would be a reflection of God's own being.[25] Alternative created orders are alternative ways of imitating or mirroring the divine perfections. Since God's perfection is infinite, it can be imitated in an infinite number of ways. But because it is immeasurable and inexhaustible, no created order can reflect it adequately. Indeed, no matter how faithfully a particular created order were to reflect God's perfection, a more faithful reflection of His perfection would be possible.

A modern theologian puts it this way:

> An unbridgeable gap separates the infinite, uncreated good from the whole universe of created and creatable things. He is completely disproportionate to them. . . . Even for God it will never be possible to pour out the fullness of uncreated being into the vessels of created beings, or to enclose the infinite within the finite. Whatever world he decides to make, what will be manifested

of his infinite fullness will never be equivalent to what remains to be manifested. There will always be an infinite margin in which other [even more perfect] worlds could occur.[26]

No created order, then, is best; for any possible created order, there is another that is better. As Aquinas said, "The universe, the present creation being supposed, cannot be better. . . . For if any one thing were bettered, the proportion of order would be destroyed; as if one string were stretched more than it ought to be, the melody of the harp would be destroyed.[27] Yet God could make other things, or add something to the present creation; and then there would be another and a better universe."[28] God can't, then, be appropriately criticized for failing to create the best order, for there isn't any.

But could God be appropriately criticized for failing to create an order better than the order He has created? There *is* such an order and God could have created it. Nevertheless, it may be inappropriate to criticize Him for not having done so. Why is this the case?

No matter what order God were to create, there would be a better order and it would be possible for Him to create it. Thus, no matter what God did, He would be exposed to the possibility of a complaint of this type. But as George Schlesinger (1925–) has argued, a type of complaint that is always in place is never in place.[29] A complaint is legitimate only when the person whose conduct is criticized could have acted in such a way that he or she would not be exposed to a complaint of that type. For example, other things being equal, it would be unfair to blame someone for the unfortunate consequences of his or her action if all of the available alternatives would have had equally unfortunate consequences.

The situation is therefore this. The critic complains that God could have created a better order. But even if God had created a better order, He would be exposed to the possibility of a similar complaint. Indeed, no created order better than our own is such that God would not be exposed to the possibility of a complaint of this sort. The complaint is thus inappropriate. Even though there are an infinite number of possible created orders better than our own, God can't be faulted simply because He created an order inferior to other orders that He might have created in their place.

Does this defuse the problem of evil? The mere fact that one state of affairs is better than another may not imply that God ought to bring about the first state of affairs rather than the second. Perhaps God has no obligation to bring about a better state of affairs just because it is better and so doesn't stand under any obligation that derives its force from an obligation to bring about the better. (If no matter how happy sentient creatures are, they could be happier, then an obligation to bring about states of affairs in which sentient creatures would be happier than they are might be an obligation of this sort.) It doesn't follow that God has no obligations or that there is no problem of evil.

The obligation to act justly and faithfully and the obligation to respect persons don't appear to derive their force from an obligation to choose the better. God may be under no obligation to choose the better. He may, however, be obligated to act justly and fairly, to fulfill His promises, and to respect the integrity of human personality. If He is, there is still a problem of evil. In this life, at least, happiness and misery aren't distributed according to worth or merit. Furthermore, some evils seem utterly inimical to the integrity of human personality (senility, for example, or the conditions obtaining in the Nazi death camps). The problem might, however, be more tractable. The theist may find it easier to respond to the charge that God has acted unjustly or without regard to the integrity of human personality than to show that no other created order would have been better.

But does this approach even mitigate the problem of evil? It might seem not. Consider the following possible obligations:

1. An obligation to act in such a way that the state of affairs that results from one's action contains no pointless evil

2. An obligation to act in such a way that the state of affairs that results from one's action contains no unnecessary evils

3. An obligation to act in such a way that the state of affairs that results from one's action contains no evil.

In God's case the relevant states of affairs are created orders. Now "For every created order there is a better" doesn't entail "All created orders contain evil."[30] If some of them do not, God could have created a world without evil. Similarly, "For every created order there is a better" doesn't entail "Every created order contains pointless or unnecessary evils." If some of them do not, God could also have created worlds without pointless or unnecessary evils. God could, then, have acted in such a way that He wouldn't be exposed to complaints based on His failure to discharge these obligations. Furthermore, the obligations in question don't clearly derive their force from an obligation to choose the better. But if God does stand under these obligations, the problem of evil seems as difficult as it would be upon the assumption that there is a best created order and God is obligated to actualize it. We must therefore examine these obligations more closely.

God may not stand under the third obligation. That one state of affairs is better than another doesn't entail that the first contains fewer evils than the second but only that the overall value of the first is greater than the overall value of the second. For example, if a created order contains more good than evil, then the state of affairs consisting in its existence would be better than the state of affairs consisting in the nonexistence of *any* created order. (The first has positive value while the second has neither positive nor negative value.) But the first state of affairs contains evils and the second doesn't. That one state of affairs is better than another does not, therefore, entail that it contains fewer evils. Thus, the ascent from worse states of affairs to better ones may not be an ascent from states of affairs with more evils to ones with fewer evils. We cannot, then, simply assume that as we ascend from worse to better created orders, we will eventually reach a point after which all created orders will be free from evil. But without this assumption there is no reason to think that if God could have created an order without evil, He should have done so. Why is this the case?

If there is no point after which all created orders are free from evil, then for any order O that contains no evil, there will be some other order O' that is better than O and does contain evil. (If there weren't, then O would be a point after which all created orders are free from evil—which is contrary to our supposition.) But if for every world free from evil, there is a better world that contains evil, then it isn't obvious that God ought to have created an order without evil. Nor will it seem obvious to many theists. Some Christian theists, for example, talk as if a created order that includes the atonement and redemption (and therefore sin and suffering) is somehow better or more splendid than any order that is free from sin and suffering but, as a consequence, fails to include this great good. They therefore implicitly deny that all orders that contain evil are inferior to some orders that don't. It isn't clear, then, that God stands under the third obligation.

On the other hand, some of the theists we are discussing admit that God stands under the first obligation. George Joyce (1864–1943), for example, argues that God's goodness precludes the creation of an order containing pointless evils—evils that are purely gratuitous, in no way contributing to good.[31] If God has only this obligation and not the other two, then the problem of evil is more tractable. Theists needn't claim that evils are necessary to the goods to which they contribute or that no other goods are greater but only that God can and does bring good out of them. For example, it may be sufficient for theists to show that our susceptibility to pain has a biological function and thus isn't pointless. They need not show that it is a logically **necessary** condition of some good or that no other biological arrangement would have been better.

There are, however, reasons for thinking that God stands under the second obligation as well as the first. Suppose that I can cure Smith's illness in either of two ways. Each mode of treatment is equally effective, but the first is quite painful and the second is not. I opt for the first treatment. The infliction of pain has a point, for it is a concomitant of a mode of treatment that produces a great good. We may even suppose that the cure is a much greater good than the pain is an evil. Nevertheless, I am surely at fault. I am at fault because the pain was unnecessary.[32] It thus isn't sufficient that evils have a point. They must in some sense be necessary to the goods to which they contribute. (Nor does this obligation derive its force from an obligation to choose the better. Even if I don't have a general obligation to bring about a better state of affairs when I might have brought about a worse, I ought not to bring about states of affairs that include unnecessary evils.)

Perhaps, then, God stands under the second obligation as well as the first. If He does, then the theists we are discussing must contend that evils or their permission are necessary conditions of some good that outweighs them (where the necessity in question is a reflection of the constraints imposed by logic, principles of value, and—perhaps—conditionals describing how free persons would behave if they were created).

But if that is the case, does the assumption that for every created order there is a better help solve the problem of evil? It does. While the theists in question must contend that evils are necessary to goods, they needn't deny that there are alternative goods, which don't include those evils, that would be greater. In their view, there are an infinite number of better alternatives to any given created order. Some of these may be free from the evils included in that order. There may, then, be alternative orders better than our own that don't include the evils found in the actual world. But it doesn't follow that God has an obligation to actualize one of these alternatives. For why should one think that He does? The only obvious reason is that God has a general obligation not to bring about a worse state of affairs when He could bring about a better. If the view we are examining is correct, God has no such obligation.

Our discussion suggests the following conclusions:

1. God isn't obligated to create the best possible order if there isn't any.

2. It is doubtful whether God has a general obligation not to create a worse order when He can create a better. A person stands under an obligation only if he or she is able to perform it. But if for every created order there is a better, God couldn't discharge the general obligation in question. (No matter what order God were to create, He could have created a better and would thus have failed to meet it.)

3. There may not be a created order that contains no evil and is better than all that do. If there isn't, God has no obligation to create a world without evil.

4. But while God may not stand under these obligations, He does stand under others. In particular, God appears obligated to act justly and faithfully, to respect the integrity of human personality, and to permit only those evils that not only have a point but also are such that their permission is a necessary condition of some good that outweighs them. Since the necessity of some evils is not obvious, the problem of evil isn't resolved.

5. Nevertheless, if God doesn't have a general obligation to choose the better, the problem is more tractable since the theist needn't claim that no alternative order is better than the one God has created.

GRATUITOUS EVIL

We have examined some of the more important accounts of the sorts of reason that an omnipotent, omniscient, and morally perfect being might have for permitting evil. None of these accounts fully explains evil. The free will defense doesn't account for natural evil, and greater goods defenses don't seem to satisfactorily account for the quantity of evil.[33] (Even if moral development, compassion, forgiveness, significant freedom, and other goods could not occur in a world without evil, it is difficult to see why so much evil is necessary.)

Furthermore, in some cases, theists don't actually explain evil. They instead explain how evil *could* be explained if certain assumptions that might be true, but are not known to be true, were true. They show, for example, how moral evil's pervasiveness could be explained if it were true that every free person whom God could create were such that if that person were created, he or she would perform at least some bad actions. Or they show how the problem of evil would be mitigated if each created order were surpassable. This may be sufficient if the theist's intention is simply to show that his or her position is consistent.[34] Nevertheless, unless reasons are provided for thinking that the assumptions are true or that other explanations of evil (including those offered by atheists) are less adequate, these accounts are possible rather than actual explanations.

In spite of the theist's explanations, much evil seems purely gratuitous. John Hick puts it this way:

> Let the hypothesis of a divine purpose of soul-making be adopted, and let it be further granted that an environment which is to serve this purpose cannot be a permanent hedonistic paradise but must offer to man real tasks, challenges, and problems. Still the question must be asked: Need the world contain the more extreme and crushing evils which it in fact contains? Are not life's challenges often so severe as to be self-defeating when considered as soul-making influences: man must (let us suppose) cultivate the soil so as to win his bread by the sweat of his brow; but need there be the gigantic famines . . . from which millions have so miserably perished? . . . These [evils] reach far beyond any constructive function of character training. Their effect seems to be sheerly dysteleological and destructive. They can break their victim's spirit and cause him to curse whatever gods there are. When a child dies of cerebral meningitis, his little personality undeveloped and his life unfulfilled, leaving only an unquenchable aching void in his parents' lives; or when a charming, lively, and intelligent woman suffers from a shrinking of the brain which destroys her personality and leaves her in an asylum . . . when such things happen we can see no gain to the soul, whether of the victim or of others, but on the contrary only a ruthlessly destructive process which is utterly inimical to human values. It seems as though "As flies to wanton boys, are we to the gods, they kill us for their sport."[35]

Although God may have good reasons for permitting these evils, we have little idea of what they might be. Many of us will wonder whether anyone *could* have morally sufficient reasons for permitting evils of this kind.

Consider, for example, the following cases of horrendous and apparently pointless evil.

E1:   A fawn is trapped in a forest fire and dies a lingering and painful death.

E2:   A child is brutally raped and murdered by her mother's boyfriend.

In a widely discussed series of articles, William Rowe argues that because

1. No goods we know of justify God's permitting *E1* and *E2*, and because

2. The probability is fairly high that we would know the goods which would justify God in permitting *E1* and *E2* if God existed.

3. It is probable that God doesn't exist.[36]

Rowe rightly contends that unless "God exists" *entails* that we would be ignorant of God's reasons for permitting *E1* and *E2*, our ignorance of those reasons lowers the probability of His existence.[37] The important question, however, is whether our ignorance of God's reasons *sufficiently* lowers the probability of His existence to make God's nonexistence more probable than not. It doesn't if our ignorance is fairly probable on the hypothesis that God exists. (Evidence that is *highly* likely on a hypothesis won't *significantly* lower its probability.) Compare this situation with another. Fred's neighbor's apartment has been burglarized. The discovery of burglars' tools in the trunk of Fred's car lowers the probability that he is innocent. Whether it *significantly* lowers the probability of his innocence depends on how likely it is that burglars' tools would have been found in his trunk even if he hadn't committed the theft. (Suppose, for example, that his nephew has been arrested three times for burglary and frequently borrows Fred's car.)

Our questions, therefore, are these: (1) Is it true that no goods we know of justify God's permitting *E1* and *E2*? (2) How probable is it that we would know the goods which would justify God in permitting *E1* and *E2* if God existed? How plausible, in other words, are Rowe's two premises?

Rowe thinks that his first premise is true because the goods we know of aren't great enough to justify evils like *E1* and *E2*, or (if they are) don't entail that God's permission of evils like *E1* and *E2* is necessary to secure them. My enjoyment of the smell of a good cigar, for instance, isn't a great enough good. And while the vision of God is great enough, neither God's permission of the fawn's suffering nor His permission of the child's brutal rape and murder is necessary to secure it.

Rowe also believes that his second premise is plausible. We have no reason to think that the goods we know of aren't a representative sample of the goods there are. So if the goods we know of don't justify evils like *E1* and *E2*, it is probable that no goods will do so. Furthermore, encounters with evils like *E1* and *E2* frequently lead to perplexity, doubt, and loss of faith. It is therefore reasonable to suppose that if God existed, He would inform us of His reasons for permitting evils like *E1* and *E2* and so reassure us of His goodness. Yet He hasn't done so.

While these considerations support Rowe's premises, they aren't conclusive. In the first place, traditional theists believe that there is an immeasurable gap between God's cognitive powers and our own. The presumption that we would understand God's reasons for permitting evils like *E1* and *E2*, if He had them, is at best weak.

In the second place, apart from revelation, we don't know what goods and evils exist in other dimensions of reality (in an afterlife, for example). Furthermore, even though humanity's well-being is presumably *one* of God's purposes, He may have others. We are less likely to be cognizant of the latter than of the former (as a small child is less likely to understand her father's desire to contribute to the ongoing discussion in philosophy, or to work for social justice, than she is to understand his love for her and desire for her welfare). If theism is true, then, it isn't unlikely that there are great goods that are dissimilar to those with which we are familiar. Some of these may justify God's permission of evils like *E1* and *E2*.

In the third place, it isn't clear that our grasp of the goods we do know of is sufficiently clear to warrant assurance that those goods don't justify God's permission of horrendous evils. Christian theists, for example, believe that the good to which things are tending is the enjoyment of God—a vision of, and participation in, God's own life. They also believe that God's intrinsic nature is unknown to us. Our grasp of the concept of the beatific vision is thus at best like a small child's grasp of the concept of sainthood or moral maturity. If these theists are right, then we have only an imperfect conception of the nature of the good most relevant to the solution of the problem of evil and thus of the things needed to secure it.[38]

In the fourth place, it is doubtful that our knowledge of the connections between goods and evils is sufficiently accurate to warrant confident assertions about the necessity or lack of necessity of the latter. There are two reasons for this. First, any good, G^*, that would justify God's permitting the world's evils would be very complex. Although we are acquainted with some of the constituents of this complex good, their value will be affected by their place in the whole. (The value of a whole isn't always a simple function of the value of its parts. The aesthetic value of Rubens' *Descent from the Cross* isn't the sum of the aesthetic value of the square foot of canvas in the painting's upper right-hand corner, the square foot immediately adjacent to it on its left, and so on.) If this is correct, then we can't consider G^*'s constituents in isolation, asking of each whether its value outweighs the disvalue of any evils that are consequences of its existence. The only good that ultimately matters is the complex whole consisting of *all* existing goods (known and unknown). We don't have a firm enough grasp of this good to speak confidently about its entailments.[39] The second reason is this. The relevant connections between goods and evils may include not only logical connections. They may also include connections that obtain in virtue of true subjunctive conditionals stating what free persons would freely do in various circumstances and true subjunctive conditionals stating what events would randomly occur under certain conditions. (For example, that if circumstance C were to obtain, a beta particle would be emitted at precisely 8:4676.) Given our comparative ignorance of complex logical connections and of the relevant subjunctive conditionals, it is doubtful that we can do more than make educated guesses as to whether the connections between goods and evils that obtain justify God's permitting horrors like *E1* and *E2*.

Finally, reflection on our knowledge of the physical universe suggests that our knowledge of goods and evils, and of the connections between them, may be very imperfect. Stephen Wykstra puts it this way:

> Around 1600, Francis Bacon . . . thought that if men would only apply his experimental method, physics could, in about twenty years, get to the bottom of what causes what. He saw our universe as being . . . "physically shallow"—as having bottom-line physical causes that are, relative to our cognitive abilities, quite near the observable surface. Newton . . . had a contrary view. Four hundred years of science have vindicated Newton. Having descended into a swarm of quarks, leptons, and other denizens of the microtheoretic deep, we are more astonished than ever. The "bottom line" micro-causes of the observable world lie very deep indeed. We realize that our world has extraordinary "physical depth."

Similarly, if God lays "the axiological foundations of our world" (is the ground of the values that govern it), it is likely that the universe has great "moral depth" as well as great physical depth. It is likely, in other words, "that many of the goods below its puzzling observable surface . . . would be 'deep' moral goods."[40]

When taken together, these considerations suggest that our cognitive relation to God may be similar to a small child's cognitive relation to her parents. Given the child's cognitive limitations, she is incapable of understanding why her father permits her to undergo a painful medical treatment, for example, or why many of the irksome restrictions he imposes on her are necessary. Her grasp of some relevant goods (such as her own physical well-being) is too imperfect for her to see why the medical treatment is necessary. Other relevant goods are currently beyond her ken. (The good of moral growth and development is an example.) Given her epistemic limitations, then, she would be unwarranted (in the first case) in concluding that the evils she experiences aren't justified by goods she knows of or (in the second) that they aren't justified by goods she doesn't know of. The implication is clear. If our epistemic relation to God is similar, we aren't justified in asserting either of Rowe's two premises.

These considerations aren't conclusive. For example, one may doubt whether the realm of values *has* a deep structure.[41] The strongest objection, however, is this:

> What happens when a loving parent intentionally permits her child to suffer intensely for the sake of a distant good that cannot otherwise be realized? In such instances the parent attends directly to the child throughout its period of suffering, comforts the child to the best of her ability, expresses her concern and love for the child in ways that are unmistakably clear to the child, assures the child that the suffering will end, and tries to explain, as best she can, why it is necessary for her to permit the suffering even though it is in her power to prevent it. In short, during these periods of intentionally permitted intense suffering, the child is *consciously aware* of the direct presence, love, and concern of the parent, and receives *special assurances* from the parent that . . . the suffering (or the parent's permission of it) is necessary for some distant good.

Yet God, Rowe argues, has not done this.[42]

While this is a powerful objection, it isn't decisive. Traditional theists believe both that God *has* assured us of His love, and that His permission of evil is justified. (This is the thrust not only of Christian revelation but of other theistic traditions as well.) Granted, *that* God has so revealed Himself isn't a matter of common knowledge. (For many disbelieve it.) On the other hand, that the prophets and saints of the theistic traditions *attest* to such a revelation is common knowledge. It is true that many disbelieve these assurances. And most of us find them especially hard to believe in the midst of our own and others' suffering. But something similar is true of small children who often refuse to accept their parent's reassurances or explanations. So it isn't clear that Rowe has located an important disanalogy between our cognitive relation to God and a small child's cognitive relation to her parents.

The conclusion of this section, then, is this. Given our cognitive limitations, the occurrence of gratuitous or apparently pointless evils probably isn't a sufficient reason for refusing to believe in God's existence.

CONCLUSION

Are the theist's responses to the problem of evil adequate? The answer to this question depends on three things—the strength of the arguments for theism; the strength of the arguments for the claim that if God existed and had a morally sufficient reason for permitting evil, we would know it; and the plausibility of the various accounts of God's reasons available to theists. If the arguments for God's existence are strong and the arguments for the claim that we would be able to understand God's reasons for permitting evil are weak, it isn't clear why theists should be particularly troubled by the incompleteness of their accounts of those reasons. Since theists have grounds for thinking that God exists, they have grounds for thinking that there are morally sufficient reasons for the permission of evil. Since they have grounds for thinking that these reasons wouldn't be fully known to them, they have grounds for thinking that the sorts of account which we have discussed are the most that could be provided if God did exist and had morally sufficient reasons for allowing evil.

Suppose, however, that the arguments for God's existence are weak and that grounds can be given for the claim that if evil had a point, we would be able to grasp it. In that case, the theist's accounts of God's reasons are probably inadequate.[43]

If these points are correct, the problem of evil shouldn't be isolated from other issues. One's assessment of the strength of the argument from evil can't be separated from one's assessment of the strength or weakness of the other considerations bearing on theism's truth. Ultimately the question is whether theism provides the best overall account of *all* the relevant facts—not only evil, but also sanctity, the world's order and beauty, religious experience, and so on. We will take up this question in Chapter 7. But before doing so, we must address another issue.

The problem of evil may not be as serious if death isn't final and this world's injustices are corrected in another. Evil's impact is at least softened if God will "wipe away all tears from all eyes" and give the righteous a share in His own unbounded and superabundant life.

But do we really survive death? Is it reasonable to believe in, or hope for, immortal life? We will discuss this issue in Chapter 4.

Notes

1. David Hume, *Dialogues Concerning Natural Religion* (Indianapolis: Bobbs-Merrill, 1947), 198.

2. Henry Mansel, *An Examination of Sir William Hamilton's Philosophy* (Boston: Gould and Lincoln, 1859), 18.

3. Peter Bertocci, *Introduction to the Philosophy of Religion* (Englewood Cliffs, N.J.: Prentice-Hall, 1951), 417f. See also Charles Hartshorne's *The Divine Relativity* (New Haven, Conn.: Yale University Press, 1948), or David Ray Griffen's *God, Power, and Evil: A Process Theodicy* (Philadelphia: Westminster Press, 1976).

4. See, for example, J. L. Mackie, "Evil and Omnipotence," *Mind* 64 (1955): 200–212.

5. To see this, consider the following. Suppose that the propositions whose consistency is in question are q and r, that p is a necessary truth, that (p and q and r) entails s, and that s is logically impossible. If (p and q and r) entails s, then p entails (if q and r, then s). Now if one proposition entails another and the first is necessary, the second is necessary. Since p is necessary, (if q and r, then s) is necessary; that is, (q and r) entails s. But any proposition that entails a logically impossible proposition is itself logically impossible. Proposition s is logically impossible by hypothesis. It follows that (q and r) is logically impossible—that is, that the conjunction of q and r is, in a broad sense, logically inconsistent.

6. Jonathan Edwards, *The Works of President Edwards,* vol. 8 (New York: Burt Franklin, 1968), 358–60.

7. ———, *Freedom of the Will* (New Haven, Conn.: Yale University Press, 1957), 411.

8. Henry Bettenson, ed., *The Early Christian Fathers* (London: Oxford University Press, 1956), 264.

9. However, this isn't entirely clear. Virtues should be distinguished from good natural dispositions. One might argue that a good disposition becomes a virtue only when it is consciously cultivated and that the conscious cultivation of a good disposition logically requires exercising it. If this is correct, then the *virtue* of compassion (as distinguished from a naturally compassionate disposition) logically presupposes the existence of suffering or misfortune.

10. One might, of course, argue that apparent evils are themselves evils (though it would be more accurate to say that the uneasy consciousness of apparent evils is an evil).

11. John Keats, *The Selected Letters of John Keats,* ed. Lionel Trilling (Garden City, N.Y.: Doubleday Anchor, 1956), 257–58.

12. C. S. Lewis, *The Problem of Pain* (New York: Macmillan, 1962), 31–34.

13. Note that the latter precludes God's simply *telling us* about natural evils. We must *experience* natural evils to appreciate them.

14. Richard Swinburne, *The Existence of God* (Oxford: Clarendon Press, 1979), chapter 11.

15. One needn't maintain that a substance's being water entails that its behavior is governed by each of these laws. One need maintain only that its being water entails that its behavior is governed by most of them.

16. In some views, value facts are themselves logical facts. For example, if there would be a prima facie objection to torture in every possible world, then "Torture is prima facie wrong" is logically necessary in the broad sense.

17. Henry Bettenson, ed., *The Later Christian Fathers* (London: Oxford University Press, 1970), 130–31.

18. See Alvin Plantinga, *God and Other Minds* (Ithaca, N.Y.: Cornell University Press, 1967), chapter 6; *The Nature of Necessity* (Oxford: Clarendon Press, 1974), chapter 9; and *God, Freedom, and Evil* (New York: Harper & Row, 1974), part 1. Plantinga uses the free will defense only to show that God's existence and the existence of evil are compatible. However, it can also be employed to explain what God's reason for permitting evil may actually be. It will be used in this way in this section.

19. A property is instantiated in a possible world if and only if an instance of the property exists in that world. Plantinga defines "essence" a bit differently, but the differences are unimportant for our purpose.

20. It isn't always true that when p entails q and A determines p, A also determines q. "I am listening to Bach's B minor mass" entails "There is such a thing as Bach's mass." And "I am running" entails "$2 + 2 = 4$." (Necessary truths are entailed by every proposition.) Nevertheless, in these cases, I don't determine the second in determining the first. But the implication often holds. For example, "I am singing" entails "I am making articulate sounds," and in determining the first I determine the second. The case in which God determines 1 and 2 seems to be one in which the implication holds. (Cases in which the implication doesn't hold are cases in which q is a necessary precondition of p [i.e., in which I can't determine p unless q already obtains], or cases in which q is a necessary truth.)

21. These are sometimes called "counterfactuals of freedom."

22. Theists have often conceded this. That our agency would be more perfect if we couldn't act badly is reflected, for example, in the belief that the blessed in heaven *can't* sin.

23. Edwards, *Freedom of the Will,* 165–66.

24. William James, "The Dilemma of Determinism," in *The Will to Believe and Other Essays* (New York: Dover, 1956), 181–82.

25. By a created order, I mean, roughly, those parts of a logically possible world in which God exists that are determined by God.

26. Charles Journet, *The Meaning of Evil* (New York: P. J. Kenedy, 1963), 110–11.

27. Aquinas's point is that the created order could not be changed for the better without altering its nature—that is, without making it a different kind of natural order.

28. Thomas Aquinas, *The Summa Theologica,* vol. 1, trans. Fathers of the English Dominican Province (New York: Benziger Bros., 1947), part I, question 25, article 6.

29. George Schlesinger, "The Problem of Evil and the Problem of Suffering," *American Philosophical Quarterly* 1 (1964): 244–47, and *Religion and Scientific Method* (Dordrecht: D. Reidel, 1977), chapters 9 and 10.

30. Except upon the dubious assumption that to be less good than something else is an evil.

31. George H. Joyce, *Principles of Natural Theology* (New York: AMS Press, 1972), chapter 17.

32. I am adapting this example from one suggested to me by William Rowe.

33. The free will defense doesn't account for natural evil except upon the assumption that all natural evil is the consequence of wicked actions.

34. This is Plantinga's intention, for example.

35. John Hick, *Evil and the God of Love* (New York: Harper & Row, 1966), 365f.

36. See, for example, "The Problem of Evil and Some Varieties of Atheism," *American Philosophical Quarterly* 16 (1979): 335–41; "The Empirical Problem of Evil," in *Rationality, Religious Belief and Moral Commitment,* ed. Robert Audi and William J. Wainwright (Ithaca, N.Y.: Cornell University Press, 1986); and "The Evidential Argument from Evil: A Second Look," in *The Evidential Argument from Evil,* ed. Daniel Howard-Snyder (Bloomington: Indiana University Press, 1996).

37. Evidence that is entailed by an hypothesis doesn't count against it.

38. The good of the beatific vision *might* justify the little girl's suffering. Marilyn Adams, for example, argues that suffering can be a means of participating in Christ's passion, thereby providing the sufferer with insight into, and communion with, the inner life of the God who is incarnate in Jesus of Nazareth. By realizing this possibility, evil is transformed into a great good. (See, for example, her "Redemptive Suffering: A Christian Approach to the Problem of Evil," in *Rationality, Religious Belief and Moral Commitment.*) In the light of the beatific vision, the raped and murdered child may retrospectively interpret (or take) her suffering in this way and rejoice in so doing. It is more difficult to believe that the good of the beatific vision justifies the fawn's suffering.

39. Thus, even if we have a firm enough grasp of the concept of the beatific vision to be confident that the little girl's enjoyment of it doesn't entail $E2$ or God's permission of $E2$, we don't have a firm enough grasp of the complex good consisting in *all* existing goods to be confident that the *latter* doesn't do so.

40. Bruce Russell and Stephen Wykstra, "The 'Inductive' Argument from Evil: A Dialogue," *Philosophical Topics* 16 (1988): 146–47.

41. See, for example, Richard Gale's "Some Difficulties in Theistic Treatments of Evil," in *The Evidential Argument from Evil.* Gale argues that morality isn't a "natural kind" like water, whose "essential nature" could be "unearthed by scientific inquiry." Morality consists of "basic principles and rules" that are "patently

obvious to . . . all participants in the moral language game." Gale also contends that we couldn't enter into relationships of love and friendship with God if His moral reasons were inscrutable. For "such relationships require significant commonality of purposes, values, sympathies, ... and the like." (Gale, "Some Difficulties in Theistic Treatments of Evil," 210.) The force of these considerations isn't clear. Even if moral *rules* don't have a "deep structure," *values* might. The value of polyphonic music, pop art, or wilderness, for example, or the disvalue of gender inequality is not "patently obvious to all participants in the moral language game." Their recognition is recent and still contentious. And even if the relevant goods and evils *were* scrutable, the connections between them might not be. Yet inscrutable connections don't preclude loving relationships. It is sufficient to know that the beloved observes the same moral rules and shares the same moral goals that I do even if I do not understand why she takes the steps she does to achieve those goals.

42. William Rowe, "The Evidential Argument from Evil: A Second Look," 276.

43. See Nelson Pike, "Hume on Evil," *The Philosophical Review* 72 (1963): 180–97.

For Further Reading

Three important recent discussions of the problem of evil are John Hick, *Evil and the God of Love* (New York: Harper & Row, 1966), Alvin Plantinga, *God, Freedom and Evil* (New York: Harper, 1974), 7–64, and Richard Swinburne, *The Existence of God* (Oxford: Clarendon Press, 1979), chapter 11. A classic statement of the skeptic's case is David Hume, *Dialogues Concerning Natural Religion* (Indianapolis: Bobbs-Merrill, 1970), parts X and XI.

The logical compatibility of God's existence and evil is discussed in Keith Yandell, "Ethics, Evils, and Theism," *Sophia* 8 (1969): 18–28, and M. B. Ahern, *The Problem of Evil* (New York: Schocken Books, 1971).

Excellent discussions of the evidential problem of evil are found in Daniel Howard-Snyder, ed., *The Evidential Problem of Evil* (Bloomington: Indiana University Press, 1996). Especially noteworthy are William Rowe, "The Problem of Evil and Some Varieties of Atheism" and his "The Evidential Argument from Evil: A Second Look;" Paul Draper, "Pain and Pleasure: An Evidential Problem for Theists;" William P. Alston, "The Inductive Argument from Evil and the Human Cognitive Condition;" and Peter Van Inwagen, "The Problem of Evil, the Problem of Air, and the Problem of Silence."

On the claim that God needn't create the best possible world see Robert M. Adams, "Must God Create the Best?" *The Philosophical Review* 81 (1972): 317–32; George Schlesinger, "Suffering and Evil," in *Contemporary Philosophy of Religion,* ed. S. M. Cahn and D. Schatz (New York: Oxford University Press, 1982); William Rowe, "The Problem of Divine Perfection and Freedom," *Reasoned Faith,* ed. Eleonore Stump (Ithaca, N.Y.: Cornell University Press, 1993); and William J. Wainwright, "Jonathan Edwards, William Rowe, and the Necessity of Creation," in *Faith, Freedom, and Rationality,* ed. Jeff Jordan and Daniel Howard-Snyder (Lanham, Md.: Rowman and Littlefield, 1996).

An important form of the problem of evil is discussed by J. L. Schellenberg, *Divine Hiddenness and Human Reason* (Ithaca, N.Y.: Cornell University Press, 1993) who argues that if a good God existed, He would make His existence more obvious. For an interesting response see Daniel Howard-Snyder, "The Argument from Divine Hiddenness," *Canadian Journal of Philosophy* 26 (1996): 433–53.

For two philosophically sophisticated Christian responses to the problem of evil see Marilyn McCord Adams, "Redemptive Suffering: A Christian Approach to the Problem of Evil," in *Rationality, Religious Belief, and Moral Commitment,* ed. Robert Audi and William J. Wainwright (Ithaca, N.Y.: Cornell University Press, 1986), "Theodicy Without Blame," *Philosophical Topics* 16 (1988): 215–45, "Problems of Evil: More Advice to Christian Philosophers," *Faith and Philosophy* 5 (1988), 121–43, and "Horrendous Evils and the Goodness of God," *Proceedings of the Aristotelian Society, Supplement* 63 (1989): 297–310; and Eleonore Stump, "The Problem of Evil," *Faith and Philosophy* 2 (1985): 392–423, "Dante's Hell, Aquinas's Moral Theory, and the Love of God," *Canadian Journal of Philosophy* 16 (1986): 181–98, "Providence and the Problem of Evil," in *Christian Philosophy,* ed. Thomas P. Flint (Notre Dame, Ind.: University of Notre Dame Press, 1990), and "Aquinas on the Suffering of Job," in *Reasoned Faith.*

CHAPTER 4

Immortality

EVERY MAJOR RELIGIOUS TRADITION proclaims the possibility of salvation—a new and transfigured life that fully satisfies our yearning for wholeness, integrity, and happiness. If death ends our existence, these yearnings will be frustrated. For as Plato (427–347 B.C.) observed, we not only want to possess the good or happiness; we want to possess it permanently. But such possession isn't possible if we don't survive death. Hence, everyone "will necessarily desire immortality together with the good."[1] It isn't surprising, then, that the major religious traditions deny that death is final. They differ, however, about the afterlife's *nature*.

Since salvation heals and completes the whole person, the whole person must survive death.[2] What a tradition believes will survive death thus depends on what it thinks a person is. The Western and Near Eastern traditions (Judaism, Christianity, and Islam) think that the body is essential to a fully human existence. They therefore believe in the resurrection of the dead—a new life with a transfigured body. (After death, a person's soul may temporarily exist in a disembodied state, but the person isn't complete until it receives a new body.) The Platonic and Asian traditions identify the person either with its mind or soul, or with some aspect or part of it. Thus, Plato believed that persons were really souls. Neoplatonism and Vedānta identify persons with the "true self." The true self is in permanent contact with the divine and is distinct from the "empirical self" that expresses itself in dreams and ordinary waking consciousness. In this view, the body is only an instrument or possession that the soul or true self temporarily uses. It may even prevent the soul from functioning properly. Plato, for example, thought that as long as the soul was embodied "she could only view real existence through the bars of a prison."[3] Since the body isn't an essential part of a person, its survival isn't necessary for continued existence. Immortality is therefore construed as the survival of a person's soul or true self.

Two philosophical questions are connected with the doctrine of immortality. Is it possible? Are there good reasons for believing it?

THE POSSIBILITY OF IMMORTALITY

One of the most discussed issues in philosophy is the "mind-body" problem. Is the mind or soul identical with its body or a part of it such as the brain, or is it distinct from its body? The resolution of this problem has important implications for the doctrine of immortality. If minds *are* bodies, they can survive only if those bodies are resurrected. If minds are distinct from their bodies, they may be capable of surviving the latter's destruction. Philosophy of religion has some bearing on this problem. For example, if classical theism is true, at least one unembodied mind exists (namely, God). While this doesn't entail that *human* minds can exist without bodies, it might make it more plausible. Philosophers of religion have devoted most of their attention, however, to another issue.

Death involves dramatic changes. Can a person preserve his or her identity through them? Suppose, for example, that some of my thoughts and feelings survive the destruction of my body. Why should I identify these things with *me*? Why should their continued existence be of any more interest to me than the survival of my skull? Or suppose that at the general resurrection a resplendent person will appear who looks like me and claims to be me. Why should I think of this future person as myself? Why not instead regard him as a *replica* who will resemble me exactly but won't *be* me? The answer to these questions depends on the nature of personal identity.

"Empiricist theories" assert that personal identity consists in such things as bodily continuity, "apparent memory," and similarity of characters.[4] Suppose that A at t_1 is the same person as B at some later time t_2. Their identity is constituted by the fact that B's body is spatio-temporally continuous with A's body, or the fact that B seems to remember doing or experiencing many of the things A did or experienced, or the fact that A and B have similar tastes, interests, purposes, and emotional makeups, or some combination of these.

Different kinds of empiricist theory have different implications for the doctrine of immortality. Many stress bodily continuity and insist that a person's continued existence depends on there being no spatio-temporal gaps between the existence of his or her body at one moment and the next. If these philosophers are correct, survival depends on the continued existence of a person's body or some portion of it such as the brain.

Other empiricist theories interpret the criterion of bodily continuity less stringently. Some philosophers think that only *temporal* continuity is needed. If someone's body is destroyed but a qualitatively identical body appears at the next moment in a different place (Mars, for example, or "heaven") and if the person who has that body displays the same character and has the same apparent memories, then the two are the same person.

Still others think that even temporal continuity is unnecessary. All we need is an appropriate causal story linking A's body and B's body. Suppose, for example, that scientists learn how to encode the pattern of a person's brain. They then destroy the brain and after a period of time impose the pattern on a new brain constructed for that purpose. When the person with the new brain recovers from the operation, we discover that he or she shares the apparent memories of the person whose brain was destroyed and exhibits the same character. Alternatively, suppose that thousands of years after a person's body is destroyed, God creates someone with a qualitatively identical body who seems to remember everything the first person did and experienced and has the same tastes, temperament, purposes, and outlook. In these cases the second body isn't spatially or temporally continuous with the first. It might nevertheless be reasonable to identify the "new" person with the "old" one.

In spite of their differences, however, each of these versions of the empiricist theory maintains that some sort of bodily continuity is essential to personal identity. If they are right, the only sort of immortality that is possible involves a resurrection of the body.

Other empiricist theories, though, deny that bodily continuity is essential. John Locke (1632–1704) asks us to imagine waking up in a body that is qualitatively different from our own and is neither spatially, temporally, nor causally connected with it.[5] For example, imagine losing consciousness and upon regaining it finding oneself in a body of the opposite sex on a different part of the globe 200 years in the future. If this scenario is coherent, bodily continuity isn't essential to personal identity. Apparent memory alone may be essential (as Locke thought) or, perhaps, memory and similarity of character. If so, we might be able to retain our identity in a disembodied state.

But is *any* empiricist theory of personal identity correct? Bodily continuity, apparent memory, and similarity of character are (normally reliable) evidence of personal identity. But do they *constitute* it? Does our identity *consist* in these things? There are difficulties in supposing it does.

Bodily continuity, continuity of (apparent) memory, and continuity of character can have degrees. Persons can survive the destruction of their limbs and even portions of their brain. I remember much of what I did yesterday and very little of what I did on this day two years ago. My character is essentially the same as it was three months ago but quite different from what it was at fourteen.

Empiricist theories maintain that personal identity consists in physical and psychological continuities. Since continuities of this sort can have degrees, advocates of these accounts must decide between two alternatives. They can conclude that personal identity also has degrees or stipulate a degree of continuity that is necessary and sufficient for personal identity. Neither alternative is attractive.

The first conflicts with our ordinary concept of a person. There are more links (apparent memories, continuity of purpose, and so on) between myself today and myself yesterday than between myself today and myself two years ago. If personal identity varies with the strength of these connections, I am less the person I was two years ago than the person I was yesterday. This is counter-intuitive. The second alternative is also problematic since any stipulation is arbitrary. Must 51 percent of my brain survive? 90 percent? How many things that my "predecessor" did and experienced must I remember? *Any* answer seems ad hoc.

Another difficulty is created by the (logical) possibility of duplication. Suppose that A's brain is severed. Half is transplanted in B's body. The other half is transplanted in C's body. Upon recovery, B and C each claim to be A. Both have the same apparent memories of what A did and experienced, and both exhibit characters continuous with A's character. If personal identity is *constituted* by bodily continuity and continuity of memory and character, then B is identical with A and C is identical with A. But things that are identical with the same thing are identical with each other. Hence, B and C are the same person. Yet this is absurd. B and C have different bodies and, once they recover from their operations, will have different experiences and live different lives.

Some empiricist theories address this problem by adding a fourth criterion—that no other person satisfies the first three requirements (bodily continuity, apparent memories, and similarity of character). This solves the problem. Since B and C both meet the first three criteria, *neither* meets the fourth. Thus, neither satisfies *all* the criteria. Hence, neither B nor C is the same person as A.

This solution seems ad hoc. Besides, it is difficult to believe that our identity over time is partly constituted by its just happening to be the case that no one else is related to our past selves by apparent memories, bodily continuity, and similarity of character.

The solution also has an odd consequence. Neither C nor B is the same person as A because the fourth criterion isn't met. Hence A doesn't survive the operation. But A would have survived if he or she had managed to ensure that only one of the transplants was successful. (Suppose that B survives the operation but C doesn't. B is linked to A by ties of memory, bodily continuity, and similarity of character. Nor is there a duplicate. All four criteria are thus satisfied. Since all four are satisfied, B is the same person as A. Hence, A survives the operation.) But could a person's survival really depend on the success or failure of an attempt of this sort? It doesn't seem so.

Because of these difficulties, many philosophers reject empiricist theories of identity. In their view, apparent memory, bodily continuity, and similarity of character are *evidence* of personal identity but don't constitute it. Some of these philosophers think that personal identity is a "primitive notion" that can't be analyzed. If they are right, attempts to define personal identity in terms of memory, bodily continuity, or anything else are misguided.

Some advocates of nonempiricist theories of personal identity postulate the existence of an enduring substance or "transcendental ego," which is the bearer of experiences and the subject of mental activity. The ego can't be identified with a material object like the brain or with a person's mental states or powers. These philosophers think that this is the only plausible alternative to empiricist theories of identity. They also believe that their hypothesis is supported by our awareness of ourselves as subjects of a variety of contemporaneous experiences and as persons persisting through time.

As I write this chapter, I am aware of the visual properties of the paper, the pressure of my hand on the pen, sounds outside my window, thoughts connected with the problem I am addressing, and so on. All these impressions and activities are experienced as *mine*—as belonging to a single subject. Again, when I reflect on the telephone call I made an hour ago, I seem to be immediately conscious of myself as identically the same subject who made the call at that time. Experiences like these can suggest that my identity consists of the persistence of something (a "soul" or "transcendental ego") which is the subject of my mental and physical activities but distinct from them. My "ego" *expresses* itself in memory, thoughts, intentions, character traits, and actions but isn't identical with them. Nor is it identical with a body or any other empirically observable object.

Many religious believers think of the self in this way. The idea of a nonempirical self or transcendental ego is deeply entrenched in Hinduism, for example, and also in neoplatonism.

The notion of a transcendental ego has difficulties of its own. Empiricist theories usually assume that meaningful questions about personal identity can be resolved by appeals to experience. Nonempiricist theories may make this impossible. Recall the case in which half of A's brain was successfully transplanted in B's body and the other half in C's body. Both B and C share A's memories and character traits. Suppose that personal identity consists in the persistence of an ego. Which of the two is A? At least four answers are possible:

1. A and B share the same ego and are hence the same person, but C's ego comes into being at the moment at which the transplant is successful. C is thus a new person.

2. A and C share the same ego and are hence the same person, but B has a new ego and is thus a new person.

3. Both B and C have new egos and are thus new persons.

4. A was really two persons. Two transcendental egos shared the same experiences and performed the same actions. After the operation, the first continues to express itself in B's personal history while the second expresses itself in C's personal history.

Which of these answers is correct? There is no obvious way of settling the issue. Does it matter? Many advocates of nonempiricist theories don't think so. After all, why should we think that every meaningful question *can* be resolved by appeals to experience? In any case, extraordinary experiences could provide an answer. If God is omniscient, He knows which (if either) of the two persons is A. Suppose the answer is "B." God could make this knowledge public by revealing it or by publicly punishing and rewarding B (but not C) for A's actions. Since God is just, He won't reward or punish a person for an action if he or she isn't responsible for it. But x is responsible for y's actions only if x and y are the same person. God's publicly punishing and rewarding B (but not C) for A's actions would thus show that B (but not C) is the same person as A. Hence, the issue could be resolved *in principle*.

Another objection is that these theories ignore the intimate connection between a self and its experiences and activities. If identity simply consists of the persistence of a transcendental ego, then a person could presumably survive the destruction of his or her body, permanent loss of memory, and a complete change of character. All that is necessary is that the ego endure. But *is* this possible? One might stipulate some degree of empirical continuity that is essential for personal survival, but this addition to the theory seems ad hoc. Or one might deny that empirical continuities are *necessary* for personal survival but concede that immortality wouldn't interest us if all of them were severed. Neither response seems fully satisfactory.

What conclusions can we draw from our discussion? Two philosophical disputes bear on the question of immortality—the mind-body problem and the controversy over the nature of personal identity.

If minds are identical with brains or if bodily continuity is necessary for personal identity, then our survival depends on some sort of bodily resurrection. Many traditions, however, reject the doctrine of resurrection. While the soul or true self is immortal, they believe the body is permanently destroyed. These traditions are therefore committed to "mind-body dualism" (the belief that minds and bodies are ontologically distinct). They must also deny that bodily continuity is entailed by personal identity. Either personal identity doesn't consist of *any* kind of empirical connection or the only relevant ones are apparent memory, similarity of character, and other psychological continuities.

In spite of their differences, though, most theories in the philosophy of mind are compatible with the possibility of *some* sort of immortality. A thing can be possible, however, without being likely. Are there reasons for thinking we actually *are* immortal?

ARGUMENTS FOR IMMORTALITY

Are there good reasons for thinking we will survive death? The empirical evidence for survival consists of such things as Jesus's alleged resurrection and mediumistic and other paranormal phenomena. The former are miraculous and their reality is disputed. Mediumistic phenomena are also problematic.

Mediums go into a trance. In some cases they claim to contact the dead. In others, they seem to be possessed by them. The "departed spirit" may reveal things about his or her past life that are apparently unknown to the medium. Sometimes they convey information that wasn't known by the deceased's acquaintances.

While this evidence can't be dismissed out of hand, it is far from conclusive. Fraud is common. Even where fraud can't be proved, one is seldom sure that the medium couldn't have acquired the information in normal ways. There are a few cases in which there is no evidence of fraud and where it is difficult to see how the medium could have been aware of what was communicated during the sitting. But even here, other hypotheses are possible. For example, the medium could be in telepathic contact with living persons who possess the information (although this may be as implausible as the hypothesis of departed spirits).

Spirit communicators are rather reticent about the nature of the next life. Insofar as it *is* described, accounts are usually childish or silly. Even if mediumistic phenomena provide evidence for *some* sort of survival, they provide little support for the splendid immortality envisaged by Plato, Christianity, or Vedānta. As Antony Flew (1923–) observes, no spirit communicator "ever seems able to give a plausible and distinctive account of his present mode of existence. What is offered always looks deplorably like the tawdry product of the medium's phantasy life, molded by the fashionable doctrines of her cultural circle (French spiritualists are often reincarnationists . . . whereas Anglo-Saxon ones know nothing of any rebirth from the 'glorious Summerland')."[6]

Are philosophical arguments any better? Some "proofs" of immortality use premises that don't depend on religious doctrines. We will examine two—an argument from the soul's simplicity and a moral argument for immortality. Other "proofs" rest on a religious outlook and will convince only those who share it. We will discuss three. The first is based on our kinship with the divine, the second on divine justice, and the third on our desire for immortality.

The Argument from the Soul's Simplicity

J. M. E. McTaggart (1866–1925) formulated the argument in this manner:

1. There are only two ways in which the soul could be destroyed—by annihilation or by the separation of its parts.

2. Science provides no instances of annihilation. Material objects, for example, don't just cease to exist. They perish when they break down into their parts or when their parts are altered or recombined to form other things. Thus, a wall perishes when it is broken up or its bricks are used to construct a porch.

3. The self doesn't have parts that could be separated from it. The self "contains a plurality" of thoughts, feelings, and sensations, but isn't a "combination" that "is built up of parts which could exist" without it. Bricks can exist apart from the wall built from them. But thoughts and feelings can't be detached from the self that has them. Nor can a person's thoughts, feelings, and sensations be recombined to form something else. Hence,

4. The self is probably immortal.[7]

McTaggart's argument isn't entirely convincing. Some philosophers think that the self *is* a combination of appropriately related mental and physical states. If it is, why can't these parts be separated? (C. D. Broad [1887–1971] thought that mediums might be in contact with detached fragments of the deceased's mental life—isolated memories, feelings, and so on.) Furthermore, there *are* cases of "annihilation." Pains stop and dreams end. Their parts aren't separated or recombined to form something else. They simply stop existing. Why couldn't the self perish in the same manner?

Nevertheless, McTaggart's argument might have some value. The self is intimately connected with its body. Hence, the body's destructibility creates a presumption that the self too is destructible. The argument from simplicity reminds us that the self *seems* very different from a body. The presumption of its destructibility may therefore be weak.

The Moral Argument for the Soul's Immortality

Immanuel Kant argued that "complete fitness of the will to the moral law is holiness" and that holiness "is a perfection of which no rational being in the world of sense is at any time capable. But since it is required as practically [morally] necessary, it can be found only in an endless progress to that complete fitness. . . . This infinite progress is possible, however, only under the presupposition of an infinitely enduring existence and personality of the same rational being."[8] Kant's argument is roughly this:

1. We are morally obligated to perfectly conform our lives to the moral law.

2. A person isn't morally obligated to do something he or she can't do.

3. Moral perfection is thus possible. (From 1 and 2.)

4. Moral perfection isn't possible in this life. The solicitations of pleasure and pain, the pull of desire, our bias toward our own happiness and the happiness of those dear to us make some failure inevitable. Therefore,

5. The moral self must survive death; moral reason requires us to postulate an eternity in which the self can endlessly progress toward perfection. (From 3 and 4.)

There are important objections to Kant's argument. Is it clear, for example, that moral perfection *can't* be attained in this life? If I am raised in a society that is careless of the truth and my temperament is such that I find it easy to lie, I will undoubtedly lie upon occasion. Total honesty is overwhelmingly improbable. But it isn't *impossible*. It would be impossible if my upbringing and natural dispositions *determined* my behavior or if I couldn't control my inclinations by exerting my will. A strong bias toward dishonesty, however, doesn't imply that I *can't* make the effort and speak the truth. Similarly, a bias toward evil makes moral perfection difficult. It doesn't make it impossible.

One can also deny that perfection is a moral obligation. We might have a duty to *strive* toward perfection. But this isn't sufficient for the argument. A duty to strive toward perfection can be discharged in this life.

Neither of these objections is conclusive. The force of the first is uncertain since it depends on the *strength* of our bias toward evil. Kant thought that our evil inclinations are very powerful. Thus, while I can exert my will and control my evil inclinations on any *particular* occasion, I can't maintain this control *permanently.* Although one might think that a person who can control his or her inclinations on any occasion can control them on all occasions, this doesn't follow. Consider an analogy. Suppose I am driving while overtired. At any moment, I can pull myself together and focus my attention on the road. However, I can't *keep* my attention on it. My mind wanders and I must again pull myself together. Similarly, a strong bias toward evil could necessitate our failing at some time or other even though it doesn't necessitate our failing on any particular occasion. If it does necessitate our failing at some time or other, moral perfection can't be attained in this life.

The second objection may also be mistaken. "Perfect truthfulness is a duty" seems equivalent to "We ought always to speak the truth." Similarly, "Perfect justice is a duty" seems equivalent to "We ought always to act justly." But in that case, "Moral perfection is a duty" should be equivalent to "We ought always to act morally." Since the latter is surely true, so is the former. Moral perfection thus does seem to be a duty.

Nevertheless, Kant's argument isn't fully compelling. He may have shown that *if* moral perfection is a duty and it can't be attained in this life, then we survive death. The antecedent of this conditional isn't unreasonable. Can it be conclusively supported, though, without appealing to religious convictions—that God commands us to imitate His own perfection, for example, or that humanity is fallen and trapped in sin? Furthermore, a person who thinks that he or she has independent reasons for believing we aren't immortal can turn Kant's argument on its head. We aren't obligated to do the impossible. If moral perfection isn't possible in this life and there is no other life, we aren't obligated to be morally perfect.

Thus while Kant's argument may have some value, it probably won't convince anyone who isn't already strongly disposed to accept a religious picture of reality. The most plausible arguments for immortality make the dependence on a religious outlook explicit. They show that a belief in immortality is reasonable *if* certain broad metaphysical assumptions about the nature of ultimate reality are true. We will discuss three examples.

The Argument from our Kinship with the Divine

Plato thought that the soul's natural habitat is the world of "forms"—a realm of eternal and immutable perfection of which the space-time world is an imperfect copy. The soul is "akin to" or "resembles" this "other world of pure, everlasting, immortal, constant being." It is "like the divine."[9] Vedānta uses the formula "satcitānanda" (being or truth, consciousness, and joy) to describe both Brahman and the self. Theists believe that human beings are made in God's image. An example is Madhva (1197–1276), who founded a theistic school of Vedānta called Dvaita. While God infinitely transcends the self, Madhva believed that the soul's eternity, consciousness, and joy are a dependent likeness of the Lord's eternal being, infinite consciousness, and perfect joy. Arguments for immortality are sometimes based on these considerations.

The soul's kinship to the divine is thought to provide assurance that it shares the divine's eternity.

This assurance of immortality isn't perfect. Even if the soul is like the divine, it needn't be like it in *all* respects. Hence, though the divine is eternal, the self may not be. Furthermore, the strength of the assurance created by our kinship to the divine varies from one tradition to another.

In Hinduism and platonism, the major division in reality is between consciousness or soul on the one hand, and "matter" (prakriti) on the other. In these systems, souls are the same kind of thing as the divine. They are either identical with ultimate reality or part of it or, if they aren't part of the divine, differ from it only in degree. In Judaism, Islam, and Christianity, however, the great division isn't between soul and matter but between uncreated and created being. In these systems, souls *aren't* the same kind of thing as the divine. They are fashioned out of nothing and are thus more like other creatures than God. The soul's kinship to the divine is thus closer in the first type of system, and the presumption of immortality is therefore stronger.[10]

Furthermore, the nature of the soul's divine kinship sometimes precludes *personal* immortality. Advaita Vedānta is an example. Advaita distinguishes between the self or "I" (ātman) and the "psychical equipment." The latter includes our senses, the mental faculties that organize and structure sense impressions, our powers of conceptual cognition, and so on. The psychical equipment itself is a mere piece of machinery. Mental activity begins only when the "I" (consciousness) comes into conjunction with it and thus animates it (turns the machine on, so to speak). This conjunction of consciousness and the psychical equipment is the empirical self (jīva). But the true self is consciousness alone, and this is identical with Brahman. Salvation consists in recognizing this identity and thus dispelling the self's mistaken identification of itself with its psychical equipment and body. Since salvation severs consciousness's conjunction with the psychical equipment, it destroys the empirical self. This has important consequences. Memory and the sense of one's self as a unique person distinct from others are expressions of powers belonging to the psychical equipment. Because the empirical self is destroyed, the liberated soul retains no memories and loses its sense of self-identity. There is thus no *personal* immortality.

We can now summarize. Our kinship to the divine may create a presumption in favor of immortality. Nevertheless, the presumption isn't conclusive. Its strength depends on how close our relationship to the divine really is. The nature of the relationship is also important. In some views, for example, immortality isn't personal.

The Argument from Divine Justice

Another argument for immortality is based on the obvious fact that in this life goods and evils aren't distributed according to people's merits. The lives of comparatively good or innocent people are often wretched, while the wicked and feckless frequently prosper. If we are immortal, however, these inequities might be corrected.

Considerations of this sort may be one reason why Plato concluded that souls are rewarded or punished in an afterlife. They also lie behind the Indian doctrine of "karma." If we confine our attention to this life, good and evil fortune seem inequitably distributed. The inequity is only apparent, however, if (as the doctrine of karma teaches) people's fortunes are the consequence of the good and evil deeds they performed in previous lives and if their present actions determine their fortunes in future lives. A doctrine of immortality is a relatively late development in the history of Israel, but it too is a response to the inequitable distribution of goods and evils in this life. A common thread runs through these teachings—the universe is just only if we survive our deaths and are rewarded or punished in another life.

Is the universe just? If classical theism is true, the world is created by a maximally perfect divine mind. Such a being would be just and any world He created would reflect His Justice. As Samuel Clarke put it, "there is plainly . . . no sufficient distinction made between virtue and vice, no proportionable and certain rewards annexed to the one, nor punishment to the other, in this present world." But "if there be a God" who is "a being of infinite justice and goodness . . . there must necessarily be a future state of rewards and punishments after this life, wherein all the present difficulties of providence shall be cleared up, by an exact and impartial administration of justice."[11]

Whether a reasonable belief in the world's justice can be grounded in a nontheistic metaphysics is a moot point. While the doctrine of karma is a firmly entrenched part of nontheistic traditions like Buddhism, Advaita Vedānta, and Jainism, they provide few systematic arguments for it. This might be significant; perhaps the doctrine isn't *supported* by their views of ultimate reality but is simply assumed without justification. (Appeals are sometimes made to such things as the Buddha's total recall of past lives and alleged recollections of experiences in previous lives, but this sort of evidence isn't very persuasive.) On the other hand, a belief in the underlying goodness of reality lies at the heart of *any* religious metaphysics whether it is theistic *or* nontheistic. It might therefore be argued that if this belief is true, the world must ultimately be just.

In short, immortality may be a necessary condition of the world's justice. If there are reasons for thinking that the universe *is* just, a belief in immortality is reasonable.

The Argument from the Desire for Happiness and Perfection

This argument appeals to our (alleged) longing for a transcendent good. What we seek in pursuing spatio-temporal things isn't satisfied by their possession. When we acquire them, we find that they aren't what we wanted or all that we wanted, and we remain restless and dissatisfied. Even the greatest temporal goods—the joys of love, beauty, extraordinary acts of human goodness—only hint at a perfection that continually eludes us. Plato thought that we are restless and dissatisfied because worldly goods are only images or symbols of what we really (although perhaps unconsciously) want—"the everlasting possession of the good." Augustine believed that a soul that doesn't turn toward God "is riveted upon sorrows, yea though it is riveted on things beautiful."[12] Plato and Augustine both thought that the sovereign good *can* be experienced in this life. But they also believed that our glimpses of it are fragmentary and imperfect. If views of this sort are correct, our deepest desires can't be satisfied if death is final.

Is there any reason to think our deepest desires *won't* be frustrated? There is if (and probably only if) some sort of religious metaphysics is true. If goodness underlies reality, it is reasonable to believe that our most heartfelt yearnings will be satisfied. Since they can be satisfied only if we are immortal, it is also reasonable to think we will survive death.

For example, theists sometimes argue that God has created us with a longing that can be satisfied only by the everlasting enjoyment of Himself. As Augustine exclaimed, "Thou madest us for Thyself, and our heart is restless, until it repose in Thee."[13] This doctrine explains our restlessness and dissatisfaction and implies that our longing for completeness and perfection can be satisfied. It thus implies our immortality. Samuel Clarke put it more simply. The "desire of immortality . . . seems to be naturally implanted in all men. . . . And it is not at all probable, that God should have given men appetites, which were never to be satisfied [or] desires, which had no objects to answer them."[14]

Thus, *if* human beings have desires which this life can't satisfy and *if* goodness underlies reality, it is reasonable to believe in, or at least hope for, immortality.

CONCLUSION

Our discussion points to two conclusions. First, the possibility of immortality depends on the outcome of issues in the philosophy of mind. For example, souls can survive the destruction of their bodies only if minds and bodies are distinct. If they aren't, survival depends on some sort of bodily resurrection. Doctrines of immortality also imply that our identity isn't destroyed by death—that *what* survives is numerically the same thing as ourselves. The possibility of immortality thus depends on the nature of personal identity; the criteria of identity must be compatible with a person's surviving the trauma of death.

Second, arguments for immortality that don't rely on a religious metaphysics aren't compelling. If a religious vision of reality is true, however, immortality is probable or at least not unlikely. Hence, if a good philosophical case can be made for a religious outlook, it can also be made for immortality.

Can a good philosophical case be made for some system of religious metaphysics? Chapters 2 and 3 examined a number of arguments for and against theism. But there are other important issues.

Our discussion so far has implicitly assumed that religious beliefs are reasonable only if they can be supported by proofs or good arguments. This may be a mistake, for properly formed religious beliefs could have other sources. Maybe religious beliefs are justified by religious experience. Or they might be legitimate expressions of faith, not reason. Or perhaps basic religious beliefs *are* rational even though believers haven't any arguments for them and can't point to public evidence that supports them. Or they might be reasonable because they provide the best overall explanation of human experience. We will discuss these important possibilities in the next three chapters.

Notes

1. Plato, *Symposium*, in *The Dialogues of Plato*, vol. 1, trans. B. Jowett (New York: Random House, 1937), 331.

2. Buddhism may be an exception to this generalization. Buddhists identify the person with the ordinary empirical self and believe it is extinguished in Nirvāna. On the other hand, Sautrāntika is the only Buddhist school that thinks of this as annihilation.

3. Plato, *Phaedo*, trans. R. Hackforth (Indianapolis: Bobbs-Merrill, 1955), 82.

4. The term "empiricist theories" is Richard Swinburne's. My discussion in this section is heavily indebted to his. See *The Coherence of Theism* (Oxford: Clarendon Press, 1977), 111–25; and Swinburne and Sydney Shoemaker, *Personal Identity* (Oxford: Basil Blackwell, 1984).

5. John Locke, *An Essay Concerning Human Understanding*, vol. 1 (New York: Dover, 1959), book 2, chapter 27, 15.

6. Antony Flew, *A New Approach to Psychical Research* (London: C. A. Watts, 1953), 67f.

7. J. M. E. McTaggart, *Some Dogmas of Religion* (London: Edward Arnold, 1906), 108–109.

8. Immanuel Kant, *Critique of Practical Reason*, trans. Louis W. Beck (New York: Liberal Arts Press, 1956), 126–27.

9. Plato, *Phaedo*, 82–84.

10. It should be noted, however, that Christianity believes that a "new birth" involving incorporation into Christ and the bestowal of the Holy Spirit "deifies" humanity and thus intensifies the likeness.

11. Samuel Clarke, *A Discourse Concerning the Unchangeable Obligations of Natural Religion and the Truth and Certainty of the Christian Revelation* (London: Printed by W. Botham for James Knapton, 1706), p. 168–69. Reprinted by Friedrich Frommann Verlag, Stuttgart, 1964.

12. Augustine, *Confessions*, trans. Edward B. Pusey (New York: The Modern Library), 62f.

13. Ibid., 3.

14. Samuel Clarke, *Unchangeable Obligations*, 188–89.

For Further Reading

The nature of personal identity is debated by Richard Swinburne and Sydney Shoemaker in *Personal Identity* (Oxford: Basil Blackwell, 1984). The issue is also discussed by Terence Penelhum, *Survival and Disembodied Existence* (London: Routledge and Kegan Paul, 1970), and H. D. Lewis, *The Self and Immortality* (London: Macmillan, 1973). For a difficult, eccentric, but very interesting discussion of the problem see Derek Parfit, *Reasons and Persons* (Oxford: Clarendon Press, 1984), part 3.

The psychic evidence for survival is sympathetically examined by H. H. Price, "The Problem of Life After Death," *Religious Studies* 3 (1968): 447–459. C. D. Broad takes a judicious but more skeptical approach in *The Mind and Its Place in Nature* (London: Routledge and Kegan Paul, 1925), chapter 12, and *Human Personality and the Possibility of Its Survival* (Berkeley: University of California Press, 1955). For a very skeptical discussion see Antony Flew, *A New Approach to Psychical Research* (London: C. A. Watts, 1953).

Oscar Cullmann, *Immortality of the Soul or Resurrection of the Dead?* (London: Epworth Press, 1958) discusses early Christian views of the afterlife. Classical arguments for immortality are found in Plato, *Phaedo*, trans. R. Hackworth (Indianapolis: Bobbs-Merrill, 1955); *A Discourse Concerning the Unalterable Obligations of Natural Religion and the Truth and Certainty of the Christian Revelation* (Bad-Cannstatt: Friedrich Frommann Verlag, 1964), Proposition IV; Immanuel Kant, *Critique of Practical Reason,* trans. Lewis W. Beck (New York: Liberal Arts Press, 1956), part 2, chapter 2, section 4; and J. M. E. McTaggart, *Some Dogmas of Religion* (London: Edward Arnold, 1906), chapter 3. Other sympathetic treatments of the doctrine are William James, *Human Immortality* (London: Dover, 1956), and A. E. Taylor, *The Christian Hope of Immortality* (London: Unicorn Press, 1930). The doctrine is sharply criticized by David Hume, "Of the Immortality of the Soul," in *The Philosophical Words*, vol. 4, ed. T. H. Green and Thomas H. Grose (Darmstadt: Scientia Verlag Aalen, 1964), Corliss Lamont, *The Illusion of Immortality* (New York: Putnam, 1935), and Antony Flew, *The Logic of Immortality* (Oxford: Basil Blackwell, 1987).

John Hick, *Death and Eternal Life* (New York: Harper and Row, 1976) is an excellent general treatment of the issues connected with personal survival. Other recent examinations of the subject include Paul Badham and Linda Badham, *Immortality or Extinction?* (London: Macmillan, 1982), Bruce Reichenbach, *Is Man a Phoenix? A Study of Immortality* (Washington, D.C.: University Press of America, 1983), and J. P. Moreland and Gary R. Habermas, *Immortality: the Other Side of Death* (Nashville: T. Nelson, c1992).

CHAPTER 5

Mysticism and Religious Experience

THE FIRST FOUR CHAPTERS have examined a variety of arguments for religious beliefs and many objections to them. Some of us will be convinced by the arguments. Others will find the objections more compelling. Many of us, however, probably think the whole discussion misses the point and that, as William James says, "Feeling is the deeper source of religion . . . philosophic and theological formulas are secondary products, like translations of a text into another tongue." James concedes that

> Conceptions and constructions are . . . a necessary part of our religion. . . . Religious experience . . . spontaneously and inevitably engenders myths, superstitions, dogmas, creeds, and metaphysical theologies, and criticisms of one set of these by adherents of another. . . . But all these intellectual operations, whether they be constructive or comparative and critical, presuppose immediate experiences as their subject-matter. They are interpretative and inductive operations, operations after the fact, consequent upon religious feeling, not coordinate with it, not independent of what it ascertains.[1]

In short, James suggests, the roots of religious belief are *experiences,* not arguments.

His suggestion is plausible. Many men and women say they have felt God's presence, enjoyed a foretaste of Nirvāna, achieved union with Brahman, or in some other way experienced ultimate reality. These experiences play an important role in the religious life of humanity. Saints, prophets, ascetics, and other exemplary religious figures frequently have them. Some traditions deliberately cultivate religious experiences. Religious doctrines often express and articulate them. Religious experiences thus lie behind many religious beliefs and practices. Do they also *justify* them? This chapter examines this question. After looking at the nature of religious experience, we will ask whether it has "cognitive value"—whether it really does provide glimpses of unseen realities.

THE NATURE OF RELIGIOUS EXPERIENCE

There are many types of religious experience. Devout theists, for example, experience gratitude, love, fear, awe, and trust, and sometimes enjoy a sense of God's reality and presence.

Visionary experiences play an important role in some religious traditions and in the lives of some religious people. For example, Jewish Merkabah mysticism sought visions of God's throne chariot and "the mysteries of the celestial throne-world."[2] "Visions of the Bodhisattvas and of the Buddhas and their paradises" are cultivated in some forms of Mahāyāna Buddhism.[3] Visions of the Virgin or Jesus are common in Christianity.

"Numinous experiences" play an especially important role in theistic traditions. Their object is experienced as overwhelmingly vital and active, a power so great that one is reduced to insignificance in its presence. The unfathomable mystery one encounters is both "dreadful" and "fascinating." It is eerie, uncanny, and potentially dangerous (though not bad or evil) but, at the same time, so splendid and wonderful that other values seem worthless in comparison.

Rudolf Otto (1869–1937) describes these experiences in this way. The soul " 'shudders,' " is "held speechless, trembles inwardly to the farthest fibre of its being," as it faces something "'uncanny' and 'aweful,' " which can only be expressed by terms suggesting "vitality, passion, emotional temper, will, force, movement, excitement, activity, impetus." The soul responds to this mystery with "blank wonder, an astonishment that strikes us dumb, amazement absolute." Completely overwhelmed, it feels that it is "impotence and general nothingness as against overpowering might, dust and ashes as against majesty." But the mystery also "allures with a potent charm." It "is experienced . . . as something that bestows upon man a beatitude beyond compare." The numinous experience is not only "fear and trembling" but also "wonderfulness and rapture."[4]

Numinous experiences are sometimes focused on a human being, a sacred place, a tree, a mountain, or some other natural object—Jesus or the Buddha, for example, Mount Sinai or the Kaaba Stone in Mecca. But their object can't always be identified with ordinary things. In many cases, a person seems to encounter a power or will that transcends nature and actively thrusts itself into his or her own life and consciousness.

Other religious experiences are "mystical." Returning home one evening, Richard Bucke (1837–1902) suddenly found himself "wrapped around as it were by a flame-colored cloud. For an instant," he said,

> he thought of fire, some sudden conflagration in the great city; the next, he knew that the light was within himself. Directly afterwards came upon him a sense of exultation, of immense joyousness accompanied or immediately followed by an intellectual illumination quite impossible to describe . . . he saw and knew that

the Cosmos is not dead matter but a living Presence, that the soul of man is immortal, that . . . all things work together for the good of each and all. . . . The illumination itself continued not more than a few moments, but its effect proved ineffaceable . . . neither did he, or could he, ever doubt the truth of what was then presented to his mind.[5]

Another speaks of an experience in which, as he lay on the seashore, "distance and nearness become blurred into one; without and within glide into each other . . . the world exhales in the soul and the soul dissolves in the world."[6]

The "disciple" in Śaṅkara's *Crest Jewel of Discrimination* offers the following description of absorption in Brahman.

The ego has disappeared. I have realized my identity with Brahman and so all my desires have melted away. I have arisen above my ignorance and my knowledge of this seeming universe. What is this joy I feel? Who shall measure it? I know nothing but joy, limitless, unbounded! . . . The treasure I have found there cannot be described in words. The mind cannot conceive of it. My mind fell like a hailstone into that vast expanse of Brahman's ocean. Touching one drop of it, I melted away and became one with Brahman. . . . Where is this universe? Who took it away? Has it merged into something else? A while ago, I beheld it—now it exists no longer. . . . Is there anything apart or distinct from Brahman? Now, finally and clearly, I know that I am the Atman [which, in this context, can be identified with Brahman], whose nature is eternal joy. I see nothing, I hear nothing, I know nothing that is separate from me.[7]

The Christian mystic Teresa of Avila (1515–82) reports that the soul is sometimes

conscious of having been most delectably wounded. . . . It complains to its Spouse with words of love, and even cries aloud, being unable to help itself, for it realizes that He is present but will not manifest Himself in such a way as to allow it to enjoy Him, and this is a great grief, though a sweet and delectable one. . . . So powerful is the effect of this upon the soul that it becomes consumed with desire, yet cannot think what to ask, so clearly conscious is it of the presence of its God.[8]

Teresa's contemporary, John of the Cross (1542–91), speaks of a state in which "the soul lives the life of God." In this state, its understanding

is now moved and informed by . . . the supernatural light of God, and has been changed into the Divine, for its understanding and that of God are now both one. And the will . . . has now been changed into the life of Divine love; for it loves after a lofty manner with Divine affection and is moved by the Holy Spirit in Whom it now lives, since its will and His will are now only one. . . . And finally, all the movements and operations which the soul had aforetime . . . are now in this union changed into movements of God.[9]

As these quotations indicate, mysticism takes different forms. Sometimes the space-time world is seen in a new way. For example, natural objects are perceived as somehow identical with each other and the mystic. The boundaries between things collapse, and the mystic finds that he or she includes, or is included in, nature as a whole. Or, as in Bucke's case, nature is experienced as a living presence, imbued with life or soul. (The first two experiences are sometimes called "nature mysticism.") Buddhism cultivates a different experience in which spatio-temporal reality is perceived as "empty"—a conceptually unstructured flow of "dharmas" (momentary events or states that resist further analysis). The object of the Buddhist's experience isn't some permanent substance or force underlying things. It is simply the process of becoming itself. But the Buddhist doesn't experience nature as we ordinarily do. He or she views it without attempting to conceptualize it and without attachment to it.

Another common experience is "monistic mystical consciousness." The mind progressively empties itself of percepts, sensations, images, and concepts until nothing remains but consciousness itself—joyous and without any object. The experience that Śaṅkara described may be an example.

In "theistic mystical experiences," the mind also empties itself of percepts, images, and all but the most general and abstract concepts such as "being," "presence," or "love." But unlike monistic experiences, these have an object or content. Their object isn't identical with any part of the space-time world, however, or the space-time world as a whole. The character or tone of the experiences is indicated by the fact that when mystics express them, they usually employ "erotic" imagery, comparing their relation to the object of their experience with that between human lovers. Teresa's and John of the Cross's experiences provide examples.

While all these experiences may have some evidential value, philosophers should be especially interested in numinous and mystical experience.

Visionary, numinous, and mystical experiences are "noetic." They involve an intuitive perceptionlike sense of objective reality or presence. For example, someone who has a vision of Krishna usually thinks that he or she is in Krishna's presence. Many numinous experiences seem to involve confrontations with an overwhelming transcendent will. The nature mystic is convinced that he or she is seeing the space-time world as it really is. Taken at face value, these experiences provide direct information about aspects or dimensions of reality that are normally hidden from us.

Visions are more problematic than numinous or mystical experiences, however, because their contents seem culturally conditioned. Buddhists don't have visions of the Virgin Mary or hear the voice of Jesus. Devout Christians don't have visions of Bodhisattvas or celestial Buddhas. Some of these experiences may be veridical, but caution is called for.

Numinous and mystical experiences, on the other hand, occur cross-culturally. For example, Christian mystics and theistic Hindu mystics have similar experiences. Monistic mystical consciousness is important in Advaita Vedānta, Yoga, and some forms of Buddhism. Numinous experiences aren't restricted to a particular time, place, or culture. It is therefore less obvious that these experiences are culturally conditioned. Are they genuine perceptions of a transcendent dimension or order? We will address this question by focusing on mystical experience.

What must be the case for mystical experiences to be veridical? A comparison with sense experience is helpful.

Suppose I see a hat on the table. We can distinguish (1) the "given"—visual sensations caused by the stimulation of the optic nerve, (2) the experience's "presentational object"—that which appears to be directly presented to my vision, namely, a hatlike surface perceived from a particular point of view, and (3) the experience's "apparent object"—what the object presented to my vision *appears* to be, namely, a hat. Since the experience has two objects, it is a basis for two perceptual claims—a claim to perceive the experience's presentational object ("I see a hatlike surface"), and a claim to perceive its apparent object ("I see a hat"). These perceptual claims should be distinguished from (4) perceptual claims that are partly based on beliefs which are indirectly connected with the experience and may not be shared by other observers. For example, thinking that the hat belongs to John, I might say "I see John's hat."

While all three perceptual claims may be correct, only the first ("I see a hatlike surface") is *immediately* warranted by the experience. That is, the first is the only one that *must* be true for my experience to be veridical. I might be mistaken in thinking that the hat is John's or even that it *is* a hat. (Perhaps it is only a papier-mâché facsimile.) Nevertheless, if I really see a hatlike surface, my perceptual experience is veridical.

When we ask whether an ordinary perceptual experience is veridical, we are thus asking whether its presentational object is really perceived. It is therefore important to distinguish its presentational object from its apparent object or its object as described by perceptual claims like "I see John's hat." It is equally important to distinguish mysticism's presentational object from its apparent object or its object as described by doctrinal systems like Buddhism or Christianity. Can this be done?

Mystics from different traditions frequently describe their experiences in similar ways. For example, theistic mystical experiences occur in Christianity, Vaiṣnavism, Śaiva Siddhānta, and Islam. Monistic mystical consciousness plays an important role in Buddhism, Advaita Vedānta, Yoga, and other traditions. Apparent perceptions of nature's unity, or its "life" or "soul," also occur cross-culturally. Furthermore, men and women who are comparatively untouched by *any* religious tradition sometimes have experiences like these (usually some form of nature mysticism or monistic mystical consciousness). These facts suggest that (1) mystical experiences aren't simply reflections of the mystic's tradition and that (2) their presentational object can be distinguished from their apparent object or their object as described by a particular tradition.

For example, the presentational object of theistic mystical consciousness appears to be an overwhelming loving presence that transcends nature and draws the mystic to itself. Its apparent object is an unembodied person or mind that various traditions then identify as Vishnu, Allah, or the triune God of Christianity. The presentational object of monistic mystical consciousness seems to be one's own empty consciousness. Different traditions identify this as the true self, the Brahman, and so on. (In this case, there doesn't seem to be an apparent object distinct from the experience's presentational object, on the one hand, and its object as described by one's tradition, on the other.)

We can now answer the question "What must be the case for mystical experiences to be veridical?" They are veridical if their presentational objects are really perceived. If empty consciousness is real and the mystic apprehends it, monistic consciousness is veridical. If the mystic is united with an overwhelming loving presence and is aware of the union, so are theistic experiences. A monistic mystic may also claim to perceive his or her identity with Brahman, and a theistic mystic may claim to apprehend an infinite mind or the triune God of Christianity. These perceptual claims too may be correct. Nevertheless, they can be mistaken without its following that the mystic's experiences are delusive. Even if they didn't perceive Brahman or apprehend the triune God, the mystics *may* have perceived their own empty consciousness or an overwhelming loving presence.

The question, then, is whether these experiences *are* veridical—that is, whether their presentational object really is perceived. We will investigate this question next.

DO RELIGIOUS EXPERIENCES HAVE COGNITIVE VALUE?

Ordinary perceptual experiences are "noetic" in the sense that (1) they are experiences *of* something (they have a presentational object) and (2) they incorporate the conviction that the presentational object exists and one is directly perceiving it. Perceptual experiences differ in this respect from feelings, emotions, and moods.

Mystical experiences are noetic. Monistic mystical experiences don't have an object distinct from consciousness but do seem to incorporate an implicit awareness of consciousness itself. Theistic mystical experiences and nature mysticism have objects and incorporate the conviction that the objects are real and one is directly perceiving them. Mystical experiences *seem*, then, to be perceptions of reality or some aspect of it. Should these apparent perceptions be accepted at face value?

There are two ways of addressing this question. The first focuses on the perceptual experiences themselves. Advaita Vedānta maintains that all apparent perceptions or cognitions are "intrinsically valid": ideas, judgments, and experiences should be accepted as valid unless they are called into question by other ideas, judgments, or experiences. Richard Swinburne makes a similar point when he appeals to the "principle of credulity": in the absence of good reasons for thinking otherwise, "if it seems (epistemically) to a subject that x is present, then probably x is present."[10]

The idea is that apparent cognitions or perceptions are *presumptively* valid—that is, they should be accepted at face value if there are no special reasons for discounting them. Thus, if it seems to me that I see a table or remember having an apple for lunch, then "I see a table" or "I remember having an apple for lunch" should be accepted in the absence of good reasons for not doing so. (Examples of such reasons are discovering that I was drugged, that there aren't any tables in my immediate vicinity, or that my memory is unreliable.)

Some principle of this kind is needed to avoid an infinite regress or circle. Why is this the case? Suppose that no apparent cognitions are presumptively valid. Each apparent cognition would then have to be justified by another apparent cognition. This cognition must in turn be justified, and so on. Either the chain of justifications goes on forever, or it eventually doubles back on itself. Both alternatives are unsatisfactory. A finite mind can't embrace an infinite chain of apparent cognitions, and a cognition can't contribute to its own support. Thus, if no apparent cognitions are presumptively valid, no cognition is ultimately justified.

So if knowledge is possible, some apparent cognitions are presumptively valid. But if some are, then all are—including mystical experiences. Restricting the principle of credulity to only some apparent cognitions is arbitrary.

The second way of addressing the question of mysticism's cognitive validity focuses on perceptual *practices*. William Alston (1921–) takes this approach.[11] A doxastic practice is a practice of forming certain kinds of beliefs under certain sorts of conditions where the content of the beliefs is a function of those conditions. For example, we form beliefs about what we did or experienced in the past when we are strongly inclined to believe that we did them or experienced them and have certain past-tinged experiences. Variations in the conditions under which our beliefs about the past are formed are correlated with variations in the beliefs themselves. Thus, the past-tinged experience associated with my belief that I had breakfast this morning is different from the past-tinged experience associated with my belief that I left my car in the parking lot. Doxastic practices also include procedures for epistemically evaluating beliefs formed under the appropriate conditions. For example, sense perceptual practice includes the procedures we use to sort out veridical sense perceptual beliefs from nonveridical ones.

Doxastic practices are basic when they provide our primary access to their subject matter. For example, memory is basic because it provides our primary access to the past. Sense perception is basic because it provides our primary access to physical objects. The reliability of basic practices can't be established without circularity. Sense perceptual practices, for instance, can't be justified by appealing to scientific theories because those theories are acceptable only if the observational data on which they are based are correct. Nor can we appeal to the fact that sense perception enables us to successfully find our way about in our physical environment because our belief that it does so is based on sense perception.

But if a basic doxastic practice like sense perception or memory can't be justified without circularity, why should we trust it? For four reasons: (1) The practice is internally consistent. Its outputs are, on the whole, mutually compatible. Most of our perceptual beliefs, for instance, are consistent with each other. (2) Its outputs are consistent with the outputs of other well-established doxastic practices. For example, our memory beliefs are generally consistent with our sense perceptual beliefs and with the beliefs we have based on inference. (3) The practice is socially established—widely accepted and deeply entrenched in the lives of those who employ it. Finally, (4) the practice is self-supporting in the sense that its outputs support its claim to reliability. Thus, sense perceptual practice displays the features it *would* have if it *were* reliable and therefore effectively controlled by the sort of objects it seems to reveal (namely, physical objects). If sense perceptual practice were reliable, for instance, we could use sense experiences to make accurate predictions about the course of future experience. (For the behavior of the physical objects that cause them is lawlike and hence predictable.) In addition, perceptual claims would be intersubjectively testable. (Physical objects are publicly accessible and their behavior regular. Hence, if I observe an accident on Route 66, other suitably situated observers should do so as well.) People would also conceptualize their experiences in roughly the same way. (For their experiences are controlled by the same sorts of objects.) So even though we can't show that our sense perceptual practice *is* reliable without falling into circularity, it displays the features it would have if it *were* reliable. In the absence of strong philosophical reasons for doubting its reliability, it is therefore reasonable to trust it.

The practice of forming beliefs about God on the basis of a sense of empowerment, guidance, or forgiveness, classical mystical experiences, and other apparent perceptions of God ("Christian mystical practice") displays similar features. (1) As a basic practice, it provides our primary access to its subject matter (God and His relations to us). As such, its reliability can't be established without circularity. Attempts to do so will appeal to beliefs about God that ultimately rest on the practice itself. (2) The outputs of Christian mystical practice are mutually consistent and (3) consistent with the outputs of other well-established practices. (Alston believes that philosophical and scientific objections to Christian beliefs can be met.) (4) The practice is socially established. It is deeply entrenched in the lives of countless men and women. (5) Christian mystical practice doesn't display the features exhibited by sense perceptual practice. It doesn't lead to a significant number of accurate predictions. Nor are its outputs intersubjectively testable. (At least not in the same way or to the same extent. As we shall see in the next section, a Christian mystic's claim to perceive God *is* subject to the tests the Christian community uses to distinguish perceptions of God from their counterfeits. But that that mystic perceived God while praying doesn't imply that other suitably situated observers would have done so if they had been praying in the same location.) Christian theists also conceptualize their experience in different ways. (There are significant differences, for example, in the ways in which Eastern Orthodox ascetics, Anglicans from south India, and fundamentalist British Baptists conceptualize the object of their religious experiences.) But these disanalogies with sense perceptual practice are irrelevant. The signs of the re-liability of a practice are determined by the nature of the practice's subject matter. And God is very different from physical objects. Christian mystical practice has the features it would have if it were reliable. If the practice were reliable, it would provide access to a God who is good but "too 'wholly other' for us to grasp any regularities in His behavior," or to adequately understand what He is like.[12] We would therefore expect to find that we couldn't predict God's behavior with much accuracy. Nor would the practice's outputs be intersubjectively testable in the way that ordinary perceptual claims are since that depends on the publicity and regularity of physical objects. And because our grasp of God is partial and inadequate, we should expect people to con-ceptualize Him differently. Finally, if the practice were to promise spiritual in-sight, sanctification, and other ethical and spiritual fruits to those who engage in it, those who do so should be (as they are) more likely to experience them.

Alston concludes that Christian mystical practice is epistemically on a par with sense perceptual practice. It is therefore arbitrary to countenance one while rejecting the other. If it is reasonable to engage in a socially established doxastic practice like sense perceptual practice, it is also reasonable to engage in Christian mystical practice.

The rationality at issue, however, isn't epistemic. Neither practice can be shown to be epistemically rational since it is impossible to establish their reli-ability without circularity. But it *is* practically or pragmatically rational to en-gage in them.[13] (The distinction between epistemic and practical rationality is roughly this. A doxastic practice is epistemically rational if we have good rea-sons to believe that it is reliable. It is practically rational if the benefits of en-gaging in it outweigh the costs.)

To sum up. The first approach to the question of mysticism's cognitive va-lidity focuses on mystical *experiences*. Since mystical experiences are apparent cognitions, they should be accepted at face value unless there are good reasons for discounting them. The second approach focuses on mystical *practices*. Mys-tical practices and sense perceptual practices display similar epistemic fea-tures. It is therefore unreasonable to engage in the latter and discount the former unless one has special reasons for believing that mystical practices are unreliable.

The following sections examine the most important reasons for discount-ing mystical perceptions and practices. Although we will focus on theistic mystical experiences and practices, most of the points made also apply to other forms of mysticism.

Dissimilarities with Sense Perception

Critics sometimes dismiss mysticism because it isn't like sense percep-tion. C. B. Martin (1924–) is an example. Perceptual claims like "I see a table" should be distinguished from first-person psychological reports like "I seem to see a table" or "I am in pain." The former are "corrigible"—a person who sincerely makes them can be mistaken. Furthermore, there are "tests and checkup procedures" for determining whether the person is mistaken or not. (These include his or her own future observations and the observations of others.) First-person psychological reports are "incorrigible." I may mistakenly think I *see* a table, but I can't be mistaken in thinking that I *seem* to see one. Perceptual claims and first-person psychological reports also differ in another way. Perceptual claims are public claims about objective reality. First-person psychological reports are private claims about the contents of our own mind, how things seem to us, and so on. Martin believes that the mystics' claims are incorrigible because they allow nothing to count against them. They are thus more like first-person psychological reports than perceptual claims. He concludes that mystical experience tells us nothing about objective reality.[14]

Martin bases his argument on a factual mistake. Mystics are often certain of the validity of their experience, but neither they nor their communities believe that the experiences are incorrigible.

A comparison with ordinary perceptual experience may be helpful. Suppose I am certain that I see a hat. There are two ways of showing I am mistaken. One could show that no hat is there. (Suppose other suitably situated observers don't see it.) Alternatively, one could show that, whether or not the hat is there, I don't *see* it. (Perhaps I am looking in the wrong direction or suffer from a neurological disorder that makes me susceptible to hat illusions.)

There are also two ways in which mystics' claims can be shown to be mistaken. Their claims are false if the reality they allegedly perceive doesn't exist. Their claims should also be withdrawn if it can be shown that, whether or not a divine reality exists, they aren't perceiving it. Mystics and their communities believe this can sometimes be done. For example, the Christian tradition employs a variety of tests to determine whether a mystic really is perceiving God. These include the consequences of the experience for the mystic and others. (Does it promote charity and humility? Is its effect peace and psychological integration or, on the contrary, psychic disintegration? Do the mystic's experiences build up the community?) The tests also include the depth, profundity, and spiritual "sweetness" of what the mystic says on the basis of his or her experiences, its agreement or disagreement with known truths, and a comparison of the mystic's experiences with others generally acknowledged to be genuine. (In a traditional community, "known truths" include orthodox religious teaching, and the experiences with which the mystic's states of consciousness are compared are those regarded as paradigmatic by his or her community.) In some cases, the judgments of authority are decisive (authority being the mystic's spiritual director, for example, or an official representative of the mystic's community).

Martin is thus mistaken in thinking that the mystics' claims are incorrigible. Nevertheless, there *is* a significant difference between the tests used by mystics and their communities and the tests used to assess ordinary perceptual claims. Suppose a woman in Brooklyn claims she saw a bear rummaging in her garbage can. Her claim is strengthened if other suitably situated observers also thought they saw the bear. If they denied seeing it, her claim would probably be dismissed. Or suppose a man claims he sighted a new star. When others check his observations, their results are inconclusive. His claim will be strengthened if he can derive novel predictions from his observations and if these predictions are subsequently confirmed. These tests (appeals to agreement and successful predictions) play a major role in the evaluation of ordinary perceptual experience. They play only a minor role in the assessment of mystical experience.

Agreement *is* a criterion. Veridical sense experiences can be confirmed by any normal person who is placed in the appropriate circumstances. Our sense experiences are thus massively confirmed by the agreement of others. Mystical experiences aren't. Nevertheless, the mystic's experiences are often compared with other experiences that the community regards as paradigmatic. For example, a Christian's experiences may be compared with those of John of the Cross or Teresa of Avila. Because of their sanctity, these figures are regarded as "suitably situated observers." If a mystic's experience agrees with theirs, the case for its validity is strengthened. If it doesn't, the case is weakened. Agreement isn't as important, however, as the consequences of the mystic's experience for the mystic and others, and the mystic's sanity, sanctity, and orthodoxy. Successful predictions are even less important. Mystics seldom base predictions on their experiences. The accuracy of their predictions thus isn't an issue.

Does the lack of analogy between the tests used to assess mystical experience and those used to assess ordinary perceptual experience cast doubt on the cognitive validity of mystical states of consciousness? It isn't clear that it does.

As we noted in the previous section, the tests for an apparent cognition should be determined by the nature of its alleged object. Ordinary perceptual experiences provide our primary access to physical objects. Physical objects are publicly accessible, comparatively easy to discern, relatively permanent, and behave in lawlike and predictable ways. It is thus reasonable to think that veridical experiences of physical objects can be confirmed by others having similar experiences under similar conditions and by successful predictions.

The objects allegedly revealed by mystical experience are different. For example, if theistic mystics are right, the object of their experiences is God. But God is eternal and nonspatial—a self-existent, omnipotent will whose inner nature is ultimately incomprehensible. Classical theists also believe that God discloses Himself when and as He pleases and that His plans and purposes aren't fully understood. If this is correct, God's actions won't be completely predictable, and there is little reason to think that veridical experiences of Him will be confirmed by similar disclosures to most people. It is therefore unlikely that a veridical experience of God would be confirmed by massive agreement or successful predictions. Hence, these tests shouldn't be imposed on theistic mystical experiences.

Successful predictions and (massive) agreement are inappropriate tests for assessing theistic mystical experience. The tests used, however, *are* appropriate. A veridical experience of a maximally perfect being would presumably have beneficial consequences, and an encounter with it would produce profound insights rather than nonsense. Since a maximally perfect being isn't a deceiver, its disclosures would be compatible with known truths. Because it is holy, holiness is likely to be a necessary condition for being a "suitably situated observer." A comparison of one's experiences with those of the saints is therefore reasonable. Appeals to authority are also reasonable if there are grounds for thinking that their authority comes from God. In short, the tests used in evaluating theistic mystical experiences are appropriate to their alleged object. They specify conditions one would expect experiences to meet if they were perceptions of God.

Let us summarize our results. Our standard examples of perceptual experience are ordinary sense experiences. Critics think that mystical experiences aren't genuine perceptions because they aren't like them. Martin, for example, believes that mystical experiences aren't corrigible and that there are no "tests and checkup procedures" for evaluating them. They are private claims about our own thoughts and feelings rather than public claims about objective reality.

Martin is mistaken. The mystics' claims are corrigible, and there are tests for evaluating them. These tests differ from those used to evaluate ordinary perceptual claims. But differences can be explained by differences in the alleged objects of mystical experience and those of sense experience. The dissimilarity with sense perception thus isn't a good reason for discounting mystical experience.

The Absence of Independent Justification

Another common objection is that there isn't any way to check the mystics' claims. They might be acceptable if there were independent reasons for believing that the mystics' experiences provide reliable information about reality. But there aren't.

Why should one think that an independent justification is necessary? Consider the following example. I have a toothache and therefore conclude I have a cavity. Judgments of this kind are warranted because we have independent access to teeth (we can see and touch them) and know that toothaches and cavities are often connected. What is true of toothaches is true of other sensations and feelings. A person is entitled to move from first-person psychological reports about his or her private experiences to facts about the public world only if we have independent access to those facts and know that the experiences are reliable signs of them. We don't have independent access to the objects of mystical experience. Hence mystical experiences can't be independently checked. Therefore, we shouldn't rely on them.[15]

Several things are wrong with this argument. For example, we may *have* independent access to the object of the mystics' experiences. If the existence of a divine reality can be proved or the claims made for the Bible, Qurān, or some other holy book are credible, then reason or revelation provides access to the experience's object. It is also misleading to describe the subjective side of mystical experience as "having certain feelings or sensations." This description neglects mysticism's noetic quality. Mystical experiences are apparent *perceptions.* Having a mystical experience isn't like feeling pain or being depressed.

The most important point, however, is this. While toothaches provide reliable indications of cavities, the *primary* mode of access to teeth and other physical objects is sense experience. It is therefore reasonable to demand independent certification when a person claims that a toothache or other sensation provides reliable information about them. An acceptable certification will appeal to facts established by employing the primary mode of access to the kind of object that the disputed claim is about (namely, teeth).

Mystical experiences, however, aren't like toothaches. Religious experiences and impressions seem to be a basic mode of cognitive experience. That is, if these experiences and impressions are valid, they provide our primary cognitive access to the objects that the mystic's reports are about.

Now, as we saw earlier, it is doubtful whether we can independently justify *any* basic mode of cognitive experience—that is, any mode of experience which, if reliable, provides our primary access to a domain of reality. Sense perception is a case in point. We have no independent way of establishing the reality of physical objects or showing that sense experiences are systematically correlated with their presence.

Every test for establishing the existence or presence of physical objects or correlations between physical objects and human experiences directly or indirectly appeals to sense experience.

Nor can sense experience be certified "pragmatically"—by the fact that relying on it enables us to successfully deal with the external world. For this appeal is circular. That relying on sense experience leads to successful adaptation can be established only by statements about human beings and their environment that are themselves based on sense experience.

The implication is clear. If a mode of experience provides primary access to a domain of reality, it can't be independently justified. Any justification begs the question by implicitly appealing to facts established *by* that mode of experience. Hence, if *religious* experience provides our primary access to *divine* reality, a lack of independent justification casts no more doubt on its reliability than on the reliability of sense perception.

Basic modes of cognitive experience, then, needn't be independently justified; proofs of their reliability are unnecessary. Still, certain things would show that they are *un*reliable. We should distrust a basic mode of cognitive experience if (1) there are reasons for thinking that the objects to which it allegedly provides access don't exist, if (2) conclusions based on it conflict with conclusions based on other equally well-entrenched bases for beliefs, if (3) the experiences are produced by causes which suggest that they are unreliable, or if (4) claims based on the mode of experience in question are inconsistent with each other.

If the arguments for naturalism were rationally compelling, one could dismiss mysticism and other types of religious experience on the ground that their object doesn't exist and on the ground that the supernaturalistic conclusions drawn from them conflict with truths established by such deeply entrenched methods as reasoning and sense experience. Since the anti-super-naturalist's arguments aren't clearly compelling, however, this line of attack isn't promising. The third and fourth possibilities must be taken more seriously and will be discussed next.

Natural Explanations of Religious Experience

Many believe that a scientific explanation of mystical experience would discredit it. The discovery of natural mechanisms underlying these experiences would show they aren't veridical.

But why would it? There are two possibilities to consider. We know that some mechanisms are unreliable; that is, they systematically produce delusive experiences and false beliefs. Psychosis and wish-fulfillment are examples. If religious experiences and beliefs are caused by *this* sort of mechanism, we should discount them.

If this line of attack is to be effective, however, one must not only show that the unreliable mechanism is *operating,* but one must also show that it *produces* the experiences and beliefs.[16] For example, some psychotics are nature mystics. Nevertheless, psychosis may not *cause* their religious experiences. Psychotics have many experiences that can't be ascribed to their illness. (Most of their sense experiences are perfectly normal.) Furthermore, most nature mystics aren't psychotic. It thus isn't clear that the psychotic's mystical experiences should be *attributed* to a psychological disorder.

The other possibility is that the psychological, neurological, and social mechanisms underlying religious experiences *aren't* known to be unreliable. That is, they aren't known to produce delusive experiences and false beliefs. Would a discovery of mechanisms of *this* kind show that mystical experiences were untrustworthy? It isn't clear that it would.

Many philosophers think that an experience of x is veridical only if x is one of its causes. Thus, a visual experience of my desk is a perception of my desk only if the desk causes my experience. Suppose, then, that a scientifically adequate natural explanation of religious experience is discovered. Would it follow that (1) God or some other supernatural entity isn't its cause or, at least, that (2) there is no reason for *thinking* that a supernatural entity is its cause? It would not.

Classical theists believe that scientifically adequate explanations can be provided for most natural phenomena. But they also believe these phenomena are immediately grounded in God's causal activity. Hence, an adequate scientific explanation of religious experience wouldn't show that God isn't its cause. Nor would it show that God's causal activity isn't *necessary* for its occurrence.

Why is this the case? There are two senses of "x is a causally sufficient condition of y." In a broad sense, x is a causally sufficient condition of y if and only if x, together with certain background conditions, produces y. In this sense, the temperature's dropping below 32 degrees Fahrenheit is a causally sufficient condition of water's freezing. But in a stronger sense, x is a causally sufficient condition of *y* if and only if *x* *alone* (in the absence of other conditions) produces *y*. The temperature's dropping below 32 degrees isn't a causally sufficient condition of water's freezing in this sense, for many other conditions are necessary. (The water can't be salty, atmospheric pressure must be normal, and so on.) In short, "*x* is a causally sufficient condition of *y* in the strong sense" entails that nothing else is necessary for its occurrence. However, "*x* is a causally sufficient condition of *y* in the broad sense" does not.

If this is correct, scientifically adequate explanations of religious experience won't imply that God's causal activity isn't necessary for their occurrence unless the mechanisms involved in the explanation are causally sufficient in the *strong* sense—that is, unless they are capable of producing the experience even if God doesn't exist or is causally inactive. But how could one show that a natural cause is sufficient in this sense? Only by showing that the mechanisms produce the experience in situations in which God doesn't exist or is causally inactive. It is difficult to see how one could do this without establishing God's nonexistence.

Thus, the discovery of an adequate scientific explanation of religious experience wouldn't show that God wasn't its cause. Would it show that there is no justification for *thinking* that God is its cause or that the experiences are veridical? There are two reasons one might think so.

If we have an adequate scientific explanation of religious experiences, we can explain them without appealing to the causal activity of their alleged object. An inference to the latter is thus unwarranted. But if so, we have no reason for thinking that a transcendent reality is their cause and thus no reason to believe they are veridical.

This argument is unsound. In the first place, we might have *independent* reasons for thinking that God or some other supernatural reality causes mystical states of consciousness and other religious experiences. But suppose we don't. Are the mystic's claims therefore baseless? It isn't clear that they are. If the mystic's perceptual judgments and the scientific account were rival *explanations* of the experience, then the mystic's contentions might be superfluous. If natural mechanisms are sufficient for the occurrence of the experience, no other explanation seems necessary. But the mystic *isn't* offering a rival explanation. Perceptual judgments ("I see a hat" or "I perceive God") aren't *inferences* to the presence of the objects of the experiences on which they are based, and they aren't causal explanations of the experiences. We aren't, then, dealing with rival explanations or inferences but with a causal explanation and a *perceptual judgment*. Since natural causes don't preclude God's causal activity and since apparent perceptions are presumptively valid (the principle of credulity), why shouldn't the mystic's claim be accepted at face value? The discovery of an adequate scientific explanation of mystical experiences might justify concluding that there are no grounds for thinking that a transcendent reality is their cause *if* there are no other reasons for doing so. But there are—the fact that the experiences are apparent perceptions and the principle of credulity.

The second reason for thinking that the discovery of an adequate scientific explanation of religious experiences would show that they aren't veridical is this. For my visual experience of my desk to be veridical, it isn't sufficient that the desk be included among the experience's causes. Suppose I am blindfolded. A researcher notices the desk in front of me and manipulates my brain to produce impressions of it. The desk is a cause of my experience. But I don't *see* it. For the desk hasn't caused my experience in the right way. Similarly, if an apparent experience of God is to be veridical, it isn't enough that God cause it. If it were, all apparent experiences of God would be veridical. For God is a cause of everything and hence of all experiences—including the most bizarre. To be veridical God must cause them in the right way.[17] Jeff Jordan (1959–) argues that the discovery of an adequate scientific explanation of religious experience would show that it wasn't caused by God in the right way.

But why would it? An experience of God has been caused in the right way if the spiritual faculties of the person having the experience are operating as they should[18] and God's intention to reveal Himself by means of that experience is among its causes. The discovery of an adequate scientific explanation of the experience wouldn't show that these conditions aren't met.

Let us summarize. If one could show that religious experiences are produced by unreliable mechanisms, one could discount them. But the discovery of natural causes of religious experience won't discredit it if the causes aren't know to systematically produce delusive experiences and false beliefs. God or other supernatural entities can work through natural causes. The fact that religious experiences are apparent cognitions and the principle of credulity provide a reason for trusting them even if an adequate scientific explanation is available. Not only is the existence of an adequate scientific explanation compatible with God's causing religious experiences, it is compatible with His causing them in the right way.

Conflicting Claims

Critics sometimes argue that religious experience can't be reliable because it supports incompatible claims. On the basis of their experiences, men and women make claims about Brahman, Allah, Yahweh, Thor, the Tao, Nirvāna, and many other things. These claims conflict. For example, if Nirvāna is real, God isn't, and vice versa. Religious experience isn't reliable because the information it allegedly provides is inconsistent.

How strong is this objection? We must distinguish claims that are directly based on an experience from claims that aren't and claims that are incompatible from claims that are merely different.

Claims that are indirectly based upon veridical experiences can be infected with error from other sources. If I claim that the hat on the table is John's, I may be mistaken. But the mistake needn't be due to a faulty visual experience. I may just be wrong in thinking the hat belongs to John. If my wife (who is looking at the hat) says she sees Tom's hat, her claim conflicts with mine. Nevertheless, while each of our claims is (partly) based on our visual experiences, the conflict doesn't show that either of our experiences is delusive. One or both of us may simply be mistaken about the hat's owner.

The point is this. The only claim immediately warranted by a veridical noetic experience is the claim to perceive its presentational object. Other perceptual claims may also be based on the experience (for example, "I see John's hat"). But showing that these claims are mistaken doesn't cast doubt on the cognitive validity of the experience itself. Now God, or the Brahman, or Nirvāna don't appear to be presentational objects of mystical experience. If they aren't, the fact that they can't all exist is beside the point. "I perceive *Brahman*" or "I perceive *God*" could be false even though the experiences on which they are based are veridical.

Different experiences do support *different* claims—that nature is one and holy (nature mysticism), that the flow of becoming escapes our inherently abstract and static concepts (the emptiness experience), that pure empty consciousness is a reality (monistic mysticism), and that an unembodied and overwhelming loving consciousness exists (theistic mysticism). These claims are obviously different. It isn't clear they are incompatible.

The claims that are *immediately* based on *mystical* experience may therefore be consistent. Some noetic religious experiences, however, do conflict. If visions of celestial Buddhas are veridical, visions of Krishna or Jesus probably aren't.[19] Visionary experiences *are* a source of inconsistent claims and hence seem unreliable. Is religious experience in general therefore unreliable?

It probably isn't. When we spoke of religious experience as a basic mode of perceptual consciousness, we were speaking loosely. There are several kinds of religious experience and important differences between them. John of the Cross, Jonathan Edwards, and many nontheistic mystics believe that mystical, numinous, and other nonvisionary experiences provide the primary, or best, or deepest access to the transcendent. These experiences are only loosely connected with visions. (The same people often have both. Nevertheless, if people stopped having visions or believing that visions were real perceptions, there is little reason to think they would stop having or trusting numinous and mystical experiences.) If this is correct, the unreliability of visionary experience doesn't imply that more basic types of religious experience lack cognitive value.[20]

But don't claims immediately based on the more *fundamental* religious experiences conflict? It isn't clear that they do. For example, a transcendent and powerful will that thrusts itself into our life and consciousness (numinous experience), an overwhelming loving presence that draws us to itself (theistic mystical consciousness), and empty consciousness (monistic mysticism) could *all* be real. The first two might be the same reality (namely, God), and the third might be our true selves.

Let us summarize. No reliable source of information produces inconsistent results. A basic mode of perceptual experience that leads to incompatible claims should therefore be discounted. The only relevant perceptual judgments, however, are claims to perceive the experience's presentational object. Conflicts between other kinds of perceptual judgment are beside the point.

Visionary experiences do lead to incompatible claims and are consequently unreliable. But many traditions believe that visions are a relatively shallow form of religious consciousness. The deepest access to ultimate reality is provided by mystical, numinous, and other nonvisionary experiences. Perhaps, then, these deeper experiences (and not religious experience in general) are the basic mode of religious perceptual experience. If they are, the objection we are discussing loses most of its force. The perceptual claims that are *immediately* based on these experiences differ, but they aren't obviously inconsistent.

The apparent inconsistency of the claims mystics make is only part of the problem, however. Claims to perceive ultimate reality are the outputs of doxastic practices that are embedded in religious traditions such as Buddhism or Christianity. These traditions are clearly incompatible.

Doxastic practices include ways of forming beliefs. But they also include procedures for epistemically evaluating them. These involve systems of "background beliefs." Suppose I think I see a tiger in my backyard. My claim would be "rebutted" if it were determined that no tigers were in the neighborhood. For in that case my claim would be false. It would be "undermined" if it were determined that I was feverish and my mind was wandering. For under those conditions perceptual reports aren't reliable. In both cases my perceptual report would be "overridden" by other things we know. In the case of sense perceptions, our background beliefs not only include beliefs about the likelihood of tigers being in the vicinity. They also include our convictions about the nature of physical objects, the conditions under which they can be accurately perceived, and so on. In the case of Christian mystical practice, background beliefs include beliefs about the nature of God and about the circumstances under which God is likely to reveal Himself. Similarly, Buddhists epistemically evaluate mystical claims by appealing to beliefs about Nirvāna, the self's relation to it, and so on. But Christian metaphysics and Buddhist metaphysics are incompatible. Hence, Christian mystical practice and Buddhist mystical practice are also incompatible.

Alston admits that the diversity of mystical practices counts against the reliability of each of them. How strongly does it do so? The answer depends partly on whether we are already engaged in a mystical practice or not.

Suppose we are not. Christian mystical practice and Buddhist mystical practice are both socially established and are both significantly self-supporting. (Both yield the moral and spiritual fruits they promise.) Neither has been shown to be unreliable. (Their outputs appear to be consistent with each other and with the outputs of such noncontroversial practices as science and sense perceptual practice.) So I have as good a reason for engaging in one as in the other. But I can't engage in both. (The practices are incompatible.) If there are no independent metaphysical or empirical reasons for preferring one mystical practice to another, it seems that I should engage in neither.[21]

What about people who *are* engaged in Christian or some other mystical practice? It seems unreasonable for them to abandon a socially established doxastic practice that they find deeply satisfying in the absence of good reasons for thinking it unreliable. But of course there *are* reasons for doubting its reliability—the existence of incompatible mystical practices that initially at least, seem equally well supported. Whether this reason is sufficiently strong to warrant *abandoning* their mystical practice is unclear, however. Alston thinks it is not, although he admits that the diversity of mystical practices should *weaken* their confidence in their practice.[22]

Ultimately, metaphysical and empirical argumentation of a familiar sort[23] may be needed to show that commitment to a mystical practice is fully rational. Alston's case for Christian mystical practice is impressive. To be fully successful it must form part of a persuasive cumulative case argument for the Christian worldview. Similarly, commitment to Buddhist or Hindu mystical practice is fully rational only if one has good reasons for thinking that the Buddhist or Hindu worldview is superior to its rivals. Can one construct an argument for the superiority of a Christian or Buddhist or some other religious worldview? We will discuss this issue in Chapter 7.

CONCLUSION

If the principle of credulity is sound, apparent cognitions should be accepted in the absence of good reasons for not doing so. Mystical consciousness and some other forms of religious experience are noetic; people who have these experiences make perceptual claims. We should therefore accept their claims unless there are good reasons for discounting them.

The only conclusive grounds for rejecting mystical or numinous experience would be (1) proofs of the nonexistence of God or other supernatural entities, (2) evidence that the experiences are produced by natural mechanisms which are known to systematically cause false beliefs and delusive experiences, or (3) good reasons for thinking that the perceptual claims immediately based on those experiences are inconsistent. So far, critics haven't provided these grounds.

The cognitive claims of mysticism and some other forms of religious experience must therefore be taken seriously. If there is independent (of religious experience) evidence for claims about God or other supernatural realities, the argument for religious experience's cognitive validity is even stronger. Religious experience seems to provide some support for religious beliefs and thus strengthens the case for them.

Whether the support provided by religious beliefs, or by religious experience in conjunction with other evidence, is sufficiently strong to *justify* religious beliefs is another question. Philosophers as well as other men and women are divided on the matter.

Nor is it clear that most people's religious beliefs rest on either arguments *or* special experiences like mysticism. While religious belief may derive its strength from feeling, few have had the *noetic* experiences that would *support* them. Are these people's beliefs somehow improper? Or is it instead possible that their beliefs *are* justified even though they aren't grounded in noetic experiences or any other kind of evidence? We will examine this question in Chapter 6.

Notes

1. William James, *The Varieties of Religious Experience* (New York: The Modern Library, ca. 1902), 423.

2. Gershom Scholem, *Major Trends in Jewish Mysticism* (New York: Schocken Books, 1961), 44.

3. Edward Conze, *Buddhist Meditation* (New York: Harper & Row, 1969), 59f.

4. Rudolf Otto, *The Idea of the Holy* (London: Oxford University Press, 1936), 17–26, 31–33.

5. Richard Bucke, *Cosmic Consciousness* (New York: Dutton, 1956), 9–10.

6. Carl Jung, *Psychology of the Unconscious* (New York: Dodd, Mead, 1947), 360–61.

7. *Shankara's Crest Jewel of Discrimination*, trans. Swami Prabhavananda (New York: Mentor Books, 1970), 103–104.

8. Teresa of Avila, *Interior Castle*, trans. and ed. E. Allison Peers (Garden City, N.Y.: Doubleday Image, 1961), 135–36.

9. John of the Cross, *Living Flame of Love*, trans. and ed. E. Allison Peers (Garden City, N.Y.: Doubleday Image, 1962), 78–79.

10. Richard Swinburne, *The Existence of God* (Oxford: Clarendon Press, 1979), 254.

11. William P. Alston, *Perceiving God: The Epistemology of Religious Experience* (Ithaca, N.Y.: Cornell University Press, 1991).

12. ———, "Christian Experience and Christian Belief," in *Faith and Rationality*, ed. Alvin Plantinga and Nicholas Wolterstorff (Notre Dame, Ind.: University of Notre Dame Press, 1983), 129.

13. It should be noted, however, that engaging in a doxastic practice involves accepting its outputs as *true* and therefore *believing* (justifiably or not) that it is reliable.

14. C. B. Martin, *Religious Belief* (Ithaca, N.Y.: Cornell University Press, 1959), chapter 5.

15. Paul Schmidt, *Religious Knowledge* (Glencoe, Ill.: Free Press, 1961), chapter 8.

16. As Gary Gutting has pointed out in *Religious Beliefs and Religious Skepticism* (Notre Dame, Ind.: University of Notre Dame Press, 1982), chapter 5.

17. This point has been made by Michael Levine ("If there is a God, any Experience which seems to be of God will be Genuine," *Religious Studies* 26 [1990]: 207–17) and Jeff Jordan ("Religious Experiences and Naturalistic Explanations," *Sophia* 33 [1994]: 60–73).

18. She isn't insane or vicious. She sincerely loves God or seeks Him. And so on.

19. All these entities could coexist in some sense. Nevertheless, the import of visions of Christ in majesty is incompatible with the import of visions of celestial Buddhas.

20. This doesn't imply that a vision might not be caused by its alleged object or that there couldn't be independent reasons for trusting a particular vision. It does imply that visions shouldn't be trusted in the absence of independent certification. Visions are like toothaches. A person may be justified in claiming to have a cavity on the basis of his or her toothache. But pains and aches aren't reliable indicators of facts about physical objects in the absence of independent reasons for thinking the two are correlated.

21. Why not engage in (for example) Buddhist mystical practice? Since the reasons for engaging in Buddhist mystical practice are no stronger than those for engaging in Christian mystical practice, it seems arbitrary to do so. Furthermore, Christian mystical practice and Buddhist mystical practice are incompatible. Hence, any reasons for the first reasons against the second, and vice versa.

22. Alston defends this claim in chapter VII of *Perceiving God*. For a critical evaluation of Alston's arguments, see section II of William Wainwright's "Religious Language, Religious Experience, and Religious Pluralism," in *The Rationality of Belief and the Plurality of Faith*, ed. Thomas D. Senor (Ithaca, N.Y.: Cornell University Press, 1995).

23. Arguments for God's or Nirvāna's existence, evidence of Christ's or the Buddha's authority, and so on.

For Further Reading

For classic descriptions of the nature of religious experience see the following: Friedrich Schleiermacher, *On Religion: Speeches to its Cultured Despisers*, trans. John Oman (New York: Harper, 1958) and *The Christian Faith* (Edinburgh: T. T. Clark, 1956), introduction; William James, *The Varieties of Religious Experience* (New York: The Modern Library, c1902); Rudolf Otto, *The Idea of the Holy*, trans. John W. Harvey (London: Oxford University Press, 1936), and *Mysticism East and West*, trans. Bertha L. Bracey and Richenda C. Payne (New York: Meridian Books, 1957); and Evelyn Underhill, *Mysticism* (Cleveland: Meridian Books, 1955). Nelson Pike, *Mystic Union* (Ithaca, N.Y.: Cornell University Press, 1992) is an interesting analysis of the union with God allegedly experienced by some Christian mystics. An important but controversial discussion of mysticism is R. C. Zaehner, *Mysticism: Sacred and Profane* (Oxford: Clarendon Press, 1957).

Steven T. Katz, "Language, Epistemology, and Mysticism," in *Mysticism and Philosophical Analysis*, ed. Steven T. Katz (London: Sheldon Press, 1978) discusses the difficulties involved in distinguishing descriptions of mystical experience from their interpretations. For a criticism of Katz see William J. Wainwright, *Mysticism: A Study of Its Nature, Cognitive Value, and Moral Implications* (Madison: University of Wisconsin Press, 1981), chapter 1; and Robert K. C. Forman, "Introduction: Mysticism, Constructivism, and Forgetting," and Anthony N. Perovich, Jr., "Does the Philosophy of Mysticism Rest on a Mistake?" both in *The Problem of Pure Consciousness*, ed. R. K. C. Forman (New York: Oxford University Press, 1990).

The cognitive value of religious experience is defended by C. D. Broad, *Religion, Philosophy, and Psychical Research* (London: Routledge and Kegan

Paul, 1953), 190–201; Walter Stace, *Mysticism and Philosophy* (Philadelphia: J. B. Lippincott, 1960); Richard Swinburne, *The Existence of God* (Oxford: Clarendon Press, 1979), chapter 13; William J. Wainwright, *Mysticism,* chapter 3; Gary Gutting, *Religious Belief and Religious Skepticism* (Notre Dame, Ind.: University of Notre Dame Press, 1982), chapter 5; William P. Alston, *Perceiving God* (Ithaca, N.Y.: Cornell University Press, 1991); and Jerome Gellman, *Experiences of God and the Rationality of Theistic Belief* (Ithaca, N.Y.: Cornell University Press, 1991).

A frequently cited skeptical attack on religious experience's cognitive value is C. B. Martin, *Religious Belief* (Ithaca, N.Y.: Cornell University Press, 1959), chapter 5. The best recent critiques are Wayne Proudfoot, *Religious Experience* (Berkeley and Los Angeles: University of California Press, 1985), and Richard Gale, *On the Nature and Existence of God* (Cambridge: Cambridge University Press, 1991), chapter 8. For another interesting critique see Evan Fales, "Scientific Explanations of Mystical Experiences, Part I: The Case of St. Teresa" and "Scientific Explanations of Mystical Experiences, Part II: The Challenge of Theism," *Religious Studies* 32 (1996): 143–63 and 297–313.

CHAPTER 6

Anti-Evidentialism

CHAPTERS 2 AND 3 EXAMINED ARGUMENTS for and against theism. Chapter 4 discussed arguments for immortality, while Chapter 5 asked whether religious experience supports religious beliefs. Does the propriety of religious belief depend on the strength of arguments like those we discussed in these chapters?

Our beliefs aren't directly subject to our control. For example, I can't make myself believe there is an elf on my desk or stop believing that cruelty is wrong just by willing to do so. I can affect my beliefs indirectly. I can seek evidence or refuse to do so, focus my attention on some aspects of a problem and ignore others, avoid the company of people who call my beliefs into question or deliberately cultivate it. What we believe thus partly depends on what we do. What, then, are our duties with respect to believing? Upon reflection, many of us will conclude that we should only hold beliefs for which we have sufficient evidence—that as William Clifford (1845–79) put it, "It is wrong always, everywhere, and for any one, to believe anything upon insufficient evidence."[1]

John Locke was the first to clearly express this view. Locke was responding to a situation in which rival Christian sects were making incompatible claims. The modern world is even more pluralistic. We are confronted with a wide variety of conflicting religious, political, economic, and scientific opinions. Reflective members of this kind of society are likely to ask adherents of rival opinions for their evidence and conclude that they have no *right* to their opinions if they can't produce it.

The bearing of these considerations is obvious. Religious beliefs are controversial. Responsible inquirers have called them into question, and some doubts about them aren't unreasonable. It seems, then, that we shouldn't hold religious beliefs if we don't have good reasons for them. This view is called "evidentialism." Religion's critics are evidentialists. So are many believers. The former attempt to show that the evidence for religious claims is insufficient. The latter respond with proofs of God's existence, arguments for the inspiration of scripture, appeals to religious experience, and so on. Both assume that religious beliefs aren't properly held without evidence. But this assumption has its critics.

This chapter examines three forms of anti-evidentialism. The first insists that properly formed religious beliefs are expressions of faith, not reason. The second thinks they are rooted in needs and desires rather than evidence. The third suggests that religious beliefs are like memory beliefs, perceptual beliefs, and our belief in other minds; they can be rationally held without evidence.

FIDEISM

"Natural theology" attempts to support religious beliefs with arguments and evidence. "Fideists" think this is misguided. The attempt is useless because the arguments and evidence aren't compelling. It is suspect because it relies on reason. Reason isn't ultimate. Faith is superior to it and calls its pretensions into question. We will discuss three forms of fideism.

Blaise Pascal and the Sense of the Heart

The most balanced fideist may be Blaise Pascal (1623–62). He neither despises reason nor totally rejects natural theology. In Pascal's opinion, "religion is not contrary to reason" (187) and would be "absurd and ridiculous" (273) if it were.[2] He may also think that some traditional proofs of God's existence are sound and that natural reason can be persuaded by them.

But even if some proofs are sound, they are religiously inadequate. Their complexity limits their value "to a very few people; and those few . . . will always be concerned lest, once the details have slipped from memory, they might be reposing confidence in a demonstration that had been unsound."[3] And even at their best, "proofs only convince the mind." (252) They make "little impression" upon the heart. (542) A successful proof might establish the existence of "a God considered as great, powerful and eternal," but it wouldn't establish the existence of "the God of Abraham, the God of Isaac, the God of Jacob." Hence, it would only establish an abstraction. God is indeed great, powerful, and eternal, but He is also "a God of love and comfort . . . who fills the soul and heart of those He possesses"—a God who Pascal thinks can be known only through Jesus Christ. (555)

The traditional proofs are therefore inadequate; formal proofs are religiously useless. But doesn't the world provide *informal* evidence of God's reality and goodness? While it does, the evidence is ambiguous. There are traces of design, saintly lives, and some support for the occurrence of miracles and revelation. There are also, however, instances of apparent disorder, evil or wasted lives, and reasons for distrusting reports of miracles and claims to revelation. Surveying the evidence, Pascal concludes that he sees "too much to deny and too little to be sure," and is thus "in a state to be pitied." (229)

Still, the evidence for God's goodness and presence shouldn't be despised. There is enough to convince those who seek God or "have the living faith in their hearts." (242) The fault doesn't really lie in the evidence but in ourselves. The evidence is real, and it is sufficient to convince those who approach it with a recognition of their need for God and a longing for Him.

Faith is not contrary to reason, then, and it is supported by some evidence. It can also answer questions that reason asks but can't answer.

According to Pascal, only Christianity can explain our situation. An impartial assessment of human existence reveals two important facts. First, a human being is an anomalous mixture of "greatness and littleness." In spite of their pretensions and self-importance, men and women are nothing "in comparison with all existence." A human being "is but a reed, the most feeble thing in nature." Nevertheless, a person is also a "thinking reed . . . [and] if the universe were to crush him, man would still be more noble than that which killed him, because he knows that he dies and the advantage which the universe has over him." (347) In spite of their frailty and insignificance, men and women are greater than nature because they can comprehend it. Second, our life is wretched. The most carefree human lives are beset by anxiety, boredom, and unhappiness. Nothing fully satisfies us, although we try to forget our emptiness by plunging into the affairs of the world and occupying ourselves with diversions and amusements.

Christianity can explain both facts. Our littleness is a consequence of our being creatures. We are finite—part of a natural order that exists only because God wills it. But we are also great since we have a supernatural destiny; God made us so that we might enter into a relation with Him and enjoy Him forever. Why, then, are we wretched? We have turned from God and sought satisfaction in other things. The consequence of our rebellion is misery because God alone can truly satisfy us.

Christianity can also explain the ambiguity of the evidence for God's existence. Human beings belong to three "orders." Each is associated with a particular aspect of reality, and has its own objects of concern and principles of judgment. The order of "the body" is associated with the senses, natural desires and appetites, and material objects and forces. Its principle of judgment is self-interest. When our lives are dominated by this order, our criteria of judgment are shaped and distorted by our desires for power and material possessions. The order of "the mind" is that of philosophy and science. Its good is intellectual understanding, and its criterion is reason. Intellectual understanding and reason *are* good. But when this order dominates our lives, our heart withers or atrophies, and we succumb to intellectual pride. The order of "the heart" is associated with our feelings, intuitions, and affections. Its proper object is the divine goodness, and its principle of judgment is a selfless love of God and neighbor. God is grasped by the heart. The ambiguity of the evidence is partly explained by the fact that God is infinite love and can't be fully known by those who don't love Him.

Human corruption also helps explain the ambiguity of the evidence. Our fallen lives are dominated by desires for power, wealth, reputation, intellectual distinction, and so on. It is difficult for reason to disengage itself from the body and its passions. Even when it does, it isn't governed by love. Because our hearts have atrophied, we can't appreciate the force of the indications of God's presence and activity in nature and history.

Finally, the ambiguity of the evidence is rooted in God's desire to respect our freedom. "God prefers rather to incline the will than the intellect. Perfect clearness would be of use to the intellect" but "would harm the will." (580) Since God wants our response to be free, He withholds evidence of His reality that would overwhelm us and so compel us to acknowledge Him.

The ambiguity of the evidence is thus explained (1) by the fact that the divine is accessible only to the heart, (2) by sin, and (3) by God's desire to respect our freedom.

In its broadest sense, natural theology is any attempt to show that religious beliefs are rational. As we shall see in Chapter 7, one can make a rationally persuasive case for a theory or hypothesis by showing that (1) a range of data requires an explanation, that (2) the theory or hypothesis explains the data, and that (3) it does so more successfully than alternative theories and hypotheses. Pascal thinks that Christianity provides an illuminating explanation of a range of facts that would be otherwise puzzling—humanity's greatness and littleness, its wretchedness, and the ambiguity of the evidence for God's reality. Pascal also thinks that atheists can't adequately explain these things. (Atheism doesn't adequately account for our greatness since we are of little significance if naturalism is true. Nor does it adequately explain our sense of homelessness, the fact that nothing that the world provides truly satisfies us. Finally, if God does *not* exist, why do we find as much apparent evidence of His presence and activity as we do?) Christianity thus provides the best explanation of the relevant facts, and this is a good reason for accepting it. Hence, if Pascal is correct, a rationally persuasive case *can* be made for Christianity, and at least one type of natural theology is successful.

Theism is also rational in another sense. Rational actions and rational beliefs are closely connected. In general, actions are rational when they are based upon rational beliefs, and rational beliefs make rational actions more likely. Nevertheless, the criteria for assessing an action's rationality differ from those used to assess a belief's rationality. Roughly speaking, actions are rational when they make the achievement of reasonable ends more likely. Beliefs are rational when they meet the appropriate "epistemic" standards—consistency, due consideration of the relevant evidence, and so on. "Practical" rationality thus differs from "epistemic" rationality.

Although fideists often question the epistemic rationality of religious beliefs, they sometimes speak as if *adopting* religion is a rational action. Pascal, for example, employs a "wager" to show it is prudentially reasonable to embrace theism:

> "God is, or He is not." But to which side shall we incline? Reason can decide nothing here. . . . A game is being played . . . where heads or tails will turn up. What will you wager? According to reason, you can do neither the one thing nor the other; according to reason, you can defend neither of the propositions. . . . but you must wager. It is not optional. You are embarked. Which will you choose then? . . . Your reason is no more shocked in choosing one rather than the other, since you must of necessity choose. This is one point settled. But your happiness? Let us weigh the gain and the loss in wagering that God is. Let us estimate these two chances. If you gain, you gain all; if you lose, you lose nothing. Wager, then,

without hesitation that He is.—"That is very fine. Yes, I must wager; but I may perhaps wager too much."—Let us see. Since there is an equal risk of gain and of loss, if you had only to gain two lives, instead of one, you might still wager. But if there were three lives to gain, you would have to play . . . , and you would be imprudent, when you are forced to play, not to chance your life to gain three at a game where there is an equal risk of loss and gain. But there is an eternity of life and happiness. . . . And thus, when one is forced to play, he must renounce reason to preserve his life, rather than risk it for infinite gain, as likely to happen as the loss of nothingness. (233)

Pascal's wager is addressed to people who are dominated by the body with its associated passions and desires. It is pointed out that the evidence is ambiguous. One should therefore assign equal probabilities to the hypothesis that God exists and will reward those who believe in Him with eternal life and to the hypothesis that God doesn't exist and there is no eternal life. But though the probabilities of the two hypotheses are equal, the values associated with them aren't. If one adopts the first hypothesis and it proves to be true, one achieves an infinite gain. If it proves false, one only loses a finite good (some worldly gratifications one might otherwise have enjoyed). If one adopts the second hypothesis and it proves to be true, one achieves a finite gain. If it proves false, however, one loses an infinite good. Pascal concludes that even if we view the matter from the perspective of worldly prudence, the most rational policy is to adopt theism.

The wager can be criticized on several counts. Perhaps the most important is that there are more alternatives to the theistic hypothesis than Pascal has considered. Both Christian theism and Advaita Vedānta, for example, promise eternal life to their adherents. Since they are incompatible, one can't bet on both. So what should one do? If one were more probable than the others, it might be reasonable to bet on it. But if the evidence is as ambiguous as Pascal sometimes suggests, Christian theism is neither more nor less likely to be true than Advaita Vedānta. In that case there is no prudential reason for choosing Christianity rather than Advaita Vedānta, or vice versa.[4]

The important point, however, is that Pascal thinks that the adoption of theism is prudentially rational. Of course, prudential considerations alone won't produce sincere religious convictions. My control over my beliefs is limited. I might therefore recognize that it is in my interest to believe something without being able to believe it. Furthermore, *sincere* theistic beliefs are an expression of a heart that loves God, not of a self egoistically concerned with its own gains and losses. Finally, faith is a product of *grace*—not of human endeavor. Nevertheless, a person who is governed by considerations of self-interest can be made to realize that the religious life is preferable even when judged by the criterion of self-interest. As a result, that person may become more receptive to religious influences, or may engage in devotional exercises and other practices that make it more likely that he or she will eventually acquire sincere and selfless religious convictions.[5]

The relations between faith and reason are therefore complex. Faith does not contradict reason. Although faith may not meet the epistemic standards of science and philosophy, religious beliefs are *compatible* with true scientific and philosophical beliefs. There is also *evidence* for religious beliefs although it appears ambiguous to the eyes of naked reason. In addition, Christianity can account for features of human existence that aren't adequately explained by other systems and thus answer questions reason raises but can't answer. Finally, because the evidence *is* ambiguous, it is prudentially rational to "bet on" theism.

In short, faith isn't opposed to reason. Nevertheless, the two belong to different orders. Properly formed religious beliefs are expressions of a heart transformed by God's love. Prudential calculations may induce people to place themselves in positions where God will stir their affections, but they can do no more than this. The evidence is sufficient to convince those whose eyes God has opened, yet until this happens it remains ambiguous.

In the last analysis, then, reason and faith aren't fully commensurable. The construction of arguments is an expression of the "mind," while faith is an expression of the "heart." Furthermore, faith transcends and judges reason. The order of the heart is superior to the order of the mind. The love that God infuses in the heart is the criterion in terms of which *all* human activities must be judged and their adequacies and inadequacies assessed. It is therefore the criterion in terms of which *rational* activity must be evaluated.

Pascal's attitude toward reason is thus ambiguous. We will next examine a fideist whose suspicion of reason sometimes verges on hostility.

Søren Kierkegaard and Religious Commitment

Søren Kierkegaard (1813–55) bases his account of the relation between faith and reason on a rich analysis of human existence.[6]

According to Kierkegaard, existing individuals are beings in time—persons in the process of "becoming." Our natures aren't imposed upon us by our genes or culture; we create them. Who we are, and what we are, is a product of our freedom—of many decisions made over the course of time. As a consequence, the most significant questions for an existing individual are "What should I do?" or "What sort of person should I become?" Kierkegaard calls these "ethico-religious questions." We can address them objectively or subjectively.

Objective thinking is disinterested and impartial. It wants to free itself from the distortions that arise when we look at things from particular personal or cultural perspectives. This is an ideal that can never be fully realized. One can, however, approximate it by abstracting from one's personal and cultural idiosyncrasies—from everything that distinguishes one from others. The thinker as a concrete existing individual, with a particular set of concerns and passions and a particular way of looking at things, shouldn't be involved in his or her question. Thinkers should detach themselves from their existence or "subjectivity" and assume the role of impartial onlookers.

Kierkegaard believes that objective thinking is appropriate only in areas like science. When we think about our own lives and their meaning, we aren't capable of the sort of detachment required in science, historical research, and philosophy. Even if we *could* abstract from our subjectivity, we shouldn't do so. The question at issue is "How are ethical and religious categories related to *me* as just the person I am—a person with precisely *my* passions, concerns, and way of looking at things?" If I abstract from my concrete existence, issues are distorted. For the question isn't "How would a disinterested observer deal with these matters?" but "How should *I* do so?" A person who always tries to think objectively about his or her own life does "his utmost to forget that he is an existing individual, by which he becomes a comic figure, since existence has the remarkable trait of compelling an existing individual to exist whether he wills it or not." (109)[7]

For example, I can think about death objectively. I can examine its nature and causes, the way in which different societies deal with it, or the most cost-effective or humane way of treating the dying. There is a sense, however, in which this misses the point. The questions I need to ask are questions about my *own* death—"What if I should die tomorrow?" or "How should I live in the face of the fact that *I* must die?"

Subjective thinking is "self-related." For example, suppose I consider the question of immortality. (Perhaps I reexamine the arguments contained in Chapter 4.) I conclude that from the standpoint of objective reason, immortality is uncertain. Having recognized this, however, I shift my point of view and bring the doctrine to bear on my own life. I ask questions like, "What should I do if I *am* immortal?" or "Should I act as if I were immortal?" and "Dare I believe that I am immortal?" I can't think about these matters dispassionately. Since my destiny is at stake, I am involved in the questions, and my answers will express my deepest concerns and commitments. "The subjective thinker [thus] adds to his equipment aesthetic and ethical passion," and "this gives him the necessary concreteness." (313)

The difference between objective and subjective thinking can be brought out in another way. The conclusions of objective thinking are propositions that are objectively true or false; that is, their truth or falsity can be assessed by intersubjective scientific or philosophical standards. They are thus impersonal. The conclusion of subjective thinking, on the other hand, is a decision or commitment—ultimately a decision to be a certain kind of person or adopt a certain way of life. Decisions and commitments are expressions of one's passions and concerns and can't be detached from the person who makes them. Nor are impersonal scientific or philosophical norms the proper standards for assessing them. Nevertheless, a person's response to ethical and religious questions may or may not be appropriate. If it *is* appropriate, he or she has the "subjective truth."

The question, then, is "How should the individual respond to the ethical and religious question—that is, what way of life should a person adopt?"

Although existing individuals are confronted with a dizzying array of alternatives, Kierkegaard thinks that they can be roughly grouped in three categories—the "aesthetic stage," the "ethical stage," and the "religious stage."

The aesthetic stage is governed by the "principle of enjoyment" ("Be happy"). Although lives governed by this principle take different forms, they have two things in common. A person at this stage flees the burdens of society, the call of duty, and the demands of God—for society, moral duty, and God may require one to relinquish happiness. Also, people who live aesthetically don't reflect on the principle that rules their lives ("Be happy"). It thus isn't consciously chosen. As a result, lives at this stage don't adequately express human freedom.

The ethical life is governed by the principle of duty. Men and women at this stage freely choose to stand under ethical principles and attempt to carry out the ethical idea in the public world of family, work, and society.

The most important forms of the religious stage are "Religion A" and "Religion B." The first is based upon the idea of "Eternity" (God and eternal life) but not on a historical revelation as Christianity or Islam are. One embraces Eternity rather than duty as one's task by attempting to bring one's life into perfect conformity with God's requirements. A person must "submit his entire immediacy with all its yearnings and desires" for natural happiness to God. "If he finds a single hard spot, a point of resistance, it means he does not have a relationship to an eternal happiness." (353) Eternal life is thus willed with "infinite passion." This expresses itself in suffering and guilt.

Why is this the case? A person who accepts Eternity as a task, attempts to bring the idea of Eternity to bear on his or her life in all its triviality—to hold the idea of God and eternal life fast at all times and in all places. He or she must at *one and the same time* engage in ordinary human affairs (write a letter, perhaps, or take the children to the amusement park) and yet never let the idea of Eternity go. But the Eternal and the finite are essentially incommensurable; the former transcends and opposes the latter. The demands of Eternity are incompatible with our desire for natural happiness. Because of this incommensurability, the attempt to bring the Eternal and finite together results in inner tension. The tension is experienced as suffering.

The "decisive" expression of Religion A, however, isn't suffering but rather guilt. One can't fully conform one's life to Eternity; *some* failure is inevitable. One's guilt is therefore total. God requires *perfect* conformity. Hence, *any* failure means His demand hasn't been met. "The very least guilt—even if from that time on the individual were an angel—when it is put together with a relationship to an eternal happiness, is enough" to make one totally guilty. (471f)

Still, this is only part of the story. Though one suffers, one *rejoices* in the midst of one's suffering and guilt. One rejoices because one's suffering "signifies that [one] has a relationship to [eternal] happiness." (406)

"Religion B" is Christianity. It differs from Religion A in three ways. First, its governing idea isn't simply Eternity (God and everlasting life) but a paradox—that Eternity has entered time in the person of Jesus of Nazareth. Second, guilt consciousness is replaced by sin consciousness. Finally, one depends not only on God but also upon another human being. In Religion A, the individual stands alone before God. Each person has to work out his or her relationship to Eternity without another's help. In Religion B, however, one's relationship to Eternity is established with the help of a "Teacher" (Christ).

What accounts for these differences? Eternity is the "Truth," and we "have the truth" when we are properly related to Eternity. Guilt expresses our recognition that we haven't met the demands of Eternity and hence aren't properly related to it. When we reflect on this situation, however, we realize that God, being good, wouldn't have created us without the Truth. We must therefore have lost it, and so our failure is our own fault. We also realize that we can't reestablish a proper relationship to Eternity. Since any attempt to do so will be affected by our distorted relationship to the Truth, our efforts are bound to fail. With these reflections, the guilty consciousness of Religion A becomes sin consciousness.

The problem of sin can be resolved only with the help of a "Teacher." For "if the learner is to acquire the Truth, the Teacher must bring it to him; and not only so, but he must also give him the condition necessary for understanding it" by restoring his power to recognize and embrace it. "But one who gives the learner not only the Truth, but also the condition for understanding it, is more than teacher." He is "God himself."[8]

Yet how can God teach us? "The union might be brought about by God's showing himself to the learner and receiving his worship, causing him to forget himself over the divine apparition." If God were to appear in His glory and majesty, however, He would overwhelm us and reduce us to nothing. God wants our *love,* and love must be freely given. To elicit love, God must therefore hide His glory and make Himself our equal. And "in order that the union may be brought about," with even the "lowliest," He "must . . . become the equal of such a one, and so he will appear in the likeness of the humblest. But the humblest is one who must serve others, and God will therefore appear in the form of a *servant.* But this servant-form is no mere outer garment," like the beggar's cloak with which kings disguise themselves in fairy tales. "It is his true form and figure." "Therefore God must suffer all things, endure all things, make experience of all things." "For this is the unfathomable nature of love, that it desires equality with the beloved, not in jest merely, but in earnest and truth."[9]

A person who responds appropriately to the ethico-religious question has the "subjective truth." Kierkegaard clearly believes that this is a decision to accept Eternity as one's task. Ultimately, it is a decision to embrace Christ. How could one justify this decision? Kierkegaard sometimes speaks as if one can't but that this shouldn't surprise us since the same is true of *any* basic commitment. The principles defining the stages are ultimate. We can use *them* to justify other decisions. For example, we might justify a decision to remain in a low-paying but socially useful job by appealing to the principle of duty. There is no further standard, however, that can be used to justify the principles themselves. *Any* decision to embrace a form of life is an unsupported act of freedom; one must choose without objectively good reasons for doing so. A decision to live religiously *is* a free commitment but so is a decision to live aesthetically or ethically.

This, however, is misleading. Committing ourselves to the principle of happiness or duty doesn't commit us to a particular set of factual beliefs. But committing ourselves to Religion A commits us to beliefs about God and eternal life, and committing ourselves to Religion B commits us to the claim that

Eternity has entered time. Commitments to Religion A or B are thus exposed to a criticism that can't be directed at a commitment to happiness or duty—namely, that the factual beliefs one is committed to are unsupported or false. One would therefore expect Kierkegaard to show that a belief in Eternity or in Eternity's entry into time isn't unreasonable. Instead, he does the opposite.

Eternity is "objectively uncertain." That is, objective thought can neither prove nor disprove God's existence and the reality of eternal life. A person who stakes everything on Eternity thus stakes his or her life on something that (if considered objectively) is equally likely to be true or false. The risk is therefore tremendous. Religion A requires us to relinquish temporal happiness for the sake of Eternity. But if we relinquish temporal happiness and there turns out to be no eternal happiness, we lose everything. "The enterprise is madness. To be sure it is madness. It is always madness to venture, but to venture everything for the sake of an eternal happiness is the height of madness." (381)

A commitment to Religion B is even "madder." The Eternal is objectively uncertain but it isn't "absurd." Although it isn't supported by the evidence, the evidence doesn't rule it out. Christianity, however, asks us to believe that the Eternal has entered time and that a person's eternal salvation depends on his or her relation to a historical event occurring a long time ago in an obscure corner of the globe. And this, says Kierkegaard, flies in the face of reason. It is a "scandal" and an "offense." (To see the point of his remark, imagine being told that a young man in Duluth is God and that everything depends upon believing in him.)

Kierkegaard thinks that uncertainty or absurdity is necessary to faith. "Suppose a man who wishes to acquire faith; let the comedy begin. He wishes to have faith, but he wishes also to safeguard himself by means of an objective inquiry. . . . What happens?" As a result of his inquiry, "the absurd becomes something different; it becomes probable, it becomes increasingly probable, it becomes extremely and emphatically probable. . . . Now he is ready to believe it; and lo, now it has become precisely impossible to believe it. Anything that is almost probable, or extremely and emphatically probable, is something he can almost know, or as good as know, or extremely and emphatically almost *know*—but it is impossible to *believe.*" (189)

Why is this the case? For two closely related reasons. "Without risk there is no faith." (182) Faith is an act of freedom, a venture, and there is no venture without risk. But "faith is [also] the highest passion" (118), and Kierkegaard thinks that passion or "inwardness" varies in proportion to the risk's enormity. Socrates, for example, views the arguments for immortality with some skepticism. "He puts the question objectively in a problematic manner: *if* there is an immortality." But "on this 'if' he risks his entire life, he has the courage to meet death, and he has with the passion of the infinite so determined the pattern of his life that it must be found acceptable—*if* there is an immortality." (180)

The risk is greatest, however, when faith's object is not only uncertain but absurd. "When Socrates believed that there was a God, he held fast to the objective uncertainty with the whole passion of his inwardness." But "the Socratic ignorance is a witty jest in comparison with the earnestness of facing the absurd; and the Socratic existential inwardness is as Greek light-mindedness in comparison with the grave strenuosity of faith." (188) The most authentic form of subjectivity, and the most perfect expression of inwardness, is thus found in Christian faith.

Kierkegaard's fideism is more extreme than Pascal's. Kierkegaard is convinced that religious truths can't be justified by reason. Pure reason succeeds only in establishing abstract truths like those of logic and mathematics. Abstract truths tell us nothing about real existence. The reasoning employed in historical research, physics, and other empirical disciplines does tell us about real existence but it can't establish anything with certainty. Even if objective thinking *could* show that religious truths are probable, it wouldn't be enough since faith is *certain* of what it believes. But, as a matter of fact, reason *can't* make religious beliefs probable. From its standpoint, even God's existence is objectively uncertain.

The problem isn't only that the evidence is ambiguous. That Eternity has entered time is a "paradox." Kierkegaard doesn't believe that the Incarnation is logically impossible, but he does think it absurd in the sense that every rational consideration counts against it.

The uncertainty and absurdity of religious belief are irreducible. Pascal suggested that the evidence of God's reality and goodness and of the truth of Christianity becomes clear to those whose hearts are purified by love. The evidence appears weak only when viewed without faith. Kierkegaard, however, seems to think that the ambiguity of the evidence can't be overcome. Even in the eyes of faith, God and eternal life appear objectively uncertain, and the Incarnation absurd.

Pascal thought that reason and faith belong to different orders. The "head" may be rationally convinced of the truth of some religious claims, but its knowledge of God is general and abstract and doesn't touch the "heart." Still, Pascal didn't suggest that a rational knowledge of some truths about God is *inconsistent* with a proper religious attitude. But Kierkegaard does. A proper religious attitude is faith, and faith requires risk. Evidence would eliminate risk and thus destroy faith.

Kierkegaard's fideism is thus more extreme than Pascal's. In spite of their disagreements, however, the two share one important assumption. Both think that believers are committed to factual claims—that God exists, for example, or has appeared in the guise of a servant. The tension between faith and reason is created by the fact that these claims appear to be unsupported by, or even opposed by, reason. Now we will examine a version of fideism that rejects this assumption. It claims that faith is a rationally unsupported commitment to a way of life, but that faith isn't committed to factual assertions.

D. Z. Phillips and the Autonomy of Religion

The modern era subjects religious belief to many pressures. Scientific theories of human origins and historical research call biblical claims into question. Philosophers and nonreligious humanists attack theism. Traditional religion is forced to compete with secular worldviews. As a result of this pressure, many believers suspect that their convictions are intellectually unwarranted. They are attracted to fideism because it seems to justify retaining religious beliefs in the face of rational criticism. If faith and reason belong to different orders, then perhaps they don't have to take rational criticism too seriously.

But traditional fideism doesn't really remove the pressure. Neither Pascal nor Kierkegaard denies that believers are committed to controversial empirical and metaphysical claims. These claims have important implications for our understanding of human beings, history, and nature. It is thus difficult to believe that philosophy, historical research, and other forms of objective thinking are irrelevant. For example, the philosophical debates concerning the nature of personal identity have an important bearing on the truth of the doctrine of immortality.

Suppose, however, that faith *has* no factual content—that religious beliefs aren't really factual claims. If this is true, philosophical or scientific attacks upon the truth of religious assertions are based on a misunderstanding of the nature of religious belief. They are therefore irrelevant. This is the position of D. Z. Phillips (1934–).[10]

Phillips thinks it "superstitious" to treat religious beliefs as factual assertions. For example, a *religious* belief in immortality is concerned with the quality of one's *present* life—a quality indicated by such expressions as "participating in the life of God" or "living in God's presence." "The belief that we shall all meet again beyond the grave," for instance, is "an expression of the belief that people should act towards each other, not according to the status and prestige that people have acquired or failed to acquire during the course of their lives, but as children of God, in the equality which death will reveal." A belief in literal survival, however, is superstitious. It misunderstands the doctrine of immortality, flies in the face of obvious facts, and betrays a selfish preoccupation with one's own future. Similarly, a *religious* belief in the Last Judgment "is the expression and embodiment of a reflection on, or vision of, the meaning of life and death." It isn't a superstitious "prediction that certain things are going to happen."[11]

What, then, does Phillips think the status of religious beliefs is? Claims like "God exists," "We are immortal," and "There will be a Last Judgment" are the basis of religious life and practice. They can be used to justify other religious beliefs. For example, a basic belief in the reality of divine love might be used to justify the conviction that God forgives me or the belief that He forbids us to take innocent lives. Nonbasic beliefs like "God forgives me" can be evaluated as true or false because there is a standard (the basic beliefs) that can be used to assess them. Basic beliefs, however, can't be rationally assessed since there is nothing more ultimate in terms of which they could be judged true or false. Phillips believes this has two consequences.

The first consequence is that basic religious claims aren't factual assertions. Why is this the case? A factual claim is either true or false. But Phillips thinks a claim can't be true or false unless there is a standard in relation to which its truth or falsity can be assessed. Basic claims, however, are ultimate; there are no further standards that can be used to determine their truth value. They thus aren't true or false and hence aren't factual assertions.

If basic religious beliefs don't express facts, what is their function? Phillips thinks they articulate "pictures." The Christian creeds, for example, summarize the story of redemption. In doing so, they present a vision of reality. Pictures, of course, aren't true or false. They can, however, be deep or profound, and those that are give life meaning by providing new ways of looking at ordinary empirical facts. Believing in God isn't assenting to factual propositions, then, but viewing one's life from the perspective of religious pictures. "It has to do with living by them, drawing sustenance from them, judging oneself in terms of them." "To ask someone whether he thinks these beliefs are true is not to ask him to produce evidence for them, but rather to ask him whether he can live by them, whether he can digest them, whether they constitute food for him."[12] Similarly, atheists aren't rejecting factual beliefs but a way of life. An atheist is a person who thinks that a life governed by religious pictures is pointless or irrelevant—who "sees nothing in it."

The second consequence of Phillips's analysis is the autonomy of religion. There are no nonreligious standards for evaluating it. This doesn't mean that religion is an "esoteric game" isolated from the rest of life. "Religion has something to say about aspects of human existence which are quite intelligible without reference to religion: birth, death, joy, misery, . . . fortune and misfortune," and our relation to people.[13]

Religion can also succumb to outside pressures. Changes in our personal histories, or in society, may weaken the hold religious pictures have over us. Someone who thought she was religious, for instance, might find the consolations of religion meaningless in the face of personal tragedy. Or the technological transformation and exploitation of nature may make it difficult to view it as God's creation. Religious pictures sometimes lose their power when subjected to the pressure of competing pictures. Religious ideals of humility and selfless love, for example, are easily subverted by the ideals of success and control that permeate technologically advanced commercial cultures.

The autonomy of religion, then, doesn't mean that religion is isolated from life and culture. It is, however, *logically* autonomous. The relation between a religious belief and the nonreligious facts impinging upon it isn't a relation between a factual assertion and evidence that confirms or disconfirms it. While the technological transformation of nature can weaken our belief in creation, for example, it has no *logical* bearing on its truth. People who try to support their beliefs with rational evidence don't understand the nature of religious belief. Faith is neither justified nor refuted by nonreligious facts.

Phillips's position is a form of fideism.[14] He thinks that natural theology is based on a mistake. Religious belief is a commitment to a picture of reality and form of life. There are no independent standards of truth that can be used to assess its rationality. Faith, in his opinion, shouldn't be confused with "reason" (science, philosophy, and historical research); it is autonomous and has its own criteria of assessment. Pascal and Kierkegaard made similar claims.

But Phillips's position is more radical since he deprives religious beliefs of their factual status while Pascal and Kierkegaard did not.

How should his proposal be evaluated? Phillips often speaks as if he were simply describing what devout people mean when they speak of God, eternal life, or the Last Judgment. But are ordinary believers *simply* articulating pictures and expressing commitments? Don't traditional Christians, Jews, and Muslims, for example, believe that the doctrine of immortality implies they will *literally* survive death?

Natural theology is also an important part of traditions like Christianity and Islam. Natural theology, however, assumes that basic beliefs like "God exists" are either true or false and that their truth or falsity can be assessed by universally shared rational criteria. It thus assumes that there *are* independent standards by which basic religious claims can be evaluated.

In Phillips's view, the differences between Christianity and Buddhism, Judaism and Islam, and religion and secularism, are like those between opposed ideals or between pessimistic and optimistic visions of life. They aren't differences over the factual nature of reality but differences in attitude, commitment, and picture preference.

There is some truth in this. A religion like Christianity or Buddhism *does* foster unique attitudes, commitments, and picture preferences. Hīnāyana Buddhism, for example, encourages us to view the world as empty of value. Christianity does not. Buddhists and Christians also tell different stories and commit themselves to different ways of life. Christians are nourished by the story of Jesus and Buddhists by the story of the Buddha. Prayer and worship are important features of Christian life, while meditation is more important in Buddhism. These differences are real and important. Nevertheless, Christians and Buddhists talk as if the differences in attitude and picture preference were rooted in *further* disagreements over empirical and metaphysical facts—that God exists and raised Jesus from the dead, for example, or that the space-time world is composed of transitory dharmas. Phillips thus *seems* to misrepresent what ordinary Christians and Buddhists believe.

Nor is it clear that one can adopt Phillips's analysis and retain important theistic attitudes and practices. Prayer and worship are forms of personal communication. One can't attempt to communicate with another, however, if one doesn't believe in his or her factual existence. For example, I can't attempt to communicate with Peter Rabbit even though I can pretend to do so. If Phillips is correct, belief in God isn't a factual belief but a commitment to a picture that deeply affects the way we look at ordinary empirical facts. One can't understand one's belief in this fashion, however, and think of God as an independently existing factual reality. Can one, then, pray and worship? Although one can speak and act *as if* one were doing what traditional believers do when they pray and worship, isn't one really doing something different—contemplating the picture, perhaps, or reaffirming one's commitment to the way of life associated with it?[15]

Phillips's fideism deprives religious beliefs of their factual status. Although this protects faith from the attacks of its critics, the price may be too high. Traditional believers appear to be making factual claims. Many of their attitudes and practices would also seem impossible if they didn't *think,* for example, that it is factually true that the God to whom they pray exists. It is thus doubtful that one can adopt Phillips's proposal and retain traditional religious faith.

Perhaps the most sympathetic way of viewing Phillips's proposal is to think of it as a recommendation. Sophisticated Christians or Muslims who no longer believe that their creeds express factual truths may still find the Christian or Muslim stories nourishing and the Christian or Muslim way of life rich and deep. People of this sort can continue to use religious language if they construe it as expressing profound and moving pictures and a commitment to live by them. While it is doubtful whether this captures the meaning of traditional religious belief, Phillips's proposal is an option for modern believers. Many regard it as the only *serious* option for religiously sensitive but intellectually honest people. The truth of this contention depends on whether treating such claims as "God exists," "Jesus rose from the dead," and "There is no permanent substance" as factual assertions really does lead to intellectual absurdities and debased religious attitudes.

Now that we have examined three types of fideism, we will compare them and draw some general conclusions.

Conclusion

Fideists are often accused of irrationalism. Although there is some justice in the charge, it oversimplifies their position.

Pascal, for example, clearly thinks that adopting Christianity is prudent and hence reasonable. He also thinks that an informal case can be made for the truth of Christianity and that hearts which have been healed of their corruption will find the evidence sufficient. Does Pascal's fideism violate epistemic principles? It does, *if* it is epistemically irrational to firmly hold beliefs that one knows would be rejected by some equally intelligent and informed people. But this principle is controversial. Is it epistemically irrational for me to be an indeterminist, for example, or a mind-body dualist, just because I know that many intelligent philosophers hold different views? If it isn't, the principle is false.

Kierkegaard seems more willing to flout reason. He usually talks as if commitments to a way of life can't be independently justified and are therefore nonrational. He doesn't use the wager, for instance, nor does he explicitly appeal to other prudential considerations. On the other hand, his account of human existence implies that some commitments are more appropriate than others. Kierkegaard thinks that "the task of the subjective thinker is to transform himself into an instrument that clearly and definitely expresses in existence whatever is essentially human."[16] What distinguishes us from other existents, however, and is therefore essential to us, is subjectivity and freedom. Since Religion B involves the greatest risks, it places the most demands on freedom and awakens the most passion. Religion B, then, is human nature's highest expression. Its adoption is therefore reasonable in the sense that by adopting it we live most authentically.

But even though adopting Christianity might be a rational *action*, Christian *beliefs* are epistemically irrational. Some of them are "absurd" in the sense that the evidence is against them. The rest are objectively uncertain.[17]

The question of faith's epistemic rationality doesn't arise for Phillips. Phillips tends to reduce religious belief to religious commitment. In his view, "Is it reasonable to believe religious claims?" and "Is it reasonable to adopt a religious form of life?" ask the same question. Theism and atheism aren't factual issues. Questions about epistemic rationality are really about the rationality of adopting a way of life.

But these questions can't be answered either. Assessments of practical rationality depend on standards that vary from one form of life to another. Practical rationality is thus relative. Phillips does imply that religion meets important human needs. It helps us come to terms with life and provides it with depth and significance. Should we conclude then that it is reasonable to live religiously? Phillips is reluctant to do so since he finds no "common evaluative yardstick" by which the worth of actions and forms of life can be assessed.[18] That is, Phillips finds no neutral standards in terms of which one way of life could be judged better or worse than another. Nor does he provide an account of human existence that could be used to evaluate actions or forms of life. (Pascal and Kierkegaard both do this.) In Phillips's opinion, it is misleading to speak as if adopting religion is rational or irrational since there aren't any standards for making these judgments.

Fideists thus differ in their attitudes toward the epistemic rationality of religious belief and the practical rationality of religious commitment. Pascal, Kierkegaard, and Phillips deny that a good evidential case can be made for the truth of religious belief, but they do so for different reasons. Pascal denies it because he thinks the evidence is ambiguous in the eyes of natural reason. Kierkegaard denies it because he believes the evidence is either objectively uncertain or against it. Phillips denies it because he thinks that religious beliefs aren't factual and that evidence is therefore irrelevant.

They also differ with respect to the possibility of rationally justifying a religious commitment. Pascal thinks that a Christian commitment is prudentially reasonable. Although Kierkegaard denies this, his analysis of human existence implies that a Christian life is most authentic. If this is true, there is reason to adopt it. Phillips is reluctant to speak of religious commitments as either rational or irrational although he does think they enrich life by providing it with depth and significance.

There is thus no clear answer to the question, "Is fideism a form of irrationalism?" Pascal's fideism doesn't intentionally violate principles of practical rationality and involves few if any departures from epistemic rationality. Although Kierkegaard denies it, his fideism may satisfy at least some standards of practical rationality. It is, however, epistemically irrational. Epistemic principles are irrelevant to Phillips's fideism since it makes no factual claims. Practical standards *are* relevant, but Phillips thinks they are relative and concludes that no way of life can be objectively more rational than another. In spite of his disclaimers, however, Phillips's account of religion implies that living religiously *is* reasonable in the sense that it effectively serves rational ends. It does this by providing life with depth and meaning and by enabling us to come to better terms with it.

In short, while fideism sometimes flouts principles of epistemic rationality, it needn't do so in a wholesale way. (Pascal's fideism is an example.) Furthermore, fideism implicitly satisfies principles of practical rationality. Fideists think the religious option provides the best or most authentic human life, or (at the very least) a significant and satisfying way of dealing with life's contingencies. If they are right, there are good prudential reasons for choosing it. Fideism may therefore be prudentially reasonable even if it isn't epistemically rational.

Whether or not fideism is ultimately defensible, it has grasped two closely related facts. First, religious belief is much more than intellectual conviction; it involves the "heart" or will. Sincere belief commits one to a whole way of life. Second, arguments and formal proofs play a minor role in forming religious beliefs. It is doubtful, for example, whether anyone has been converted by "proofs" of God's existence. Religious belief has other sources. A person is moved by the preaching of the Buddha or Jesus, for instance, or seems to experience God in his or her life, or is deeply impressed by someone's sanctity. Proofs and arguments come later if at all.

It doesn't follow, however, that religious belief is epistemically irrational. Why do fideists think it is? They usually assume that religious beliefs aren't epistemically rational unless they are supported by proofs, formal arguments, and public evidence. But the arguments for God's existence, the immortality of the soul, or the validity of religious experience aren't universally compelling. Many intelligent people find them unconvincing. Furthermore, most fideists share their skepticism. Recognizing that the arguments aren't universally compelling and sharing the skepticism of the arguments' critics, fideists conclude that faith is epistemically irrational or, at least, nonrational.

Are they right? Not necessarily. (1) Some arguments for religious belief may be stronger than skeptics think. Some of us, for example, think that the cosmological proof *is* strong enough to establish its conclusion. (2) A more important point, however, is this. Few interesting arguments in philosophy, the humanities, or the social sciences are universally compelling. But it doesn't follow that conclusions in these areas aren't epistemically rational. Skeptics and fideists may have an unduly rigorous idea of "proof." If we adopt looser standards, perhaps a good case *can* be made for the truth of some religious beliefs. Furthermore, (3) epistemic rationality does not always depend on having proofs or arguments. Perhaps religious beliefs are epistemically rational even though they aren't based on evidence.

We have already discussed the proofs. The second possibility will be examined in Chapter 7. We now discuss the third.

WILLIAM JAMES AND THE WILL TO BELIEVE

William Clifford thought that one is entitled only to beliefs that are backed by good evidence or that are self-evident like simple mathematical truths and the deliverances of our senses. William James thinks that Clifford's policy for forming beliefs is misguided. In his opinion, a person can be rationally entitled to beliefs that aren't "intellectually warranted"—that is, are neither self-evident *nor* backed by sufficient evidence.

Why does he think this? For one thing, Clifford's policy fails to satisfy its own standards. Its legitimacy isn't self-evident. Nor is it supported by good evidence.

James also thinks that Clifford's policy is mistaken. In some cases, it is unreasonable to follow it. For example, an intellectually unwarranted belief can sometimes help bring about the truth of what is believed. The unfounded belief that another likes me, for instance, may help elicit that liking. Or suppose that several of us are engaged in a cooperative endeavor—arranging a picnic, perhaps, or organizing a relief effort. If we don't know each other very well, we have little evidence that others will do their part if we do ours. Nevertheless, if each of us believes that everyone will cooperate, we are more likely to do our share and thus bring about the truth of what is believed. Again, someone fleeing an attacker may be able to leap a chasm that is wider than anything the person has jumped before only if he or she is confident of successfully doing so.

None of these beliefs is intellectually warranted. They aren't self-evident, and they aren't supported by good evidence. If we adhere to Cifford's rule for belief formation, we will therefore refuse to indulge in them. We will "stand aloof" from others until we have objective evidence that they like us. We won't cooperate with others until we have proof that they will cooperate with us. We won't believe that we can leap the chasm—and will either let ourselves be captured or leap and fall on the rocks below. But to behave in these ways is absurd.[19]

There are also some *general* hypotheses about the nature of life that are neither self-evident nor supported by compelling objective evidence but that should nevertheless be believed since believing them can help make them true. Examples are "optimism" (the belief that the world isn't a bad whole), and "meliorism" (the belief that life can be improved by human effort). If we believe these hypotheses, we are more likely to act in ways that help bring about their truth.

Another kind of case in which it is unreasonable to follow Clifford's policy is the case where one must believe something in order to acquire evidence for it. For example, some have argued that experiences confirming religious truths can be obtained only if one initially accepts them without adequate warrant and acts on their basis. Clifford's policy would prevent us from obtaining grounds for truths of this kind. A policy with this consequence is irrational.

Finally, a blind adherence to Clifford's rule may prevent us from acknowledging some important truths. The point of an epistemic practice is to place us in touch with reality. Rational epistemic practices are those that successfully do this. A commitment to Clifford's policy could defeat this aim.

For example, the religious hypothesis contains two affirmations. First, "the best things are the more eternal things . . . the things . . . that throw the last stone, so to speak, and say the final word." Second, "we are better off even now if we believe [the] first affirmation to be true."[20] James thinks that the truth of the religious hypothesis is neither self-evident nor supported by compelling objective evidence. Clifford thus forbids us to believe it. Nevertheless, there aren't any *decisive* objections to the religious hypothesis, and there is some evidence in its favor. It *may* be true. If it *is* true, it is the most important truth about reality, and a life that isn't based on it is a failure. An adherence to Clifford's rule could thus prevent us from accepting a truth that is vital to us and could thereby frustrate the aim of *any* sound epistemic policy (to put us in touch with reality). As James says, "A rule of thinking which would absolutely prevent me from acknowledging certain kinds of truth if those kinds of truth were really there, would be an irrational rule."

Suppose we concede that Clifford's policy is inadequate. What should we put in its place? His rule shouldn't be discarded altogether. It is an appropriate policy in science and in most ordinary affairs of life. Indeed, when the issues aren't momentous and it makes little practical difference whether we believe or not, we shouldn't make up "our minds at all till objective evidence has come." Nevertheless, there *are* circumstances in which people have a right to intellectually unwarranted beliefs. According to James, they are entitled to exercise this right when two conditions are met.

First the choice between the belief and its alternatives is "living," "momentous," and "forced." The choice is living if each alternative "appeals as a real possibility to him to whom it is proposed"—that is, if one has some inclination to believe and thus act upon it. For example, the choice between determinism and indeterminism is a living option for many of us since we have some tendency to believe it and some tendency to deny it.

A choice is momentous if the opportunity presented is unique, the stake is significant, and the decision is irreversible "if it later prove unwise." James's example is a person who has the opportunity of going on a long polar expedition. The opportunity won't recur. He wishes to go but will have to sacrifice other interests to do so and, once embarked, he can't go back.

The choice is forced if it is unavoidable. "Call my theory true or call it false" doesn't present me with a forced option because I can do neither. But "Either accept this truth or go without it" does. I may deny it or suspend judgment. But in either case, I go without it.

Second, the issue "cannot by its nature be decided on intellectual grounds."

James thinks that the choice between the religious hypothesis and its denial meets these conditions. Most of us have some tendency to believe the religious hypothesis and some tendency to deny it. The choice is thus living.

It is also momentous since "we are supposed to gain, even now, by our belief, and to lose by our non-belief, a certain vital good."[21] Furthermore, the choice is forced "so far as that good goes" since one loses the good, if there is one, whether one rejects the religious hypothesis as false or merely suspends judgment. (The choice presented to us isn't "Call the religious hypothesis true or call it false" but "Accept it or go without it—that is, live in accordance with it or don't.")

The truth or falsity of the religious hypothesis isn't self-evident. James also thinks that the evidence is inconclusive. The issue cannot, then, be decided on intellectual grounds.

Both conditions are thus met. We are therefore within our intellectual rights in believing the religious hypothesis (or rejecting it).

Belief in these circumstances is primarily an expression of will rather than intellect. But by "will," James means something broader than "choice." I can't choose to believe just anything I please. I cannot decide to believe that I have a hundred dollars in my pocket and find myself believing it. I have no tendency to believe it (partly because I know the evidence is against it) and can't make myself believe it by trying. What, then, does James mean?

Belief in metaphysical hypotheses like determinism or supernaturalism is an expression of our "willing" or "passional" nature—that is, of our temperament, needs, concerns, fears, hopes, passions, and emotions. Choice (conscious volition) can play a role in the formation of these beliefs. For example, we might deliberately decide to commit ourselves to the religious hypothesis. If deliberate choice is to be effective, however, it must be supported by our passional nature.

James's point, then, is that where the conditions for exercising our right to believe are met, we aren't behaving irrationally when we follow the promptings of our passional nature. He isn't providing a license for wishful thinking. We are only entitled to exercise our right when the issue is intellectually undecidable; we have no right to beliefs that are obviously false or ruled out by good evidence. There is thus no place for absurd beliefs. Furthermore, we have no right to believe arbitrarily or to adopt the hypothesis we may superficially wish to be true. Our "choice" should be reflective, and it should be made rationally.

But the demands of reason are "practical" as well as "theoretical." "In the lower forms of life no one will pretend that cognition is anything more than a guide to appropriate action . . . and although it is true that the later mental development . . . gives birth to a vast amount of theoretic activity over and above that which is immediately ministerial to practice, yet the earlier claim is only postponed, not effaced." Intelligence evolved so that we might act successfully and enter into satisfactory relations with the world. Hence, the only views that will permanently satisfy intelligence are those that make action possible and meaningful and enable us to satisfactorily adjust to the "cosmos in its totality" as well as to our immediate environment. To do this, a view must not only satisfy our "theoretical intellects" but must also meet our deepest needs and respect our most heartfelt emotions. No view will content us long if it "essentially baffles and disappoints our dearest desires and most cherished powers" or refuses "to legitimate and to legitimate in an emphatic manner, the more powerful of our emotional and practical tendencies."[22]

James thinks that intellectuals have too narrow a view of rationality. The "sentiment" (feeling) of irrationality is a cognitive disturbance—an "inhibition" or "arrest" of thought that occurs when thinking encounters obstacles. Some difficulties are "theoretical" or "intellectual." One discovers that one's views are inconsistent or that one's predictions turn out to be mistaken. Or perhaps one encounters new phenomena that can't be fitted under familiar categories.

Other difficulties are "practical." A view can fail to satisfy our emotional demands. For example, life may seem meaningless to a person who is convinced that reality is only "atoms moving in a void." There can also be a tension between our theoretical views and cherished patterns of behavior. For instance, we might have difficulty reconciling our views on social justice with beliefs and attitudes implicit in our affluent lifestyles. Or we may be struck by an apparent incoherence or lack of fit in our beliefs. For example, many people feel that their religious and scientific beliefs don't hang together. Although they recognize that these beliefs aren't formally inconsistent, religion seems to them somehow out of place in the world described by science.

The impression or "sentiment" of rationality occurs when these disturbances are successfully overcome. The most rational view, therefore, is that which best meets the demands of our nature and thus encounters the fewest "inhibitions" or "arrests." Some of these demands are intellectual. We want views that will simplify experience by bringing it under general categories and laws, explain a wide range of phenomena, and accurately predict the future. Views that are inconsistent or incompatible with obvious facts frustrate these demands and won't satisfy us in the long run. But satisfactory views must also accommodate our passional nature. They must assure us that the world makes moral sense—that life has a meaning, that human action makes a difference, and so on. In short, the most rational view is that which best enables us to come to terms with existence as a whole. While no view that frustrates our intellectual demands will ultimately be found satisfactory, neither will any view that frustrates our deepest emotional demands or our need for significant action.

There are a number of important alternative hypotheses about the ultimate nature of life and reality. Examples are determinism or indeterminism, pessimism or optimism, and naturalism or supernaturalism. These "generic and broad" hypotheses express our "total reaction upon life"—our "sense of what life honestly and deeply means . . . our individual way of just seeing and feeling the total push and pressure of the cosmos."[23] James thinks that the choice between these hypotheses can't be made on intellectual grounds. None is self-evident, and the objective evidence isn't sufficient to decide between them. We should therefore adopt the hypotheses that best enable us to feel at home in the universe and engage in significant action. Reflection is needed to determine which hypotheses most effectively do so. The reasoning involved in this reflection won't, however, primarily consist in an examination of objective evidence but in a consideration of the hypotheses' "congruence" or "incongruence" with our passional nature.

How should we evaluate James's proposal? While anti-evidentialists think that people are sometimes justified in holding beliefs for which they lack adequate evidence, they usually concede that people aren't justified in holding them when they have, or should have, good reasons for rejecting them. James, for example, insists we have no right to beliefs when the weight of the evidence is against them. One may, then, have reasons for thinking that one's belief is false and, if so, should reject it.

But one might also have reasons for thinking that one's belief was produced by an unreliable psychological mechanism. There may be no decisive evidence against the claim that purple lemons grow some place in the universe. Yet if I believe this because I dreamed it, I have no right to my belief. Fancy and dreams are more likely to produce false than true beliefs and thus aren't reliable belief-producing mechanisms.[24]

Since the beliefs with which we are concerned are intellectually undecidable, we don't have good reasons for thinking them false. But don't we have good reasons for thinking that our passional nature (emotion, desire, fear, hope, and so on) is an unreliable belief-producing mechanism—one that is at least as likely to produce false as true beliefs and thus distort our relations with reality?

James appears to think that when the needs and emotions are deep and widely shared and the beliefs are beliefs in "generic and broad" hypotheses about the ultimate nature of reality and human life, we do *not* have good reasons for thinking that our passional nature is an unreliable belief-producing mechanism. True beliefs are those that enable us to effectively deal with reality. A system of beliefs that expresses our *whole* nature (intellectual *and* passional) is more likely to lead to effective relations with reality than one that expresses only part of it.[25]

James's appeal to our passional nature is similar to Pascal's appeal to the heart and Kierkegaard's appeal to subjectivity, will, and passion. But James isn't a fideist. In his opinion, religious beliefs *are* rational. We fail to see this because we mistakenly equate "rational beliefs" with beliefs that are self-evident or backed by compelling objective evidence. In actuality, the most rational system of beliefs is that which most effectively enables us to deal with reality and hence involves the fewest cognitive disturbances. To do this, beliefs must satisfy passional as well as intellectual needs.

James's point isn't just that our lives will be happier or more meaningful if our beliefs are partly shaped by the demands of our passional nature. Our beliefs are more likely to be *true.* True scientific, moral, or metaphysical beliefs are those that place us in touch with reality. In James's opinion, the only plausible criterion for being in touch with reality is successful action and proper adjustment to the cosmos. He therefore concludes that epistemic standards should be "practical" as well as "theoretical."

James thinks that a system of beliefs that meets these requirements will include religious convictions. Religious beliefs, then, aren't just prudentially rational. They are also *epistemically* rational.

James's plea for a broader understanding of rational believing should be taken seriously. Many of us, though, may still wonder whether our passional nature has much to do with epistemic rationality. Is the fact that a view meets our deepest emotional and volitional needs any real indication of its truth?

If God has created us and fitted us to the world in which He has placed us, then both our intellectual *and* practical capacities are probably trustworthy. One can't appeal to these alleged facts in the present context, however, because the belief that they obtain is a *religious* belief, and what is at issue is the epistemic rationality of religious beliefs in general. James's own position is that our intellectual and practical capacities would not have evolved as they have if the beliefs they produce egregiously misrepresented reality.[26]

Next we turn to an anti-evidentialist who seems to avoid appeals to the heart, the will, or our passional nature.

ALVIN PLANTINGA AND PROPERLY BASIC BELIEFS

One of the most important recent challenges to evidentialism is Alvin Plantinga's. Plantinga contends that a belief in God can be like a belief that there is a desk in front of me or a belief that I had breakfast this morning. Although these beliefs aren't conclusions from evidence, there are circumstances in which I am rationally entitled to hold them.[27]

Evidentialists are usually "foundationalists." Foundationalists maintain that a rational belief is either supported by evidence or "property basic." A belief is basic if it isn't accepted on the basis of other beliefs. It is *properly* basic when it is formed in circumstances that rationally entitle a person to hold it. My belief that $2 + 2 = 4$ or my belief that I am now in pain are examples of properly basic beliefs. I am entitled to beliefs that aren't properly basic only if I have evidence for them. My evidence must ultimately rest on my properly basic beliefs.

Most foundationalists have been "classical foundationalists." Classical foundationalists maintain that a belief is properly basic if and only if it is self-evident, incorrigible, or evident to the senses. The statements "$2 + 2 = 4$" and "A whole is greater than its parts" are examples of self-evident propositions. Incorrigible beliefs are beliefs that can't be mistaken. For example, if I believe that I am in pain, I am in pain; and if I believe that I am not in pain, I am not in pain. My belief that I have a pen in my hand is one that is evident to my senses.[28]

If classical foundationalism is true, evidentialism is true. Religious beliefs are neither self-evident, incorrigible, nor evident to the senses. We are thus entitled to them only if we have evidence for them.

Plantinga's objection isn't to foundationalism as such but to *classical* foundationalism. Its criterion of proper basicality should be rejected.

The classical foundationalists' criterion of proper basicality fails to satisfy the classical foundationalists' own standards. "Only beliefs that are self-evident, incorrigible, or evident to the senses are properly basic" isn't self-evident. (Plantinga, for one, doubts it.) It isn't incorrigible. (Classical foundationalists may be mistaken.) Nor is it evident to the senses. Hence, it isn't properly basic. But neither is it supported by evidence. Attempts to show that the criterion follows from propositions that are self-evident, incorrigible, or evident to the senses have been unsuccessful. The classical foundationalists' criterion of proper basicality is thus neither properly basic nor supported by evidence. Hence, if their standards of rationality are correct, we aren't entitled to believe it.

The classical foundationalists' criterion of proper basicality is also *false*. Plantinga asks us to consider such beliefs as

I see a tree,

I had breakfast this morning, and

That person is angry.

These beliefs spontaneously arise in certain characteristic circumstances. Upon having a familiar sort of visual experience, I find myself immediately believing that I am seeing a tree. The belief that I had breakfast this morning is spontaneously formed in circumstances that include a strong inclination to believe this together with a certain "past-tinged experience." When I see a person behaving angrily, I simply take it that he or she is angry.

These beliefs aren't "groundless." The characteristic circumstances in which they arise "confer on me the right to hold" them. For example, having a certain kind of visual experience in standard conditions (I am not too far away, the light is good, and so on) is the ground of the belief that I see a tree and justifies my holding that belief. My belief is also "defeasible"—that is, I can be mistaken. For example, what I take to be a tree might be an artificial tree. Nevertheless, if I have no reason to think there are artificial trees in the area and no reason to think that my visual equipment is defective, simply having the belief in those circumstances entitles me to it.

Even though these beliefs have grounds and are defeasible, they are basic. They aren't inferred from other beliefs that are taken as evidence for them. For example, I don't *infer* that I had breakfast this morning from the fact that I am inclined to believe that I did and am having a certain "past-tinged experience." Indeed, I wouldn't normally even *think* of this fact. While having the belief in those circumstances justifies my holding it, I don't reason *from* those circumstances *to* my belief.[29]

The three beliefs are also *properly* basic. I am rationally entitled to hold them in the circumstances in question. But only the first satisfies the classical foundationalists' criterion of proper basicality.[30] Their criterion is thus false.

It doesn't follow that *evidentialism* is false. Even if some properly basic beliefs are neither self-evident, incorrigible, nor evident to the senses, theistic beliefs may require evidence. Nevertheless, Plantinga thinks that theistic beliefs too can be properly basic.

Upon contemplating the heavens, the theist may spontaneously form the belief that they were created by God. "Upon reading the Bible, one may be impressed with a deep sense that God is speaking to him. Upon having done what I know is cheap, or wrong, or wicked I may feel guilty in God's sight and form the belief *God disapproves of what I've done.* Upon confession and repentance, I may feel forgiven, forming the belief *God forgives me for what I've done.*"[31] These beliefs are spontaneously formed in the circumstances in question. They aren't inferred from other beliefs that the theist takes as evidence for them. They are thus basic.

Are they *properly* basic? Once we abandon the classical foundationalists' criterion of proper basicality, we have no reason to think they aren't. They *are* defeasible, and sophisticated theists are aware of objections to them such as the problem of evil. If they can't meet these objections, they might not be entitled to retain their beliefs. But if they can meet them or have reasons for thinking they can be met, they have a right to hold on to them. Their beliefs continue to be *basic* since they aren't inferred from the considerations they use to meet objections to their beliefs. Their beliefs are *properly* basic since they are formed in the right sort of circumstances, and objections to them can be defeated.

The most common objection to Plantinga's proposal is that it licenses absurdities. Anyone who can't provide evidence for his or her favorite beliefs can call them properly basic. Doesn't such a person have as much right to do so as the theist? Suppose, for example, that members of a new sect claim that their belief in the Great Pumpkin is properly basic. Don't we have as much reason to accept *their* claim as to accept similar claims by theists? Plantinga thinks not.

Our rejection of the classical foundationalists' criterion for proper basicality doesn't commit us to endorsing just any belief as properly basic. To think that it does supposes that we must first have a criterion before we can determine whether a belief is or is not properly basic. This is false. We don't have an adequate criterion of proper basicality and yet we know, for example, that some memory claims are properly basic and that claims about the constitution of the atom are not. We also know that a belief in the Great Pumpkin isn't properly basic. Of course, disagreements exist concerning which beliefs are and are not properly basic. But this isn't relevant. People disagree about all sorts of things.

"There is [also] a relevant *difference* between belief in God and belief in the Great Pumpkin."[32] God has created us with a disposition to believe in Him in certain characteristic circumstances but not with a disposition to believe in the Great Pumpkin. The "Great Pumpkin objection" can thus be dismissed.

But *is* the fact that people disagree on examples of proper basicality irrelevant? Suppose that those who disagree with the theist are equally sane, intelligent, and well informed. Perhaps they are even as religiously sensitive. Doesn't their disagreement provide the theist with a reason for distrusting his or her own examples ("God made all this," "God has forgiven me," and so on)? Gary Gutting (1942–) argues that it does.[33]

Two sorts of disagreement are possible. First, a person in the appropriate circumstances may fail to spontaneously form theistic beliefs. Atheists look at the starry heavens but have no inclination to believe that God made them. Or someone may read the scriptures without finding it immediately obvious that

God is speaking through them. Second, a person may think that a belief that is incompatible with theism is properly basic. Atheists seldom claim that their disbelief in God's existence is basic. But people *have* regarded beliefs as properly basic that seem to entail that theism is false. For example, upon reading the Iśa Upanishad or having a monistic mystical experience, Advaitins may find themselves spontaneously believing that differences are unreal or that the impersonal Brahman is ultimate. If these beliefs are true, theism is false. Each type of disagreement creates problems.

Gutting argues that "Belief that *p* is properly basic for *A* in circumstances *C*" entails "When *A* is in *C*, *A* is in an epistemic situation which gives *A* privileged access to the truth of *p*." For example, "I see a tree" is properly basic for me only if I am in a set of circumstances "in which there is good reason to think that my non-inferential judgment . . . will be correct." If someone convinces me that I am not properly positioned to see the tree or have been given a drug that induces hallucinations, I shouldn't regard my belief as properly basic.

Gutting thinks that theistic beliefs aren't properly basic because the "characteristic circumstances" that Plantinga describes don't provide privileged access to the truth of theistic propositions. If they did, any properly qualified person would discern their truth when placed in those circumstances. Some theists do find themselves spontaneously forming theistic beliefs when they contemplate the beauty of a flower or are overcome with guilt. But many of their "epistemic peers" (people who are equally intelligent, honest, well informed, and sensitive) do not. The truth of theistic propositions isn't immediately obvious to *them* when they gaze on the starry heavens, or read the Bible, or repent. While they are in the same epistemic situation, they don't spontaneously form theistic judgments. Thus, the epistemic situations Plantinga describes (gazing at the heavens, reading the Bible, and so on) don't provide privileged access to theistic truths. Theistic beliefs, therefore, aren't *properly* basic.

The second type of disagreement creates a different problem. Adherents of nontheistic religions seem to regard beliefs that are incompatible with theism as properly basic. As a Christian or Jewish theist reads the Bible, it may seem immediately obvious that God is addressing him or her through the words of scripture. An Advaitin may find it immediately obvious that the Iśa Upanishad is a revelation of eternal truth. Both think that their beliefs are not only basic but also *properly* basic. Why, then, should theists trust their own "intuitions" rather than those of Advaitins? If both are equally intelligent, informed, and religiously sensitive, it seems arbitrary to privilege one set of intuitions rather than the other.

Why is this the case? The theist's beliefs and the Advaitin's beliefs appear to be formed in similar ways. The same type of belief-producing mechanism seems involved in both cases. Thus, if one is reliable, so is the other. But the mechanisms can't both be reliable since they produce conflicting beliefs. Hence, neither is reliable.

Plantinga has a response to both difficulties. In creating us in His image, God has given us epistemic faculties that reflect His own cognitive excellence.

Beliefs produced by these faculties are warranted,[34] and are thus likely to be true, provided that they are aimed at truth,[35] and are functioning as God designed them to in the epistemic environment for which He intended them. Familiar examples are memory, sense perception, our power of rational inference, and so on. But God also created us with what John Calvin (1509–64) calls a *sensus divinitatis,* a disposition to believe in Him when placed in appropriate circumstances (contemplating the starry heavens, say, or experiencing remorse). Theistic beliefs produced in these circumstances are not only basic. They are *properly* basic—and that in two senses. First, one violates no epistemic duties in holding beliefs produced by the *sensus divinitatis* in those circumstances. Second, the beliefs are warranted because they are produced by a cognitive faculty (the *sensus divinitatis*) that is aimed at truth, and is functioning as it was designed to function in the cognitive environment for which God intended it.

Our cognitive faculties can malfunction, however. Blindness can impair our perceptual faculties. Amnesia can affect memory. Mental disorders can weaken or destroy our reasoning capacities. Our capacity for religious discernment can also malfunction. A person whose *sensus divinitatis* is operating according to its "design plan" will find himself or herself spontaneously forming true beliefs about God in a wide variety of circumstances. But sin has damaged this capacity. The result is that many do not find themselves spontaneously forming theistic beliefs when confronted with their own moral inadequacy, say, or the beauties of nature.[36]

Plantinga's response to the first sort of disagreement is therefore this. Those who don't form basic beliefs about God in the appropriate circumstances *aren't* the epistemic peers of the men and women who do. While they may be as intelligent, well informed, honest, and sensitive as theists whose beliefs about God are basic in those circumstances, the operation of their *sensus divinitatis* has been impaired by sin.

It should be noted, though, that atheists and agnostics aren't the only ones for whom belief in God isn't basic. Many *theists'* belief in God isn't basic either. While they believe (for example) that God has created the heavens, they don't find this immediately obvious when they contemplate them. Their belief is based on *inference* from a variety of evidence, or (as in Kierkegaard's case) is the expression of a *willed commitment* to a truth that is thought of as objectively uncertain and therefore epistemically unwarranted. A consequence of Plantinga's position is that the cognitive capacities of these theists, too, are malfunctioning. Even if their belief in God is strong, stable, and central to the way they view the world and conduct their lives, their power of religious discernment has been impaired by their own or another's sin.[37] Hence, they too aren't the epistemic peers of theists whose belief in God is properly basic.[38] Many theists find this consequence counter-intuitive.

How could Plantinga respond to the second sort of disagreement? There are at least two possibilities. The first is to concede that the Advaitin's beliefs *are* partly produced by the *sensus divinitatis* but argue that its functioning has been impaired by sin so that its deliverances are general or inchoate. The Advaitin's *sensus divinitatis* prompts him to correctly believe that the spatio-temporal world is rooted in a divine reality but fails to convince him that the divine reality in question is *God*. The Advaitin's other beliefs (that distinctions are unreal, that Brahman alone is real, and so on) are based on mistaken testimony (traditional interpretations of the Vedas, for example) and faulty inferences.

The second possibility is that the Advaitin's beliefs aren't produced by the *sensus divinitatis* at all but by other belief-producing mechanisms that either aren't aimed at truth or aren't functioning properly in the epistemic environment for which God designed them. Plantinga could argue, for instance, that Advaita Vedānta is a joint product of monistic mystical experiences, faith in the Vedas and other allegedly authoritative texts, and inference. Our capacity for empty-consciousness experiences isn't aimed at truth, however. It is either the product of autoconditioning, which deranges our faculties, or (more charitably) the product of faculties that are designed to quiet the mind and prepare it for theistic mystical experiences. Our tendency to rely on testimony and our powers of inference *are* aimed at truth but have malfunctioned in this case. The Advaitin has been misled by his tendency to rely on testimony because the testimony he relies on is in error, and his inferences are demonstrably faulty.[39]

How plausible is Plantinga's position? Stephen Wykstra argues that religious beliefs are "evidence essential"—they are rationally held only if one has reason to believe that someone in one's intellectual community has good evidence for them. Religious beliefs are like scientific and metaphysical beliefs in this respect, and unlike memory beliefs or perceptual judgments. (I am entitled to believe that there are quarks, for example, but only because I have reason to believe that physicists have evidence for them.) If this is correct, religious beliefs aren't properly basic.[40]

A second problem is the position's potential for circularity. Plantinga argues that if his theistic metaphysics is true,[41] then belief in God is sometimes properly basic. To show that belief in God is never properly basic, one must therefore show that Plantinga's theistic metaphysics is false. So theistic belief is properly basic and hence rationally justified (or warranted) if theological claims like Plantinga's are true. It probably isn't properly basic if they aren't. While this seems correct, a consequence is that only those already disposed to accept a theistic metaphysics like Plantinga's will be persuaded by his defense of the rationality of theistic belief.[42] And if the theistic metaphysics is, in turn, supported by appeals to the proper basicality of belief in its key components (that God exists, is all powerful, is benevolent, and so on), then Plantinga's defense of the proper basicality of theistic belief is also circular.[43]

To summarize: Evidentialists maintain that one is entitled to religious beliefs only if one has evidence for them. Evidentialism derives much of its force from classical foundationalism. According to the latter, we are immediately entitled to beliefs that are self-evident, incorrigible, or evident to the senses. Other beliefs must be justified by evidence. Since religious beliefs are neither self-evident, incorrigible, nor evident to the senses, evidence is required for them.

Plantinga maintains that classical foundationalism is false. Many beliefs, including theistic ones, are immediately justified (properly basic) even though they aren't self-evident, incorrigible, or evident to the senses. In certain circumstances, we may simply find ourselves believing that God wants us to do something or that He has forgiven us and be justified in doing so even though we have no evidence for our beliefs.

The problem, however, is that some don't find theistic propositions obvious when placed in the appropriate circumstances, and others seem to regard beliefs that are incompatible with theism as properly basic. The first suggests that Plantinga's characteristic circumstances don't provide privileged access to theistic truths. (If they did, everyone in those circumstances would discern them.) The second suggests that the disposition to form theistic beliefs in the characteristic circumstances may be an unreliable belief-producing mechanism. (If it were reliable, the beliefs it produces shouldn't conflict with other beliefs produced in the same way.)

The first difficulty can be met by citing relevant differences between the epistemic qualifications of those who find a belief in God immediately obvious in the appropriate circumstances and those who don't—the possession of a properly functioning *sensus divinitatis* by the former, for example, and its absence in the latter. The second can be met by arguing, for instance, that (1) the Advaitin's *sensus divinitatis* is impaired or that (2) his religious beliefs are produced by other mechanisms that either aren't aimed at truth or are malfunctioning. But problems remain. Many theists think that beliefs about God are "evidence essential" and so can't be properly basic. Others are troubled by the potential circularity of Plantinga's defense of the rationality of theistic beliefs.

The most significant feature of Plantinga's position may be its challenge to a model of rationality (classical foundationalism) that has dominated discussions of religious issues for several hundred years. But Plantinga shares certain assumptions with his opponents. He too is a foundationalist, though not a classical foundationalist. An ideally rational person's beliefs will be structured in a certain way. His or her basic beliefs (those accepted without evidence) will be *properly* basic. They won't be groundless; for they will be formed in circumstances that justify one's holding them, and they will be the expressions of reliable belief-producing mechanisms. The ideally rational person's other beliefs will be based on evidence.

Plantinga, then, has a more traditional conception of epistemic rationality than James does. But Plantinga must explain why theists whose belief in God is properly basic are in an epistemically superior position. If he claims they are freer from sin, or are spiritually more mature, then he may be closer than he seems to Pascal, Kierkegaard, and James. The difference between mature theists and others will ultimately be a difference in the state of their hearts or subjectivity or passional natures.

CONCLUSION

The five philosophers discussed in this chapter are all anti-evidentialists. They are convinced that properly formed religious beliefs needn't be based on good arguments or an impartial appraisal of objective evidence.

But there are also important disagreements. Phillips thinks that religious claims aren't factual assertions. The others think they are but differ over the role reason plays in forming religious beliefs.

Plantinga insists he isn't a fideist. Human beings have a natural capacity to "apprehend God's existence and to grasp something of his nature and actions. This natural knowledge can be and is suppressed by sin but the fact remains that a capacity to apprehend God's existence is as much a part of our natural noetic equipment as is the capacity to apprehend perceptual truths, truths about the past, and truths about other minds."[44] A mature theist's belief in God is as rational as his or her memory beliefs, perceptual beliefs, or beliefs about other minds.

Kierkegaard and Pascal would disagree. Kierkegaard believes that properly formed religious beliefs go beyond the evidence or even against it, and lack the kind of objective certainty that many memory and perceptual beliefs have. Pascal thinks that mature theistic beliefs *can* be based on accounts of miracles, the growth of the church, apparent fulfillment of prophecies, and other evidence. This evidence won't seem sufficient, however, if God hasn't opened the believer's eyes to its force. Both Kierkegaard *and* Pascal think it misleading to call religious beliefs "rational" since this obscures the role our subjectivity or heart plays in forming religious beliefs. For example, they both think that conclusive arguments wouldn't leave any room for our wills.

Why do they think this? Some arguments are so conclusive that we cannot reject their conclusions. Examples are a simple geometrical proof that the sum of the angles of a Euclidian triangle is 180 degrees, and the evidential case for the claim that Great Britain is an island. Many of our perceptual and memory beliefs are equally compelling. It seems, then, that if the objective evidence for God's existence was conclusive, or if our belief in God was as inescapable as our belief that we had breakfast this morning, we couldn't help but assent to God's existence. Belief would thus be forced. God, however, wants the heart's *free* response. Pascal and Kierkegaard conclude that compelling arguments, or the kind of objective certainty that many of our perceptual and memory beliefs have, are incompatible with faith.

This is doubtful. Religious faith includes an assent to religious truths. But it also includes trust in, love of, and fidelity toward the good to which one has assented. Fidelity, trust, and love involve voluntary movements of the will. The intellect's assent, however, does not always *determine* the will. We sometimes voluntarily reject goods that we believe to be rationally certain. For example, I might continue to smoke even though I am rationally convinced that it will injure my health and that health is a greater good than smoking. Thus, even if one's intellect thinks the divine good is rationally certain, one's will may be able to reject it by refusing to love it, trust in it, or submit to it. Rational certainty isn't clearly incompatible with the freedom that is essential to faith.

Still, Pascal and Kierkegaard are right in thinking that the will may play a role in eliciting assent to religious truths. One can willfully reject the conclusion of an argument that should convince a fair-minded person. The possibility of doing so arises when an argument isn't absolutely conclusive, or when it is complex or difficult to follow. For example, although most of us are familiar with the case against smoking, some of us minimize the force of the evidence and continue to believe that smoking won't harm us. We are able to do this because the case is complex and its conclusion only probable. Since we wish to smoke, we don't attend to the evidence too carefully or very often. We seize on every consideration that casts doubt on the case and comfort ourselves with the thought that the conclusion is only probable. The important point is that our inattention and self-deception are partly willful—an expression of our desire to find the conclusion false. Now many of the arguments for God's reality are also complex, and none is entirely conclusive. Thus, even if the evidence isn't as ambiguous as fideists think, a person who wants to avoid the conclusion can willfully reject it.

In evaluating evidence that is complex or somewhat inconclusive, one reaches a point where what is crucial isn't further investigation but one's general sense of the strength of the evidence as a whole. Like James, Pascal and Kierkegaard recognize that a person's assessment of the force of evidence is influenced by his or her "passional nature" or "heart" or "subjectivity."

But Pascal and Kierkegaard also differ from James. Their conceptions of rationality are heavily influenced by classical foundationalism. It thus doesn't occur to them that the requirements of epistemic rationality might be practical as well as intellectual.

Suppose it did. Would they then agree that religious beliefs can be epistemically rational in James's sense? Probably not. For both Pascal and Kierkegaard think that a properly formed religious belief isn't *just* an expression of the demands of our intellectual and passional natures. It is a *supernatural* act—the expression of a heart that has been transformed by God's grace and infused with divine love. Even when "reason" is construed very broadly, faith transcends it.

How should we assess the anti-evidentialists? While many of their points are controversial, two seem clearly correct.

1. Character and will play an important role in forming properly held beliefs. Intellectual integrity, a willingness to examine objections, and a concern for truth are clearly necessary. But James, Pascal, and Kierkegaard suggest that more is needed. James thinks that the demands of our passional nature should be taken into account. Pascal believes that a longing for and love of God are necessary. Kierkegaard argues that a properly formed religious belief expresses a freely chosen and passionate commitment.

2. We must broaden our conception of reason. Pascal's wager reminds us that rationality is practical as well as theoretical and that it might be prudentially rational to cultivate certain beliefs. Plantinga shows that influential models of epistemic rationality such as classical foundationalism are seriously flawed. Kierkegaard calls our attention to the importance of "subjective" thinking, and James argues that a rational person should take account of the demands of his or her passional nature.

These points seem correct. Nevertheless, evidence is more important than our authors seem to think. For one thing, adherents of *rival* religious systems speak as if some of their beliefs were properly basic, imply that their own views best meet the demands of our passional nature, and cite reasons of the heart. Once we recognize the diversity of religious systems and the similarity of the appeals on which they are based, it isn't clear that we can rationally retain our own beliefs unless we investigate the alternatives and discover good reasons for discounting them. This involves comparing and weighing complicated chains of evidence.[45]

Chapter 7 explores this problem. After examining what is needed to have a good evidential case, we will apply our results to disputes between rival systems of religious belief.

Notes

1. William Clifford, "The Ethics of Belief," in *The Ethics of Belief Debate*, ed. Gerald D. McCarthy (Atlanta: Scholars Press, 1986), 24.

2. Quotations are from W. F. Trotter's translation of Pascal's *Pensées* (New York: Random House, 1941). The *Pensées* is a collection of fragments assembled after Pascal's death. The numbers in the text refer to the number of the fragment (in the Brunschvicg ordering).

3. Terence Penelhum, *God and Skepticism* (Dordrecht: D. Reidel, 1983), 89.

4. It doesn't follow that the wager is useless. For it might justify committing ourselves to the generic hypothesis that there is "a higher and more spiritual universe" (see "William James and the Will to Believe" later in this chapter) provided that one has reasons for thinking that believing this much (and acting accordingly) is sufficient to secure an "infinite" good if the higher universe exists. Indeed, if the generic hypothesis and its denial are equally probable, and the payoff of the former is greater than the payoff of the latter, then it is prudentially reasonable to bet on the religious hypothesis even if its payoff is not infinite.

5. The practices don't produce faith but remove obstacles to it, thus making God's bestowal of faith more likely.

6. An excellent selection from Kierkegaard's works can be found in *A Kierkegaard Anthology*, ed. Robert Bretall (Princeton: Princeton University Press, 1973).

7. Søren Kierkegaard, *Concluding Unscientific Postscript*, trans. David F. Swenson (Princeton: Princeton University Press, 1944). Page numbers in the text refer to this volume.

8. ———, *Philosophical Fragments*, trans. David F. Swenson (Princeton: Princeton University Press, 1936), 9–10.

9. Ibid., 22, 24–25.

10. For a good introduction to Phillips's position, see his *Faith and Philosophical Enquiry* (New York: Schocken Books, 1971).

11. D. Z. Phillips, *Death and Immortality* (New York: St. Martin's Press, 1970), 67.

12. Ibid., 68, 71.

13. Phillips, *Faith and Philosophical Enquiry*, 97.

14. It should be noted that Phillips denies that his work expresses a form of fideism. In his view, it merely describes the way religious utterances are used. The fact remains, however, that religious *belief* as described by Phillips *is* fideistic.

15. For this point see Edward Henderson, "Reductionism and the Practice of Worship," *International Journal for Philosophy of Religion* 10 (1979): 25–40.

16. Kierkegaard, *Concluding Unscientific Postscript*, 318.

17. Does this imply that the *adoption* of Religion B is irrational? Perhaps. But one should notice that even though one can't adopt Religion B without *embracing* an irrational belief, the adoption of Religion B isn't *based* on an irrational belief. (The truth of the doctrine of the Incarnation isn't offered as a reason for adopting Christianity.) Thus, a decision to adopt Religion B isn't irrational because it is *grounded* in an irrational belief, although it may be irrational for other reasons.

18. D. Z. Phillips, "Belief, Change and Forms of Life," in *The Autonomy of Religious Belief*, ed. Frederick Crosson (Notre Dame, Ind.: University of Notre Dame Press, 1981), 62.

19. One might object that Clifford's rule doesn't entail that we shouldn't act *as if* we believed these things, but only that we shouldn't *believe* them. It thus doesn't require us to stand aloof from others, refuse to cooperate with them, and so on. But can we effectively act as if we believed these things if we don't believe them? In some cases we probably can (the case of cooperative endeavors, for example). In others, we can't. Nothing short of the belief that one can leap the chasm will be effective. In any case, it isn't easy to consistently act as if one believed something when one doesn't.

20. William James, "The Will to Believe," in *The Will to Believe and Other Essays*, 25. All quotations in this section are from this essay unless otherwise noted.

21. The choice is clearly significant but is it unique and irreversible? Can't I postpone the decision, and can't I reverse it once I have made it? Perhaps uniqueness and irreversibility are important only because they sometimes contribute to the significance of our choices. Or perhaps there is a sense in which the decision to embrace or reject the religious hypothesis *is* irreversible and unique. Embracing or rejecting it largely determines a person's character and the shape of his or her life. Having created one's character and life, one must suffer the consequences for better or for worse. One's decision isn't easily reversed. The decision is also pressing; death could intervene at any moment. So it can't really be postponed either.

22. James, "The Sentiment of Rationality," in *The Will to Believe and Other Essays*, 82, 84–85, 88.

23. James, *Pragmatism* (New York: Meridian Books, 1958), 17f.

24. A belief-producing mechanism is (roughly) a disposition to believe certain things under certain conditions. For example, when two things have been conjoined in our experience, we are disposed to expect the second when we encounter the first. Again, we are disposed to formulate beliefs about the past when we have past-tinged experiences.

25. James sometimes speaks as if individual temperaments color our passional demands and determine whether an individual will be responsive to determinism rather than indeterminism, to supernaturalism rather than naturalism, and so on. But, on the whole, he seems to think that certain demands (that life have a meaning, for example, or that constructive action be possible) are shared by almost all of us. James also believes there are good reasons for thinking that views like indeterminism, supernaturalism, and optimism satisfy these demands better than their rivals.

26. James also thinks that trust in the reliability of our powers is itself a basic need or demand of human nature. As such, a belief in our powers' reliability will encounter fewer "inhibitions" or "arrests" than a belief in their unreliability. It is therefore more reasonable to trust our powers than to mistrust them.

27. Plantinga's views are developed in a number of essays. See especially "Is Belief in God Rational?" in *Rationality and Religious Belief,* ed. C. F. Delaney (Notre Dame, Ind.: University of Notre Dame Press, 1979); "Is Belief in God Properly Basic?" *Nous* 15 (1981): 41–51; "Reason and Belief in God," in *Faith and Rationality,* ed. Alvin Plantinga and Nicholas Wolterstorff (Notre Dame, Ind.: University of Notre Dame Press, 1983); and "Epistemic Justification," *Nous* 20 (1986): 3–18.

28. Ancient and medieval foundationalists assumed that ordinary perceptual judgments are properly basic. Following Descartes, modern foundationalists usually restrict properly basic beliefs to beliefs that are either self-evident or incorrigible. Perceptual beliefs, such as my belief that there is a pen in my hand, are warranted only if they can be derived from incorrigible beliefs about how things seem to me.

29. But reasoning and the consideration of evidence aren't totally irrelevant to basic beliefs. If someone suggests that my memory is faulty, I may have to consider his or her reasons. If they are good, I am no longer entitled to my belief. If they aren't, I am justified in retaining it. My belief, however, *remains basic.* Even though I used reason to repel an attack upon my belief, my belief isn't inferred *from* my reasons for rejecting the suggestion that my memory is faulty.

30. More accurately, it satisfies the criterion of ancient and medieval foundationalism. It doesn't satisfy Descartes' criterion since it is neither self-evident nor incorrigible.

31. Plantinga, "Is Belief in God Properly Basic?" 46. Strictly speaking, all basic theistic beliefs are of this type ("God made this," "God forgives me," and so on). But because these beliefs include a belief in God's existence, the latter too can be regarded as basic.

32. Ibid., 50.

33. Gary Gutting, *Religious Belief and Religious Skepticism* (Notre Dame, Ind.: University of Notre Dame Press, 1982), chapter 3, section 1.

34. A person can truly believe *p* without knowing *p*. Thus, while I may truly believe that a fair coin will turn up heads, I don't know that it will; my belief is unwarranted. Warrant is what distinguishes knowledge from (mere) true belief.

35. Rather than comfort, say, or some other nonepistemic good. For example, God may have designed us so that, when seriously ill, we tend to believe that our chances of recovery are greater than they are. For God knows that if we believe that, we are more likely to recover.

36. For a sketch of these views, see, for example, Alvin Plantinga, "Justification and Theism," *Faith and Philosophy* 4 (1987): 403–26.

37. A bad upbringing or a hostile environment may warp or stunt the development of one's *sensus divinitatis.* The sin in this case isn't one's own, however, but another's (those responsible for one's education or for an environment that is hostile or indifferent to religious belief).

38. It should be noted, though, that Plantinga believes there is little difference between himself and those who think that theistic belief is the product of inferences from the glories of nature, the promptings of conscience, and so on, that are *spontaneous, compelling, and direct in the sense that they involve few or no intermediate steps.* This concession may not amount to much. For the fact remains that the beliefs of many committed theists are neither properly basic nor the result of simple immediate inferences of this sort. Theists whose beliefs rest on complicated chains of argument or assessments of complex bodies of evidence are examples.

39. Of course, this response is plausible only if one can identify the testimony's errors and show where the Advaitin's inferences go wrong.

40. Stephen J. Wykstra, "Toward a Sensible Evidentialism: On the Notion of 'Needing Evidence,' " in *Philosophy of Religion: Selected Readings,* 3rd ed., ed. William L. Rowe and William J. Wainwright (Orlando, Fla.: Harcourt Brace, 1998).

41. That is, if God exists, has designed us so that our cognitive faculties produce basic theistic beliefs when functioning properly in a suitable epistemic environment, and so on.

42. Note that the unpersuaded will include theists as well as atheists and agnostics. Most theists think that God has equipped us with cognitive faculties that are sufficient to know Him if properly used. There is no consensus, however, that the faculty in question is a *sensus divinitatis* rather than (for example) our ability to reason from evidence.

43. Whether circles of this kind are always vicious is another matter. For an argument that they aren't, see William J. Wainwright, *Reason and the Heart* (Ithaca, N.Y.: Cornell University Press, 1995), chapter 4.

44. Plantinga, "Reason and Belief in God," 90.

45. Plantinga probably wouldn't deny this. In his view, theistic belief is defeasible and evidence may be needed to meet potential defeaters such as the existence of rival religious systems. He would insist, however, that the mature theist's belief doesn't *rest* on this evidence. Even if this is true, it may diminish some of the interest of his position. The most obvious way of meeting the defeater is by showing that there are more serious objections to rival systems than to one's own. But there doesn't seem to be much difference between doing *this* and showing that one's system of beliefs is more rational than the alternatives because it provides a better overall explanation of the facts.

For Further Reading

The reader should consult the works by Pascal, Kierkegaard, Phillips, James, and Plantinga cited in footnotes 2, 6, 7, 8, 10, 11, 20, 22, 27, and 36. An interesting defense of Pascal is provided by Nicholas Rescher, *Pascal's Wager*

(Notre Dame, Ind.: University of Notre Dame Press, 1985). Also useful is Jeff Jordan, ed., *Gambling of God: Essays on Pascal's Wager* (Lanham, Md.: Rowman and Littlefield, 1994). A critical but sympathetic and historically informed discussion of fideism is provided by Terence Penelhum, *God and Skepticism* (Dordrecht: D. Reidel, 1986). (Penelhum's account of sixteenth and seventeenth century fideism is especially valuable.) For a persuasive argument that Kierkegaard's attitudes towards reason are more balanced than sometimes thought, see C. Stephen Evans, *Passionate Reason: Making Sense of Kierkegaard's Philosophical Fragments* (Bloomington: Indiana University Press, 1992). *The Concept of Prayer* (New York: Schocken Books, 1966) is another good example of D. Z. Phillips's approach to religious language and practice. Those interested in Phillips's take on Plantinga should consult his *Faith After Foundationalism* (London and New York: Routledge, 1988). For a critique of Phillips see William J. Wainwright, "Theism, Metaphysics, and D. Z. Phillips," *Topoi* 14 (1995): 87–93. Phillips's reply is in the same issue (*Topoi* 14: 95–105).

Historical and contemporary defenses of, and attacks on, evidentialism are found in Gerald D. McCarthy, ed., *The Ethics of Belief Debate* (Atlanta: Scholar's Press, 1986). For a useful critical examination of the possibility and value of using one's will to produce religious belief, see Louis P. Pojman, *Religious Belief and the Will* (London and New York: Routledge and Kegan Paul, 1986).

For a recent and widely discussed attack on evidentialism, see Nicholas Wolterstorff, "Thomas Reid and Rationality," in *Rationality in the Calvinian Tradition*, ed. H. Hart, J. Van der Hoeven, and Nicholas Wolterstorff (Lanham, Md.: University Press of America, 1983); "Can Belief in God Be Rational If It Has No Foundations?" in *Faith and Rationality*, ed. Alvin Plantinga and Nicholas Wolterstorff (Notre Dame, Ind.: University of Notre Dame Press, 1983); and "The Migration of the Theistic Arguments: From Natural Theology to Evidentialist Apologetics," in *Rationality, Religious Belief, and Moral Commitment*, ed. Robert Audi and William J. Wainwright (Ithaca, N.Y.: Cornell University Press, 1986). William J. Wainwright, *Reason and the Heart* (Ithaca, N.Y.: Cornell University Press, 1995) argues that while evidentialism may be correct, a properly disposed heart is sometimes needed to assess the evidence properly.

Is Theism the Best Explanation? Assessing Worldviews

ANTI-EVIDENTIALISTS DENY THAT properly held religious beliefs must be *based* on good evidence. But they needn't deny that there *is* good evidence for them. Plantinga, for example, thinks there is. Most anti-evidentialists, however, do not. They believe that the (alleged) failure of cosmological and design arguments as well as other traditional proofs of religious assertions shows that the evidence is inadequate.

But these anti-evidentialists take an unduly narrow view of "good evidence." Many of the arguments we use in ordinary life, the humanities, and even the sciences don't meet rigorous formal standards. Nevertheless, some of them are good arguments. This chapter examines the claim that arguments of this kind can be used to justify religious beliefs.

CUMULATIVE ARGUMENTS

Sound reasoning doesn't always meet the rigorous standards of deductive or inductive logic. A conclusion is sometimes warranted even though it isn't entailed by one's premises and can't be derived from the evidence by inductive extrapolation (for example, by generalizing from the character of a fair sample of the population one is examining, or by inferring that an event will occur because similar events have occurred under similar conditions in the past). Many good arguments are "cumulative case" arguments. These arguments attempt to establish a conclusion by introducing a variety of diverse considerations. When taken singly, none of the considerations is sufficient to justify the conclusion. When taken jointly, however, they make an impressive case for it.

John Henry Newman (1801–90) invites us to consider our belief that Great Britain is an island. Our conviction is well founded. We have no doubt that it is true. But if asked to give our evidence for it, we can only respond that

> first, we have been so taught in our childhood, and it is so in all the maps; next, we have never heard it contradicted or questioned; on the contrary, every one whom we have heard speak on the subject of Great Britain, every book we have read, invariably took it for granted; our whole national history [Newman was British], the routine transactions and current events of the country, our social and commercial system, our political relations with foreigners, imply it in one way or another. Numberless facts, or what we consider facts, rest on the truth of it; no received fact rests on its being otherwise.[1]

Our belief that Britain is an island isn't based on a rigorous deductive or inductive argument. Nevertheless, it is reasonable; a diverse variety of independent considerations support it and nothing supports its denial.

In some cases, the evidence may conflict. Basil Mitchell (1917–) tells the story of an officer on watch "in a ship at sea in stormy weather." The lookout "reports a lighthouse on a certain bearing. The navigating officer says he cannot have seen a lighthouse, because his reckoning puts him a hundred miles away from the nearest land. . . . Shortly afterwards . . . the lookout reports land on the starboard bow. The navigating officer . . . says it must be cloud—and it is indeed very difficult to distinguish cloud from land in these conditions." The lookout makes further sightings of what appears to be land, and these too could be clouds. Nevertheless, as the signs of land accumulate, the watch officer concludes that "he had better assume that" the navigator has miscalculated, and "that he is where the sightings place him." His assessment is based on his "overall appraisal of the situation." The navigator's reckoning provided a reason for distrusting the initial sighting. "But the other reports, although their evidential value, taken singly, is slight . . . do cumulatively amount to a convincing case" that the ship is close to land.[2]

Mitchell also invites us to consider disputes in literary criticism, historical research, and philosophy. In interpreting a poem, a critic selects a certain passage as a "clue to the author's overall meaning." He recognizes that the meaning of other passages seems to conflict with his interpretation of the poem but either shows how they can be construed so as to fit his interpretation or offers reasons for thinking that the discrepancy is unimportant. Another critic takes issue with the first, arguing that the latter's interpretation distorts the meaning of the poem. The second critic thinks that *other* passages provide the key to the meaning of the whole, and she attempts to show that the first critic's handling of discrepancies is implausible. "In the end," the two critics "will need to take one another right through the text, and the argument will consist in each trying to convince the other of the need to give each passage the weight and significance that, in terms of his own interpretation, it ought to bear."[3]

Disputes between historians or philosophers are also frequently over which interpretation makes the most sense of a range of facts. Here, too, conclusions are based on a diverse variety of independent considerations. For example, a historian's interpretation of the French Revolution's Reign of Terror will be determined by the documentary and nondocumentary evidence at his or her disposal, assessments of the general trustworthiness of the evidence, beliefs about what people would be likely to do in the relevant circumstances, perceived analogies with other revolutions, and so on.

Or consider the philosophical debate between determinists and indeterminists. Many things are relevant to this dispute—the social sciences' success in predicting certain aspects of human behavior and their failure to predict others, the correct analysis of the language of moral responsibility, the proper interpretation of hypothetical cases in which a person's behavior is *clearly* determined, and so on. Once again, the dispute is over which interpretation of a phenomenon (in this case human behavior) makes most sense in view of all the relevant considerations.

Scientists engage in similar disputes during periods of "scientific revolution." Thomas Kuhn (1922–96) defines "paradigms" as "standard examples" of scientific work that "embody" a set of assumptions about the proper methods of a science and the nature of its subject matter.[4] Examples are Newton's work in mechanics or Dalton's work in chemistry. Paradigms create "research traditions" by implicitly defining "for a given scientific community the types of question that may legitimately be asked, the types of explanation that are to be sought, and the types of solution that are acceptable." Thus, Newton's work in mechanics illustrated the way in which problems in physics should be defined and solved ("for instance, by analysis in terms of masses and forces"). It even molded "the scientist's assumptions as to what kinds of entity there are in the world. (Newton was interested in matter in motion.)" The normal practice of science is governed by these paradigms. For example, Newton's work dominated physics for two centuries.[5]

Paradigms aren't discarded lightly. Observations that seem to falsify a paradigm or the theories it generates aren't conclusive. Sometimes they are corrected in the light of theory. "Newton, for example, told the Astronomer Royal . . . to correct some astronomical data because it disagreed with theoretical predictions." Sometimes auxiliary hypotheses are added to the theory to explain recalcitrant data. At other times, troublesome observations are set aside as anomalies—problems awaiting future solution. For example, Newton admitted there was a discrepancy between his predictions and the observed motion of the moon. The scientific community didn't conclude that this falsified Newton's theory, however, although the discrepancy wasn't explained until sixty years later.[6]

But paradigms or theories aren't immune to falsification. As discrepancies accumulate, more and more auxiliary hypotheses must be added to the theory, and more and more observations must be set aside as anomalies. Eventually a point is reached where members of the scientific community begin to suspect that the theory, and perhaps the research tradition that generated it, is in trouble. Even then, a theory or paradigm won't be discarded if there aren't promising alternatives, for a theory or paradigm that has led to the successful solution of many problems is better than no theory or paradigm at all.

The shift to a new paradigm is a scientific "revolution." An example is the shift from Newtonian physics to relativity. There are no clear-cut decision procedures for determining whether a new paradigm is superior. Nevertheless, debates between adherents of old and new paradigms *are* governed by certain scientific "values." Both sides prize simplicity, precise explanations, comprehensiveness, and so on. Each party will thus try to show that its paradigm more effectively realizes one or more of these values. For example, advocates of the new paradigm may appeal to its ability to solve some of the problems that the old paradigm set aside as anomalies. Defenders of the old paradigm will point to its long history of successes. The "revolutionaries" may claim that the new theories are simpler, while the "conservatives" may argue that the established theories explain more. Each side attempts to show that its research program has the greatest chance of future success.[7]

The important point is this. The conclusion that one paradigm is better than another can be reasonable or unreasonable. Nevertheless, it doesn't stand in a precise formal relation to the considerations that support it. There are no clearly defined rules that can be mechanically applied to determine whether one's conclusion is the most reasonable that might be drawn from the considerations in question. One's decision is ultimately a matter of judgment.

All these examples of reasoning are "inferences to the best explanation." In each case, a conclusion is accepted because it makes more sense of a range of facts than its alternatives do. For example, the most natural explanation of the fact that everyone speaks of Great Britain as an island, that maps depict it as an island, and so on, is that Great Britain *is* an island. The watch officer concludes that land is near because this provides a better explanation of the relevant evidence than the hypothesis that the navigator's reckoning is accurate and the sightings of land are only apparent. The literary critic argues that his or her interpretation does more justice to the poem's features than those proposed by other critics. A philosopher embraces indeterminism because it seems to make more sense of human moral behavior, the predictive successes and failures of the social sciences, and people's intuitions about hypothetical cases. An advocate of a new scientific paradigm attempts to convince fellow scientists that the new paradigm generates better accounts of their common subject matter.

There are no "algorithms" (mechanical decision procedures) for evaluating inferences of this kind. There *are* general rules and guidelines, and some of these will be discussed in the next section. Their application, however, requires judgment.

As Newman points out, our estimate of the force of a body of evidence often depends on a host of considerations too "numerous" and "delicate" to be fully articulated. A historian's conviction that the *Aeneid* couldn't be a thirteenth-century forgery, for instance, is partly based on his or her knowledge of the capacities of the medieval mind. While this knowledge depends on a lifetime of reading and study, many of the considerations that shaped it have been forgotten and others have merged into a general impression of what the medieval mind could and could not do. "We do not pretend to be able to draw the line between what the medieval intellect could and could not do; but we feel sure that at least it could not write the classics. An instinctive sense of this [as well as] a faith in testimony, are the sufficient, but the undeveloped argument on which to ground our certitude."[8]

Experience is also a factor. For example, one's assessment of a witness's trustworthiness is affected by one's encounters with people's truthfulness and dishonesty. The doctor's diagnosis is influenced by his or her experience as well as by formal training and knowledge of the latest scientific findings. When values are at issue, character or taste may be needed. Intelligence and information being equal, a good man or woman is more likely to accurately assess a morally ambiguous situation than someone who is indifferent to moral values. A person who is aesthetically insensitive is less likely to make a contribution to our understanding of art.

In short, a type of reasoning is employed in diverse forms of human inquiry that is neither deductive nor inductive but an inference to the best explanation. Conclusions are drawn from a variety of independent considerations. None is itself sufficient to establish the conclusion. They can't always be fully articulated. Nor do they stand in deductive or inductive relations to the conclusion. Nevertheless, when taken together, they entitle us to infer that some hypothesis or interpretation makes more sense of a range of facts than its alternatives. There are general rules and guidelines for inferences of this kind. Their application, however, requires judgment. The quality of a person's judgment is affected by learning and experience, familiarity with the subject matter, and, in some cases, character or taste.

How is this relevant to the philosophy of religion? Basil Mitchell suggests that the "intellectual aspect" of a traditional religion "may be regarded as a worldview or metaphysical system"—a comprehensive picture that attempts to make sense of human experience as a whole.[9] In this respect, systems of religious belief resemble worldviews like Marxism and philosophical systems such as Stoicism or platonism. Metaphysical systems are supported and attacked by cumulative case reasoning. Their advocates insist they make more sense of the relevant facts than their alternatives do. Critics attempt to show that they don't.

Can *religious* worldviews be supported by this sort of reasoning? We will explore this issue in the next two sections.

COMPARING RIVAL WORLDVIEWS

A variety of criteria are used to assess rival metaphysical systems. We will discuss the most important ones and illustrate their application by examining the dispute between theism and naturalism.

The Criteria

Good metaphysical systems must meet a number of criteria. For example, (1) *the facts that the system explains must actually exist.* Some metaphysical systems, for instance, offer explanations of the objectivity of moral and aesthetic values. If values *aren't* objective, these systems are defective.

In addition, (2) *a good metaphysical system should be compatible with well-established facts and theories.* For example, philosophical accounts of the mind-body relation mustn't contradict the findings of biology and psychology. Generally speaking, metaphysical systems should be compatible with accepted theories in other disciplines. If they aren't, the burden of proof is on the metaphysician to show why those theories are inadequate. Systems that are incompatible with the theory of biological evolution, for instance, begin with a strike against them.

An adequate system must also meet four formal criteria. (3) *It must be logically consistent,* and (4) *it shouldn't be "self-stultifying."*[10] While most worldviews meet the first formal requirement, some seem to fail the second. A view is self-stultifying if its assertion implies that it can't be known to be true, or its assertion implies that it is false or can't be expressed. Mādhyamika Buddhism and Advaita Vedānta may fail this test. Mādhyamika, for example, seems to assert that all views are false. But if *all* views are false, then its own view is false (that is, it is false that all views are false). Advaita maintains that reality is inexpressible. If reality is inexpressible, however, one can't *express* this by saying "Reality is inexpressible." For in saying "Reality is inexpressible," you *have* expressed it. (We will consider responses to these criticisms in the next section.)

(5) *Adequate metaphysical systems should also be coherent.* Their parts ought to "hang together." A system should thus display a certain amount of interconnectedness and systematic articulation. Monotheism, for example, seems more coherent than polytheisms that posit a number of gods but don't clearly explain the connections among them.

Other things being equal, (6) *simpler systems are preferable to complex ones.* A system may be simpler because it employs fewer basic concepts or makes fewer basic assumptions, or because it uses fewer explanatory principles or isn't committed to as many kinds of reality. For example, physicalism and idealism posit only one kind of reality (bodies and minds, respectively). They are thus simpler than dualisms that assert that matter and mind are equally real and can't be reduced to each other. Monotheism is simpler than polytheism in the sense that it posits fewer explanatory principles.

But good metaphysical systems not only must meet formal criteria. They must also possess explanatory power. This involves several things—avoiding ad hoc hypotheses, precision, scope, fruitfulness, and a system's ability to "illuminate" the facts it explains.

(7) *Good metaphysical systems should avoid ad hoc hypotheses.* An ad hoc hypothesis has no independent plausibility and is neither implied by the theory nor naturally suggested by it. Its only function is to explain away apparent counter-evidence. For example, when confronted with evidence of geological and biological evolution, some nineteenth-century biblical literalists tried to preserve their version of Christianity by adding a hypothesis. They suggested that God had deliberately created a world containing fossil traces and other misleading indications of geological and biological evolution; the empirical evidence points to evolution but the evidence is deceptive.

(8) *Metaphysical explanations should be precise.* An explanation is more precise when it accounts for more features of a phenomenon or provides a more detailed explanation of the mechanisms responsible for it. For example, a theory of art that explains various kinds of aesthetic value (beauty, expressiveness, sublimity, and so on) is more precise than one that only accounts for aesthetic value in general. Or suppose two metaphysical theories trace phenomena back to an absolute mind. One is more precise than the other if it provides a more detailed account of the absolute spirit and its relation to other things.

(9) *A system's scope is also important.* Other things being equal, metaphysical theories are better when they explain a wider range of phenomena. A system that illuminates humanity's scientific, moral, aesthetic, and religious experience, for example, is superior to one that illuminates only science.

Furthermore, (10) *one should consider a system's fruitfulness.* There are several ways in which theories can be fruitful. They may predict new phenomena or previously unnoticed aspects of known phenomena. They may also generate interesting new problems and solutions or suggest illuminating interpretations of facts the theories didn't anticipate. Metaphysical theories don't generate predictions. However, they can generate new problems and solutions and interesting interpretations of new facts. Platonism, for example, was used to illuminate the data of Christian revelation and romantic love, although it didn't anticipate either of these phenomena.

(11) *Good metaphysical systems provide illuminating explanations of the phenomena within their explanatory range.* There are several ways in which theories can illuminate facts. A puzzling phenomenon can sometimes be subsumed under general principles. The phenomenon is explained by showing how it follows from the system's postulates and theorems or from hypotheses that either are suggested by the system or are easily incorporated in it. For example, classical theists make sense of revelation by inferring the likelihood of a revelation from God's desire to enter into relations with His creatures and humanity's weakness and need for God. Theists frequently attempt to illuminate evil by showing how its occurrence follows from hypotheses that easily cohere with theism (the lawfulness of the created order, for instance, or the desirability of moral growth and independence). If the theist's postulates, theorems, and hypotheses are plausible, the puzzling phenomenon is "illuminated."

When a metaphysical theory integrates a set of apparently unrelated phenomena, it sometimes illuminates them. For example, a system may interpret historical, sociological, psychological, and moral facts as diverse expressions of humanity's drive toward transcendence. Other systems interpret the same facts as expressions of sinful self-reliance. Still others think it more helpful to view them as products of the interaction between an innately good human nature and a corrupt social environment.

One of the most effective ways of illuminating a phenomenon is by drawing analogies with phenomena that are better understood. Edward Schoen (1949–) discusses an important example of this. Many theistic explanations account for a pattern of phenomena by postulating the activity of an entity that is relevantly similar to entities that are known to be responsible for analogous patterns of phenomena. Thus, I may notice an apparently providential pattern in my life or in the history of a religious community. Noting similarities between these patterns and patterns in the lives of those who are cared for by others, I postulate a loving will to account for them.[11]

In short, a good metaphysical system explains real facts, is consistent with other things we know, meets formal criteria, and possesses explanatory power. It may also have to satisfy a pragmatic criterion.

Paul Tillich argues that (12) *philosophical theories should be judged by "their efficacy in the life-process of mankind."*[12] According to Frederick Ferré (1933–), an adequate metaphysical system must be "capable of 'coming to life' for individuals . . . becoming . . . a usable instrument for our coping with the total environment." It must have a "capacity for ringing true with respect to" those who use it, enabling them to "cope successfully with the challenges of life."[13] William James makes a similar point. Adequate metaphysical systems must meet practical as well as intellectual demands. (See the discussion of James in Chapter 6.)

The best metaphysical system, then, is that which best satisfies these criteria. One should note that the criteria are comparative; they are used in deciding *between* competing theories. The question, therefore, is "*On the whole*, does theory A satisfy the criteria better than theory B?" Theory A might do this even if it doesn't fully satisfy *some* of the criteria (perhaps it includes some ad hoc hypotheses) and even if B satisfies a few criteria better than A. As an example of the complex issues involved in comparing systems, we will briefly look at theism and naturalism.

An Example: Theism and Naturalism

Theists believe in a supernatural reality that transcends nature. Naturalists think that the space-time world is all there is. Theism and naturalism, then, are very different metaphysical systems. Does one satisfy our criteria better than the other?

Both systems are consistent and reasonably coherent. Both can accommodate new knowledge, and adapt themselves to new historical and cultural situations. Alvin Plantinga, however, believes that naturalism is self-stultifying. If naturalism is true, our cognitive faculties are products of mindless evolutionary forces. If they are, we have no reason to think that the probability that they are reliable is greater than fifty-fifty. We should therefore distrust them. But if so, we should *also* distrust the beliefs that they produce—including the belief in naturalism. Hence, if naturalism is true, we have no reason to think that it is.[14]

Gary Gutting thinks that naturalism is more precise.[15] However, this is doubtful. *Scientific* explanations may be more precise than theistic explanations, but naturalism isn't science; it is a metaphysical hypothesis like theism. Naturalists can *use* scientific explanations to fill out their picture of the world, but so can theists. (Theists are only committed to rejecting *reductive* scientific accounts of things like religious experience or miracles and, even then, only in some cases.) Furthermore, many theistic explanations *are* precise. Some theological accounts of mystical experience, for instance, are as detailed as "scientific" ones.[16]

Naturalism is simpler in the sense that it denies the existence of transcendent reality and thus postulates fewer entities. On the other hand, theism seems superior in scope. The existence of contingent being falls within the explanatory range of any comprehensive metaphysical system.[17] Theism can explain it and naturalism can't.

The most significant question, probably, is, "Which system provides the most illuminating explanations and most effectively enables its adherents to come to terms with life?"

Theism may provide more illuminating accounts of apparent design (Chapter 2), religious experience (Chapter 5), and our dissatisfaction with temporal goods (Chapter 4). Theists also believe that their worldview provides illuminating accounts of phenomena like sanctity and the apparent objectivity of moral value. For example, George Mavrodes (1926–) argues that objective values are more "at home" in a theistic universe than in the sort of world envisaged by naturalism. The existence of objective value is less surprising if maximal perfection exists and goodness is therefore embedded in the structure of things.[18]

On the other hand, naturalists think that their account of evil is more illuminating. The occurrence of suffering and wickedness isn't particularly surprising if the space-time world is all there is. It is regrettable that natural causes have this consequence, but there is no reason why they shouldn't. If *God* had created the world, however, one wouldn't expect so much evil. Naturalists conclude that suffering and wickedness are more intelligible within their framework. The force of their point, of course, depends on the success or failure of the theistic strategies discussed in Chapter 3.

Determining which system best satisfies the pragmatic criterion is also difficult. For one thing, assessments reflect people's values, and their values are influenced by their metaphysical commitments and predilections. Persons who are sympathetic with theism won't be happy with systems that seem to frustrate our spiritual aspirations and deprive life of overall meaning. In deciding between theism and naturalism, however, they must be careful not to beg the question by appealing to values that couldn't be acknowledged by nontheists. For similar reasons, those who are sympathetic to naturalism shouldn't base their decision on claims that are plausible only if naturalism is true (for example, that the most important values are temporal).

Furthermore, secularization is a comparatively recent phenomenon. While every civilized society has included those who are indifferent or hostile to religion, the modern West may be the first in which some form of naturalism is held by many people from all walks of life. William James thinks that the relevant question is, "In the long run, which system best enables humanity to come to terms with life?" If it is, the verdict may still be out. On the other hand, it *is* relevant that religious skeptics often feel that life without God or the holy is stunted, incomplete, or in some other way unsatisfactory. It is also relevant that each of us is exposed to the threats of meaningless, guilt, and death, and that we experience these threats in anxiety. It isn't obvious that anything short of transcendence can meet these threats or allay this anxiety.

Our brief comparison of theism and naturalism illustrates the difficulty of applying our criteria. They aren't very precise, and there are disagreements concerning their relative weight. (Is scope, for example, more important than simplicity?) The relevant evidence is also complex, and much of it is "delicate." For example, a person who doesn't appreciate moral values or is insensitive to the richness and complexity of our moral life is a poor judge of explanations of moral value.

The application of the criteria thus calls for judgment. The quality of one's judgment is a function of knowledge, intelligence, and the care with which one has considered the issue. It is also a function of the depth of a person's experience and his or her sensitivity to the relevant evidence. It isn't surprising, then, that intelligent men and women apply these criteria and come to different conclusions. Each of us must nonetheless form the best judgment he or she can in the light of all the relevant considerations.

Conclusion

This section has examined criteria for assessing worldviews. These criteria aren't peculiar to metaphysics. All except the pragmatic criterion are relevant to the assessment of *any* inference to the best explanation. The criteria are imprecise, however, and can't be applied mechanically. Their application can thus be expected to produce disagreements. The dispute between theists and naturalists is an example. Nevertheless, some assessments *are* more reasonable than others. Theism, for instance, may be more reasonable than naturalism (or vice versa).

The next section applies the criteria to some issues involved in disputes between rival religious systems. Our discussion will introduce an important set of new problems and illustrate points made in this section in more detail.

COMPARING RIVAL RELIGIOUS SYSTEMS

William James thinks the religious hypothesis contains two affirmations. First, there is a "higher universe"; the space-time world isn't the whole of reality. Second, we are better off if we believe this and act accordingly. (See Chapter 6.) Many find the religious hypothesis more plausible than naturalism. But even if they are right, how should the hypothesis be filled out? What is the nature of the higher universe and our relation to it? Buddhism, Christianity, and so on, answer these questions in different ways. Do some of these systems satisfy our criteria better than others?

A worldview should be consistent with the rest of what we know. One might think that religious worldviews fail this test, since traditional theologies often contain pieces of antiquated science. Most of these errors, however, aren't essential to the worldviews in which they are incorporated, and, on the whole, the major traditions have successfully accommodated new scientific knowledge.

The question of historical accuracy may be more important. Historical events are essential to some systems. For example, Christianity is a response to God's alleged revelation in Christ. It therefore depends on the accuracy of the main outlines of the gospel's accounts of Jesus's life and teachings. Although the degree of accuracy that is needed is a matter of dispute, even the most "liberal" versions of Christianity regard Jesus's existence and goodness as essential.

Historical accuracy is less important when a system emphasizes the teaching, rather than the life, of its founder. Buddhism is an example. In other cases, it isn't easy to determine whether historical accuracy is important or not. For example, Vaiṣṇavas assert that God (Vishnu) sometimes assumes an animal or human form for the benefit of creatures. These "descents" (avatāras) are grounded in God's compassion. By assuming the form of a creature, God reveals His beauty and splendor and makes Himself accessible. The descents are real (not mere appearances), and the most important (Rama and Krishna) seem to be regarded as historical figures. The accuracy of the lives of Rama and Krishna may therefore be important. On the other hand, their historical accuracy may be as unimportant as the historical accuracy of mythological or symbolic stories describing Vishnu's descent as a tortoise or a "man-lion."

The crucial point is this. The worldviews of the major religious traditions are compatible with scientific knowledge. But controversial historical claims are essential to some of them. If these claims are false or doubtful, the system is partially discredited.

On the whole, religious worldviews are consistent and reasonably coherent. However, a few may be self-stultifying. MādhyamikaBuddhism appears to assert that all views are false. But if *all* views are false, its own view is false. Advaita maintains that reality is inexpressible. Yet if reality *is* inexpressible, one can't express this by *saying* "Reality is inexpressible." (See the section on comparing worldviews.) These worldviews thus seem self-stultifying. But both have responses to this charge. Mādhyamika denies that it really is asserting that all views are false. It neither denies nor asserts that all views are false. Nor does it deny or assert the opposite (that some views are true). Mādhyamika insists it has *no* views of its own and thus isn't asserting *anything*! Advaita can evade the charge by qualifying the claim that reality is inexpressible. For example, it can withdraw to the position that reality can be expressed only by negations (saying what it is not). Since "Reality is not expressible by affirmative statements" is a negation, its assertion isn't inconsistent with the truth of what it says. In spite of appearances, then, Mādhyamika and Advaita may not be self-stultifying. In any case, most religious worldviews are free from this defect.

The major religious worldviews are also more or less equally precise, comprehensive, and fruitful. Nor does one seem more ad hoc than the others.

But some systems might seem simpler. Jewish and Muslim monotheism is simpler than the Christian doctrine that one divine nature exists in three "presentations" or "persons" (Father, Son, and Holy Spirit). Hīnāyana Buddhists say little about Nirvāna except that it is real, totally unlike the space-time world or its constituents, and the end of suffering. Hīnāyana's description of ultimate reality is thus simpler than the more elaborate descriptions of other systems.

But religious worldviews aren't just accounts of ultimate reality. They are also interpretations of reality as a whole. For example, Hīnāyana Buddhism provides elaborate analyses of the constituents of the space-time world and their interconnections. One must understand these to grasp the nature of human existence and the causes of suffering. What is crucial, then, isn't the comparative simplicity of different accounts of ultimate reality but the comparative simplicity of entire systems. It isn't clear that any religious view, *as a whole*, is simpler than others. Hīnāyana, for instance, is dualistic. Nirvāna and the space-time world are both real, and neither is the ground of the other. It is thus more complex than some systems in the sense that it posits *two* ultimate principles.

Our discussion up to this point suggests that worldviews are more or less equally successful in meeting most of the criteria for good metaphysical hypotheses.

But the two most important criteria haven't yet been discussed—the demand for illuminating explanations and pragmatic effectiveness. Disputes between adherents of different religious worldviews hinge on these criteria. Christians, for example, believe that their view provides a more illuminating account of the human situation and that its adoption leads to a better quality of existence. Buddhists and Muslims make similar claims. What sorts of issues are involved in these disputes? Let us examine a few cases in detail.

The Pragmatic Criterion: Karunā and Agape

Are some religious worldviews more effective instruments for coping successfully with life?

Over the centuries, countless men and women have found that a Christian or Buddhist or Muslim vision of reality and way of life illumines and enriches their existence. All the major traditions are viable in the sense that they enable their adherents to come to terms with the difficulties of human existence and find meaning and value in their lives. Even so, some traditions may provide more adequate objects for humanity's religious, ethical, and spiritual aspirations and may produce more attractive religious lives. If they do, they satisfy the pragmatic criterion better than others.

There is a broad ethical consensus among the higher religions. All prize justice, loyalty, compassion, and so on. Furthermore, the faithful in these traditions embody these values. Devout Hindus, for example, are neither more nor less just, loyal, and compassionate than are devout Muslims or Christians. But their ideals differ. We should therefore compare these ideals and the lives of the men and women who most faithfully exemplify them (the "saints"). For example, Christian agape should be compared with Mahāyāna Buddhism's karunā.

Agape is completely selfless love. Without counting the cost, one responds in love to one's neighbor. This response is based solely on the neighbor's need—not on advantages to oneself or on the neighbor's pleasantness, usefulness, or merit. Agape embraces friend and foe, righteous and unrighteous, without regard for personal advantage or the neighbor's objectively good or bad qualities. It thus reflects the love of God, who needs nothing but, out of His overflowing goodness, freely embraces the unworthy. The Christian, says Martin Luther (1483–1546), should live

> only for others and not for himself . . . he should be guided in all his works by this thought and contemplate this one thing alone, that he may serve and benefit others in all that he does, considering nothing except the need and the advantage of his neighbor. . . . Here faith is truly active through love, that is, it finds expression in works of the freest service, cheerfully and lovingly done, with which a man willingly serves another without hope of reward. . . . He ought to think . . . I will give myself as a Christ to my neighbor, just as Christ offered himself to me.[19]

The ideal of karunā is exemplified by the Bodhisattva. Bodhisattvas are the perfect embodiments of wisdom (prajnā) and compassion (karunā). Although destined to become Buddhas, they postpone their own final release until everyone has achieved enlightenment.[20] Bodhisattvas

> do not wish to attain their own private Nirvāna. On the contrary, they have surveyed the highly painful world of being, and yet, desirous to win supreme enlightenment, they do not tremble at birth-and-death. They have set out for the benefit of the world, for the ease of the world, out of pity for the world. They have resolved: "We will become a shelter for the world, a refuge for the world, the world's place of rest, the final relief of the world, islands of the world, lights of the world, leaders of the world, the world's means of salvation."[21]

Mahāyāna Buddhists contrast their ideal with the Arhat ideal of Hīnāyana Buddhism. An Arhat is someone who successfully puts the Buddha's teachings into practice and achieves enlightenment. Because they cherish their own "private Nirvāna," however, Arhats are still affected by the distinction between "mine" and "thine." Thus, they haven't completely freed themselves from self-seeking and egoism. Arhats are compassionate, but their primary virtue is wisdom, through which they achieve their own salvation. Bodhisattvas equally exhibit *both* virtues and place the salvation of others above their own.

Both agape and karunā are subject to similar criticisms. For example, Sigmund Freud (1856–1939) argues that a selfless love that embraces all creatures is irrational. In the first place, it is psychologically impossible. "Were all men loved equally and indiscriminately, merely because they inhabit the earth, . . . then Freud suspects that not much love could fall to any of them." There is, as it were, a fixed quantity of love, and what love gains in extension, it loses in intensity. Furthermore, while the requirement that one love one's neighbor or feel universal compassion is designed to "curtail instinctive aggressiveness," it may increase it. No one can meet the demand, and the failure to do so leads to self-hatred (that is, aggression against oneself). Finally, love should be limited to one's "intimates," or to "those who deserve it." It is irrational to try to love people for whom one has no special affection or who don't merit it.[22]

Christians respond that agape *is* possible with God's help, and Buddhists claim that karunā can be achieved through self-discipline and meditation. Both deny that it leads to self-hatred. An examination of the lives of Christian and Buddhist saints tends to support these claims. Saint Francis, for example, appears to have achieved selflessness without being burdened by self-hatred.[23]

Freud's final criticism is more telling. Isn't it unreasonable to prize something that doesn't deserve it? Plato thought so. Love is rational only when things are loved in proportion to their worth.

Plato's claim is plausible, but Christians have often incorporated it in their accounts. For example, they have argued that God should be loved above creatures, while creatures should be loved in proportion to the degree to which they reflect Him. Although some deny that Plato's claim can be coherently combined with the agape motif, it isn't obvious that it can't. That the neighbor ought to be loved regardless of his or her pleasant, unpleasant, moral, or immoral qualities seems consistent with the claim that the basis of one's regard should be the (objective) fact that the neighbor is an image of God or a potential member of His kingdom and thus reflects His glory.

Mahāyāna Buddhists would simply reject Plato's claim. Discriminations between the good and the bad or the deserving and undeserving are created by an ego that falsely believes in the reality of distinctions.

Both agape and karunā idealize selfless and indiscriminate love or compassion. Both ideals can survive Freud's criticisms. Should one be preferred to the other?

Buddhists think that persons are simply flows of momentary psychological and bodily constituents (the "dharmas"). There is no soul or self over and above one's constantly changing feelings, thoughts, volitions, and momentary body states. Hīnāyana Buddhists believe that the dharmas are real. But Mahāyāna Buddhists deny it. What we conventionally regard as persons are collections of fleeting psychological and bodily constituents that are themselves unreal. Persons are thus fictions. Therefore, "a Bodhisattva should think thus: As many beings as there are in the universe of beings . . . all these should be led by me into Nirvāna. . . . And yet, although innumerable beings have thus been led to Nirvāna, no being at all has been led to Nirvāna. And why? If in a Bodhisattva, the perception of 'a being' should take place, he would not be called an 'enlightenment being' [the literal meaning of 'bodhisattva']."[24]

But is this coherent? A "love" or "compassion" that refuses to recognize the independent reality of persons is very different from what we ordinarily think of as love or compassion. The latter is a relation between independently real persons. It would be odd to speak of having compassion for oneself or for a character in fiction. Of course, I might say that in looking back on my youth, I feel compassion for the boy I once was. In doing so, however, I distinguish my present self from my past self and treat the latter as another person. It is also true that I can be moved by the misfortunes of fictional characters. Nevertheless, an impulse to relieve their distress or a wish to remove their discomfort would indicate that I had forgotten that they *were* fictional characters. Genuine love or compassion, then, seems to presuppose a belief in the independence and reality of its object. Bodhisattvas lack this belief. Hence, while they may exhibit qualities *similar* to those indicated by "love" or "compassion," it isn't clear that the terms can properly be applied to their attitudes or that they have the same value.[25]

The karunā ideal may thus be incoherent. Is the agape ideal superior? Does it more fully embody our ethical insights and more effectively meet our ethical aspirations? It may. If an affirmative answer is to help us decide between theism and Mahāyāna, however, it shouldn't be based on views of human nature or morality that are plausible only if theism is true. One falls into a circle if one argues that a worldview is superior because it more effectively meets the pragmatic criterion and supports the latter by appealing to the worldview whose adequacy is in question.

The Illumination Criterion: The Origin of the Space-Time World

Do some religious systems provide more illuminating explanations? The sorts of issues involved can be illustrated by comparing three accounts of the space-time world's origins.

Classical Western theism ascribes its origin to the divine will. A self-existent God freely chooses to create contingent being. Some of the ramifications of this were discussed in the sections on the cosmological and design arguments. (See Chapter 2.)

Advaita Vedānta has a different account. Advaita thinks that Brahman alone is real. It also thinks that Brahman is devoid of distinctions. (See Chapter 1, "Is a Perfect Reality Personal?") Now the space-time world contains distinctions. It must, then, be unreal. Still, nature *is experienced*, and an object of experience has some kind of reality. Suppose, for example, that someone is delirious and seems to see a unicorn. While the unicorn doesn't exist, it appears to do so. It isn't real but *seems* real to the person who hallucinates. It thus has a kind of "practical" or "psychological" reality. The space-time world has a similar status. It doesn't exist. Nevertheless, it *seems* to exist. It has the same sort of reality, then, as illusory appearances. "The case is [also] analogous to that of a dreaming man who in his dream sees manifold things and, up to the moment of waking, is convinced that his ideas are produced by real perception without suspecting the perception to be a merely apparent one."[26]

The world illusion is created by avidyā or ignorance. "In dream, the mind . . . creates by its own power a complete universe of subject and object.

The waking state [too] is only a prolonged dream" produced by ignorance. Indeed, the deluded mind

> creates all the objects which [it] experiences. . . . Ceaselessly, it creates the differences in men's bodies, color, social condition and race. . . . It creates desires, actions and the fruits of actions. . . . Because of this ignorance, all the creatures of the universe are swept helplessly hither and thither, like masses of cloud before the wind.[27]

Avidyā isn't just intellectual error. A person who is trapped in it not only thinks wrongly but also feels, desires, and responds wrongly. Avidyā is a distorted understanding of oneself and the world that warps all one's reactions. It isn't easily dispelled. "The truth of Brahman may be understood intellectually. But the ego-sense [and ignorance which causes it] is deep-rooted and powerful, for it has existed from beginningless time. . . . It can be removed only by the earnest effort to live constantly in union with Brahman."[28]

The space-time world is thus produced by avidyā in the same way that hallucinations are produced by psychological disorders or dreams by repressed desires. If avidyā were replaced by Brahman-knowledge (jnāna),[29] the space-time world would disappear as the hallucination stops when the disorder is cured or a dream disappears when a person wakes up. For "the entire complex of phenomenal existence is considered as true [only] as long as the knowledge of the Brahman being the Self of all has not arisen; just as the phantoms of a dream are considered to be true [only] until the sleeper wakes."[30]

We are like someone walking in the dark who mistakes a rope for a snake. Although there is no snake, he or she experiences a shudder of fear and either runs away or takes other measures that would be appropriate if the snake were real. Just as this person ignorantly misidentifies the rope as a snake and acts accordingly, so we ignorantly misidentify reality (that is, the Brahman) as the space-time world and act as if the things in it were real. In truth, however, there is only the Brahman, and this is identical with our true self. "You may mistake a rope for a snake, if you are deluded. But, when the delusion passes, you realize that the imagined snake was none other than the rope. So also this universe is none other than the Ātman [the true self]."[31]

But if Brahman alone is real, what causes ignorance? Advaitins sometimes argue that

1. Avidyā has no beginning. (Indian thought believes that nature is beginningless. Since it is beginningless, the ignorance that continuously produces it must also be beginningless.)
2. Something that lacks a beginning can't have a cause. Hence,
3. Ignorance can't have a cause.

The demand for a causal explanation of ignorance thus rests on a failure to appreciate the implications of the world's beginninglessness.

But the argument isn't compelling. Its second premise assumes that causes must temporally precede their effects. If this is true, then anything that has a cause *follows* it and thus has a beginning. But the second premise isn't true. If I draw a circle on a chalkboard, the motion of my hand causes the appearance of the circle but doesn't temporally precede it. Even if ignorance is beginningless, some explanation of its occurrence is needed.

Another difficult question is, *"Who* is ignorant?" Only conscious subjects can be ignorant. Advaita thinks there are two subjects—the ātman or true self, which is identical with Brahman, and the empirical self or jīva. The jīva is the self that dreams, has ordinary waking experiences, and so on. It is part of the space-time world and, hence, ultimately illusory.

There are thus two possible answers to the question "Who is ignorant?"—"the true self" or "the empirical self." Neither is satisfactory. The true self can't be the subject of ignorance because it is identical with the Brahman, which is devoid of all stains and impurities. Is, then, the empirical self the subject of ignorance? The jīva is a product or creation of ignorance—part of the world-illusion. It is therefore difficult to see how it can also be its subject. (If the ignorant empirical self produces the world-illusion, it produces itself as well as everything else. But nothing can be its own cause.)[32]

Advaita has a response to these difficulties. There are only two standpoints from which the question of the nature and origin of ignorance can be approached—knowledge (jnāna) and ignorance (avidyā). Ignorance can't be understood from either perspective. A person trapped in ignorance can't properly understand anything and thus can't understand ignorance or the world it produces. But knowledge can't grasp ignorance and the space-time world either for, with the appearance of knowledge, these things vanish and consciousness becomes joyously empty. Knowledge could grasp ignorance only if it was aware of it, and it isn't. In short, if Advaita were *true,* ignorance couldn't be understood. The fact that it can't thus *confirms* the theory rather than disconfirms it.

Even if this response is satisfactory, Advaita faces another problem. Much of the theory's plausibility derives from the apparent implications of monistic mystical consciousness. During this experience, distinctions disappear. Nothing remains but consciousness itself. A person who thinks that the nature of things is revealed in the experience might easily conclude, therefore, that reality simply *is* pure empty consciousness and everything else illusion.[33] But though the conclusion is natural, it may be unwarranted.

Monistic experiences are cultivated in Buddhism because they help break up ordinary mental habits and temporarily free the mind from disturbances. Nevertheless, most Buddhists refuse to draw ontological conclusions from these experiences. All Buddhists reject Advaita's interpretation of them. Again, the Yoga school of Hinduism prizes monistic experiences as highly as Advaita. But Yoga interprets them differently. They *are* regarded as experiences of one's true self, but each person's true self is believed to be distinct. There are a *plurality of* true selves rather than a single one as Advaita thinks. Yoga also denies that the experience shows that nature is unreal.

The Advaitin account of monistic experience is thus an interpretation, and other interpretations are possible. There are also other types of religious experience—numinous experience, theistic mystical consciousness, and so on. It isn't clear why monistic consciousness should be privileged rather than these.

The Advaitin account is thus fraught with difficulties and receives less support from monistic mystical consciousness than one might think. Theists may therefore be justified in rejecting it. But they should also compare their accounts with those provided by Buddhists, Taoists, and *other theists*. One of the most interesting examples of the latter is offered by Viśiṣṭādvaita Vedānta.

In many ways, Viśiṣṭādvaita resembles classical Western theism. God is "the sum of all noble attributes." "He, the supreme one, is unique, transcending in character every other entity, because his nature is opposed to all evil and is of the sole nature of supreme bliss. He is the abode of countless auspicious attributes unsurpassed in their perfection." He is omnipotent, omniscient, and all-loving. His "grandeur is inconceivable."[34] Salvation is a consequence of grace and consists in an eternal loving union with God Himself. How is this God related to the world?

Creation myths often depict a struggle between the gods and nondivine principles or powers. The gods create the cosmos by imposing order, law, and structure on an alien material or force. But their victory isn't complete. The recalcitrance of the material or force prevents them from fully realizing their purposes.

Independent powers and principles are incompatible with God's absolute sovereignty and perfect power. Hence, as theism develops, these myths become problematic. Western theists rejected the idea of a material or stuff from which God creates the space-time world. In their view, it is created "out of nothing" (that is, there *is* no material). Indian theism retained the notion of a material or stuff but protected God's sovereignty and power by denying its independence. The material or stuff that God shapes or orders is drawn from His own being. God is like a spider who weaves a web out of the silky material it draws from its body. A sophisticated descendent of this idea is found in Rāmānuja's (eleventh-century) Viśiṣṭādvaita.

Rāmānuja thinks that "the entire complex of intelligent and nonintelligent beings (souls and matter) in all their different estates is real, and constitutes the form, i.e., the body of the highest Brahman."[35] The space-time world is thus related to God as our bodies are related to our souls. What are the implications?

Rāmānuja maintains that the "relationship of soul and body" is the

> relationship of the supporter and the supported, . . . of the controller and the controlled, and . . . of the principal entity and the subsidiary entity. That which takes possession of another entity entirely as the latter's support, controller and principal, is called the soul of that latter entity. That which, in its entirety, depends upon, is controlled by and subserves another and is therefore its inseparable mode, is called the body of the latter.[36]

God is related to the world in the same way. As Rāmānuja puts it,

> Any substance which a sentient soul is capable of completely controlling and
> supporting for its own purposes and which stands to the soul in an entirely
> subordinate relation, is the body of that soul. . . . In this sense, . . . all sentient and
> non-sentient beings together constitute the body of the Supreme Person, for they
> are completely controlled and supported by him for his own ends, and are abso-
> lutely subordinate to him.[37]

Since God is the world's support, controller, and principal, it is absolutely dependent upon Him. It has little value in comparison with Him, and He is untouched by its imperfections. God

> enters into all spiritual and physical entities as their inner self, appropriates them
> as his wondrous forms and modes and causes wondrous activities. Thus he
> flourishes in a plurality of forms. [But] having thus entered into this wondrous
> and manifold universe by an infinitesimal part of himself as its inner soul and
> controlling it all, he remains absolutely one, the repository of infinite and sur-
> passingly perfect attributes, the Lord of lords, the highest Brahman, the supreme
> Person.[38]

The Viśiṣṭādvaitin model preserves God's sovereignty, independence,
and absolute control. Is it better or worse than the Western model of creation
out of nothing? The accounts differ in one important respect. The Indian picture implies that the world is in some sense divine—part of God. It also suggests that the world is necessary. (God can't exist without His body because it
is part of Him.) The Western view implies that God and the world are radically different. The world isn't part of God and thus isn't inherently divine.
Some spatio-temporal things *are* holy (Jerusalem or Mecca, for example, or the
saints). But their holiness is freely bestowed on them by God and hence isn't
inherent. Nor is the world necessary. Its existence depends on an act of divine
will and is thus radically contingent. Therefore, if it is more illuminating to regard the world as contingent and devoid of (inherent) holiness, one should
prefer the Western view. The Indian model is preferable if it is more appropriate to think of it as necessary and divine.

We have considered some issues that arise in comparing rival explanations of the space-time world. One should ask questions like "Is the explanation as puzzling as what it explains?" "Does it receive independent support
from religious experience or other sources?" and "Does it conflict with our intuitions concerning the nature of the space-time world?" These and similar
questions must be answered before concluding that one account of the
world's origins is more illuminating than others. Comparable issues will arise
if we compare religious explanations of other phenomena.

Conclusion

The worldviews of the major religious traditions are more or less equally
successful in meeting most of the criteria for assessing metaphysical systems.
In general, they are consistent, comprehensive, compatible with commonly
acknowledged facts, enable their adherents to come to terms with life, and so

on. We should therefore focus our attention on two questions—"Are the ethical ideals of some systems superior?" and "Are the explanations offered by some systems more illuminating?" Our discussion of agape and karuṇā and of several accounts of the space-time world's origins provides examples of the sorts of problems that arise when one attempts to answer these questions. Although the issues are complex, and their resolution calls for judgment, our discussion doesn't imply that they *can't* be resolved or that a rational judgment is impossible. Suppose, however, that our best attempts to rationally adjudicate the competing claims of the world religions prove unsuccessful. How should a person respond to this failure? We will consider this question in the next chapter.

Notes

1. John Henry Newman, *A Grammar of Assent* (New York: Doubleday, 1955), 234–35.

2. Basil Mitchell, *The Justification of Religious Belief* (London: Macmillan, 1973), 112–13.

3. Ibid., 45–47.

4. Thomas Kuhn, *The Structure of Scientific Revolutions,* 2d ed. (Chicago: University of Chicago Press, 1970).

5. Ian Barbour, *Myths, Models, and Paradigms* (New York: Harper & Row, 1974), 103–104.

6. Ibid., 100–101.

7. The dispute is often complicated by the fact that what one party regards as a problem or solution isn't regarded as a problem or solution by the other. For example, Daltonian chemistry was primarily interested in quantitative changes in chemical reactions while the older chemistry was more interested in qualitative changes.

8. Newman, 235–37.

9. Mitchell, 99.

10. Keith Yandell, "Religious Experience and Rational Appraisal," *Religious Studies* 10 (1974): 186.

11. Edward Schoen, *Religious Explanations* (Durham, N.C.: Duke University Press, 1985).

12. Paul Tillich, *Systematic Theology,* vol. 1 (Chicago: University of Chicago Press, 1951), 105.

13. Frederick Ferré and Kent Bendall, *Exploring the Logic of Faith* (New York: Association Press, 1963), 171.

14. Alvin Plantinga, "An Evolutionary Argument Against Naturalism," in *Faith in Theory and Practice,* ed. Elizabeth S. Radcliffe and Carol J. White (Chicago and La Salle, Ill.: Open Court, 1993).

15. Gary Gutting, *Religious Belief and Religious Skepticism* (Notre Dame, Ind.: University of Notre Dame Press, 1982), chapter 5.

16. See, for example, Albert Farges, *Mystical Phenomena*, trans. S. P. Jacques (New York: Benziger Bros., 1925), and Auguste Poulain, *The Graces of Interior Prayer*, trans. L. L. Yorke Smith (St. Louis: B. Herder, 1950). These accounts are as detailed as the "scientific" ones of atheists like James Leuba, *The Psychology of Religious Mysticism* (New York: Harcourt Brace, 1925) or Sigmund Freud—see, for example, *The Future of an Illusion*, trans. W. D. Robson-Scott (New York: Liveright, 1949).

17. Some naturalists think that the existence of the natural world is necessary. Others maintain that questions about its origins are meaningless. Nevertheless, most naturalists concede that, in their view, the existence of contingent being is simply a brute fact that has no explanation.

18. George Mavrodes, "Religion and the Queerness of Morality," *Rationality, Religious Belief and Moral Commitment*, ed. Robert Audi and William J. Wainwright (Ithaca, N.Y.: Cornell University Press, 1986). For a theistic interpretation of sanctity, see Patrick Sherry, *Spirit, Saints, and Immortality* (Albany: State University of New York Press, 1984).

19. Martin Luther, *Christian Liberty* (Philadelphia: Muhlenberg Press, 1957), 27–30.

20. Or less dramatically: they vow to become Buddhas on the condition that, having become Buddhas, they may work for the salvation of everyone.

21. Quoted in Edward Conze, *Buddhism: Its Essence and Development* (New York: Harper, 1959), 128.

22. Irving Singer, *The Nature of Love: Plato to Luther* (New York: Random House, 1966), 311–12.

23. Although Freud tends to equate them, self-hatred should be distinguished from guilt (the painful recognition of one's distance from the ideal and one's responsibility for one's failure). One can feel guilty without hating oneself. Christian saints sometimes have an acute sense of guilt, but it is tendentious to argue that they hate themselves.

24. Quoted in Conze, 130.

25. For a further discussion of these issues, see William J. Wainwright, *Mysticism* (Madison: University of Wisconsin Press, 1981), chapter 5.

26. *The Vedānta Sūtras of Bādarāyana with the Commentary by Śaṅkara*, trans. George Thibaut (New York: Dover, 1962), part 1, 324. Advaita's position, however, is more complex than this might suggest, for there are *levels* of reality. A thing is real if it is an object of some type of experience. Something is fully real if an experience of it can't be "sublated" (that is, corrected or shown to be in error) by another type of experience. Dreams and hallucinations are sublated by ordinary waking experience. Hence, dream objects and hallucinatory objects are less real than the objects of waking consciousness. But waking consciousness is itself superseded and shown to be in error by (monistic) mystical experience. Hence, nature (the object of ordinary consciousness) isn't fully real. Still, it is *more* real than ordinary illusions.

27. *Shankara's Crest Jewel of Discrimination*, trans. Swami Prabhavananda (New York: Mentor Books, 1970), 58–60.

28. Ibid., 73.

29. Jnāna is the opposite of avidyā—an "existential" appropriation of insight into reality. One experiences the absolute oneness of Brahman and one's identity with it. (Monistic mystical consciousness provides a model of this experience.) The insight into reality's unity is appropriated when every aspect of the personality (feelings, desires, emotions, and so on) has been permeated and shaped by it.

30. *The Vedānta Sūtras,* part 1, 324.

31. *Sbankara's Crest Jewel,* 90.

32. Advaitins sometimes respond that the jīva isn't wholly illusory. The intellect, will, senses, and other bits of mental equipment are inert pieces of psychological machinery. The machine functions only when consciousness (the Ātman-Brahman) is conjoined with it. The jīva is this union of the true self with the "psychic equipment." But this doesn't solve the problem. In this view, the subject is the consciousness that is conjoined with the psychic equipment. Since consciousness is the Ātman and the Ātman is the Brahman, the latter is the real subject of ignorance. Hence, the Brahman is stained by it. See Stafford Betty, "A Death-Blow to Śankara's Non-Dualism?" *Religious Studies* 12 (1976): 281–90.

33. Advaitins argue that the experience of empty consciousness can't be sublated. One experience sublates another if it "cancels" the latter's content. Thus, the illusory experience of the snake is sublated by the experience of a rope obtained when we look at the object more closely. The content of the first experience is "cancelled" (shown to be illusory) by the second experience. Since the experience of empty consciousness has no content, its content can't be canceled. Hence, the experience can't be sublated. This argument assumes that an experience can be shown to be erroneous only by canceling its content.

34. Rāmānuja, *Vedārthasaṁgraha,* trans. S. S. Raghavachar (Mysore: Sri Ramakrishna Ashrama, 1956), 4, 11.

35. *The Vedānta Sūtras with the Commentary by Rāmānuja,* trans. George Thibaut (Delhi: Motilal Banarsidass, 1962), 88.

36. *Vedārthasaṁgraha,* 76.

37. *The Vedānta Sūtras with the Commentary by Rāmānuja,* 424.

38. *Vedārthasaṁgraha,* 83. Rāmānuja believes that the body-soul analogy is imperfect in one respect. Souls need bodies to accomplish their purposes, but God doesn't need the universe.

For Further Reading

The two best accounts of cumulative case reasoning are John Henry Newman, *A Grammar of Assent* (New York: Doubleday, 1955) and Basil Mitchell, *The Justification of Religious Belief* (London: Macmillan, 1973).

The classical discussion of agape is Anders Nygren, *Agape and Eros,* trans. Philip S. Watson (London: S.P.C.K., 1957). The reader should also consult Irving Singer, *The Nature of Love: Plato to Luther* (New York: Random House, 1966). The karunā ideal is discussed in Edward Conze, *Buddhism: Its Essence and Development* (New York: Harper, 1959), and *Buddhist Thought in India* (Ann

Arbor: University of Michigan Press, 1967). See also D. T. Suzuki, *Outlines of Mahāyāna Buddhism* (New York: Schocken Books, 1963), chapters XI and XII. For a controversial but interesting discussion see Arthur Danto, *Mysticism and Morality* (New York: Basic Books, 1972), chapter 4.

More about Rāmānuja a can be found in Ninian Smart, *Doctrine and Argument in Indian Philosophy* (London: George Allen and Unwin, 1964); and M. Hiriyana, *Outlines of Indian Philosophy* (London: George Allen and Unwin, 1932); Eric J. Lott, *Vedantic Approaches to God* (London: Macmillan, 1980); and Julius Lipner, *The Face of Truth* (Albany: State University of New York Press, 1986). See also Rudolf Otto, *India's Religion of Grace and Christianity Compared and Contrasted* (London: S.C.M. Press, 1930), and John B. Carman, *The Theology of Rāmānuja* (New Haven: Yale University Press, 1974).

CHAPTER 8

The Diversity
of Religions

CONTACT BETWEEN THE WORLD'S major religions isn't new. Educated medieval Christians knew something about Islam and more about Judaism. Buddhists, Confucianists, and Taoists coexisted in China, and Hindus, Jains, and Buddhists coexisted in India. While relations between these traditions were sometimes hostile, their adherents often learned from each other. For example, medieval Christian theologians acknowledged their debts to the great Jewish philosopher Maimonides (1135–1204), and to Muslim philosophers such as Avicenna (980–1037) and Averroës (1126–98).

Nevertheless, our situation today differs from that of our forebears in two ways. In the first place, we know more about other religions than our predecessors did. Good translations of important Hindu or Buddhist texts, for instance, are readily available. Universities and colleges regularly offer courses on non-Western religious traditions, and bookstores stock a variety of scholarly and popular works on Islam, Buddhism, Taoism, and so on. In the second place, we are more likely to know members of other traditions. Interreligious dialogue is common, and mosques and Buddhist or Hindu temples are found in most major Western cities. Increased knowledge and contact have three interrelated consequences. First, it is now easier to place ourselves in the shoes of adherents of other religious traditions—to see how the world looks through the eyes of an intelligent, educated, and religiously and morally sensitive Muslim, say. Second, awareness of the intellectual sophistication and spiritual richness of other traditions makes it more difficult to dismiss them as misguided or to retain our confidence in the superiority of our own tradition. Finally, two questions become pressing: Do the major world religions agree on essentials? And, if they do not, how should one respond to religious diversity?

It initially looks as if the first question is easily answered. At the most general level, the major traditions would agree with William James. Religion involves three beliefs:

> 1. . . . the visible world is part of a more spiritual universe from which it draws its chief significance; 2. . . . union or harmonious relation with that higher universe is our true end; 3. . . . prayer or inner communion with the spirit thereof . . . is a process wherein work is really done, and spiritual energy flows in and produces effects, psychological or material, within the phenomenal world.[1]

201

Once we descend from this level of generality, however, the appearance of unity vanishes. Westerners have usually identified the higher universe with God, but this ignores important alternatives. Advaita Vedānta identifies it with the nirguna Brahman, which is beyond space, time, causality, and the subject-object relation. Hīnāyana Buddhists believe that the higher universe is Nirvāna. Nirvāna is the end of ignorant desire, and of the suffering it causes. Positive terms like "peace," "purity," "safety," "the refuge," "the island," and "the opposite shore" are sometimes applied to it. But while these terms tell us something about what Nirvāna can mean for us (it provides safety, for example), Nirvāna itself can't really be described. In particular, it can't be described as a transcendent substance like God or Brahman. These differences between the traditions seem real and important.

How should we respond to them? One way is to apply the criteria for assessing worldviews discussed in Chapter 7 to the competing claims of the major world religions. The careful application of these criteria may lead to the conclusion that one tradition is rationally superior to the others. This conclusion would be a matter of judgment (like the conclusion that mind-body dualism is superior to materialism, or the conclusion that Keats is a better poet than Shelley), and intelligent men and women may disagree. Our conclusion may nonetheless be *justified* by our application of the criteria, and it may also be *correct*.

But we might come to a different conclusion. John Hick, for example, thinks that intellectually sophisticated versions of the major world religions meet the criteria equally well. Śaṅkara's version of Advaita Vedānta, for instance, is neither more nor less coherent, fruitful, illuminating, and so on than Aquinas's or Calvin's version of Christianity. [2] And even if our application of the criteria eliminates some systems, it might not eliminate all but one. We might eliminate nontheistic systems, for example, but be unable to decide between competing theistic worldviews. Or we might succeed in eliminating theistic systems but be unable to decide between Advaita Vedānta, Taoism, Yogācāra Buddhism, and other nontheistic accounts of the world.

So let us suppose that our application of the criteria for assessing worldviews fails to yield clear results—that, as far as we can tell, Christianity, Judaism, Advaita Vedānta, Hīnāyana Buddhism, and so on, meet the criteria equally well. This chapter discusses three responses to this possible outcome: relativism, the devaluation of propositional truth and belief, and "religious pluralism"—the view that all the great faiths are equally valid.

RELATIVISM

Relativists deny that there are neutral objective standards for evaluating rival worldviews. While each worldview has its own principles of truth and rationality, there are no *common* standards that could be used to show that one set of principles is *more* rational than another. For example, Peter Winch (1926–97) thinks that Western science and Azande witchcraft employ incommensurable norms of rationality. The magical practices of the Azande seem irrational when judged from the standpoint of Western scientific culture. Nevertheless, the Azande practices have their own kind of sense because they enable the Azande to come to terms with sickness, death, and the other contingencies of human existence. Both Western science and Azande witchcraft are rational when judged by their own principles. Neither can be said to be more rational than the other, however, for there are no objective, system-neutral standards for making this kind of judgment.[3]

Is it clear, though, that basic standards of truth and rationality really do differ from tradition to tradition? Winch argues that Azande witchcraft is rational because it enables the Azande to cope with life's contingencies. The standard that Winch is implicitly appealing to, however, is: "It is rational to do what is necessary to secure such important goods as peace and resignation in the face of life's contingencies." And *this* isn't peculiar to the Azande. On the contrary, it is "a general norm of rational action." Adopting effective means to reasonable ends is the *essence* of practical or prudential rationality.[4]

Others argue that some traditions reject logic. The occurrence of paradoxes and apparent inconsistencies allegedly shows that the traditions that include them reject the law of noncontradiction (that inconsistent statements can't both be true). But the fact that Christians, for instance, sometimes contradict themselves is inconclusive. One must also show that they are aware of these inconsistencies and aren't troubled by them. (That I sometimes unwittingly contradict myself doesn't show that I reject the law of noncontradiction. It shows only that I am not always rational.) Furthermore, not all *apparent* contradictions are *real* ones. Apparently inconsistent statements aren't always to be taken literally. They are often used to make a point that could be expressed less paradoxically. For example, "Man is a wolf" is not self-contradictory, inconsistently implying that humans are not human, because "wolf" is used metaphorically. "God neither exists nor does not exist" is sometimes used to make the (perfectly consistent) point that God isn't real in the way that spatio-temporal objects are.

One strand of Mahāyāna Buddhism does repudiate logic. Mādhyamika and Ch'an (Zen) are examples. But the significance of this is unclear. In the first place, their rejection of logic is a self-conscious and deliberate repudiation of a way of thinking that they admit is natural. Second, even the enlightened employ ordinary canons of reasoning when they practice science or engage in everyday affairs. Ordinary standards are appropriate in these realms (although not at the level of *deep* truth). Furthermore, Mādhyamika's rejection of the principles of logic is based on arguments that *employ* them. (Mādhyamika deliberately uses logic to destroy logic.) Finally, these traditions aren't interested in replacing ordinary canons of rationality with other canons but in transcending *any* kind of conceptual thinking. The upshot is that it isn't clear that these Buddhists are employing *different* standards of rationality than the rest of us are.

But even if standards of prudential rationality and logic are common to all societies, the criteria for assessing worldviews that were discussed in Chapter 7 are not. For example, they apparently weren't used in traditional African societies. The significance of this is unclear, however. The reason that these societies didn't develop the criteria wasn't that they *rejected* them (or thought they were inapplicable). It was, rather, that criteria for assessing conflicting theories are essentially *comparative,* and members of the societies in question weren't actively confronted with a plurality of worldviews that could be assessed as more or less simple, coherent, illuminating, and so on. The criteria weren't formulated or applied because there was nothing to apply them *to.*[5]

Where thinkers *are* confronted with a plurality of competing theories, however, the criteria that were discussed in Chapter 7 are implicitly appealed to. For example, Rāmānuja attempted to defend Viśiṣṭādvaita Vedānta by arguing that Advaita Vedānta is self-stultifying. Buddhists accused Hindus of construing ultimate reality and the self as permanent substances, and tried to show that the concept of permanent substance is incoherent. Augustine contended that Christianity could provide a more illuminating account of Rome's rise and fall than paganism could. Christians argued that their moral ideal is superior to Judaism's, and Confucianists criticized the Buddhist's ideal because it seemed to neglect the demands of society. The point is not that these arguments were or were not sound, but that they implicitly appealed to the criteria for assessing theories discussed in Chapter 7.

So the criteria for assessing competing theories are common to Christianity, Hinduism, Buddhism, and the other great religious traditions and are thus system-neutral; they aren't peculiar to only some of the worldviews whose claims are in question.

Are they also *objective?* Although this is a large issue, two points are important. First, if the criteria *aren't* objective, then the choice between rival religious systems isn't the only choice that is nonrational. Since choices between rival theories in the sciences and humanities are guided by the same criteria, they too are nonrational.

The second point is this. Most religions imply that their claims are objectively true and should therefore be accepted by everyone. (Exceptions are often only apparent. Advaita Vedānta, for example, maintains that theism is appropriate for some people and polytheism for others. They are appropriate for them, however, only because of their comparative lack of spiritual maturity. For the spiritually adult, there is only one truth—the unreality of distinctions and one's identity with Brahman.)[6] By denying the existence of objective standards, relativism implies that most religions lack the kind of truth that their adherents ascribe to them. Many people are attracted to relativism because it seems to respect religions equally. In fact, it devalues most of them by denying their objective truth.

To summarize: The criteria that were discussed in Chapter 7 apply to religious worldviews as well as to theories in the sciences and humanities. Since there are common standards, relativism is a reasonable response to the plurality of religions only if those standards lack objective validity. If they do, however, then many other realms of human thought are infected with relativity since they too employ them. This includes the historical, anthropological, and literary disciplines that study humanity's religious traditions, and that relativists typically appeal to support their claims. Furthermore, relativism's "tolerance" of a plurality of views (its refusal to judge) conceals an implicit adverse verdict: Religions don't have the kind of objective truth their members attribute to them.

THE DEVALUATION OF PROPOSITIONAL TRUTH AND BELIEF

Many thoughtful men and women attempt to minimize the significance of doctrinal conflicts between the world's religions by arguing that beliefs are comparatively unimportant. Propositional truth isn't the only or most important kind of truth. Truth is also personal authenticity. Ultimately, the true is the Real. God or the Transcendent is the truth, and what matters is the quality of one's relation to it (one's loyalty, trust, serenity, and so on)—not one's propositional beliefs. As Wilfred Cantwell Smith says, religion is not itself true or false but "becomes less or more true in the case of particular persons as it informs their lives . . . and shapes and nurtures their faith."[7] A person's religion can be evaluated only by the quality of that person's life, the degree to which it is "an immediate embodiment of his faith."[8] Differences in belief conceal the fact that in all of the major traditions, men and women faithfully respond to the Transcendent.

Yet doctrinal conflicts can't be set aside this easily. "True" *can* mean "authentic" or "genuine." For example, we speak of true value or false faces, of revealing one's true self, and so on. We can also apply "true" to lives that are authentic, that is, which are genuine or real in the sense that there is little or no gap between the faith a person professes and his or her life. No religion has a monopoly on truth in this sense. While the faith of some Muslims may be more authentic than the faith of some Christians (and vice versa), Muslims in general are neither more nor less authentically faithful than Christians.

But *what* faithful men and women embody is a particular set of practices, evaluations, *and beliefs*. And the quality or depth of their authenticity varies with the *adequacy* of their evaluations and beliefs. The faith of a believer in a flying saucer cult and the faith of a devout Muslim may be equally authentic in the sense that the life of each embodies his or her beliefs and values. It doesn't follow that their faith is equally authentic in the sense that it deserves equal esteem. The beliefs of the first are silly or false, and his or her values are misguided. If authenticity means more than the absence of a gap between what one professes and the way one lives, then the truth or falsity of one's doctrinal beliefs is important. Whether the faiths of Buddhists and Muslims are equally authentic in the sense of being equally valuable thus partly depends upon which of their doctrinal systems is closer to the truth.

"True" can mean "real" as well as "authentic." Ultimate reality is preeminently true because it is more real than anything else. There are several ways of understanding this. One is to distinguish levels of reality. Items at level m are more real than items at level n if all items at level n depend for their being on items on level m and no items at level m depend for their being on items at level n. In this sense, dreams are less real than dreamers, fictional characters are less real than their authors, and the space-time world is less real than God, who calls it into being.[9]

There are other ways of distinguishing the more from the less real. Advaita Vedānta claims that the Brahman is more real than the space-time world because the latter is illusory and the former is not. Again, the unreal may be equated with the contradictory or incoherent. Mādhyamika argues that the space-time world as ordinarily experienced is unreal because all conceptualizations of it break down, revealing contradictions and incoherencies. What is truly real is the process of becoming (the conceptually unstructured flow of transient reality). To see things as they are, we must stop conceptualizing them, and free our minds from attachment.[10]

It thus makes sense to equate ultimate reality with the truth if by "the truth" we mean "that which is more real than anything else." But it does so because the claim that the ultimate is more real than anything else can be articulated in propositions like "The world depends upon God although God does not depend upon it" or "All conceptualizations of the space-time world are incoherent." If propositions like these are false, then it is false that God is the truth or that the truth is the process of becoming. One can't, then, avoid questions of propositional truth by equating truth with the ultimately real.[11]

It is a mistake, then, to argue that doctrinal conflicts are unimportant because truth as authenticity or truth as reality are more important than propositional truth. Genuine authenticity presupposes that one possesses propositional truth. Ultimate reality is the truth (more real than anything else) only if certain propositions are true. If doctrinal conflicts can't be rationally resolved, then there is no rational way of determining which lives are more authentic, or whether God or Nirvāna or Brahman are the truth. Beliefs, and the truth of what one believes, are important.

RELIGIOUS PLURALISM

One of the most sophisticated attempts to come to terms with the diversity of religions is John Hick's. Hick does not deny that religious faith includes a propositional component, and that this is important. Nor does he dispute the objectivity of the criteria for assessing worldviews that were discussed in Chapter 7. But he does deny that their application enables us to decide between Buddhism and Christianity, say, or between Judaism and Islam. For, in Hick's view, the great world religions are more or less equally simple, coherent, fruitful, illuminating, and so on.

So what should we do in the face of religious diversity? Like William Alston (see Chapter 5), Hick believes that his own religious experiences, and those of his fellow Christians, are *prima facie* veridical. But he also thinks there are no epistemically relevant differences between Christian religious experiences and the religious experiences of Buddhists, Hindus, and so on. (As Alston might put it, all of these experiences, and the beliefs based on them, are products of mystical practices that [1] are socially established, [2] have outputs that are internally consistent and [3] are consistent with the outputs of other well-established doxastic practices, and [4] provide the spiritual and moral fruits they promise.) Hence, if Christian experiences are *prima facie* veridical, then so too are Hindu, Buddhist, Jewish, and Muslim experiences. These experiences, as well as the beliefs based upon them, conflict, however. For their apparent objects not only differ but are incompatible. (If God, say, is ultimate, Nirvāna is not, and vice versa.) It thus seems that the religious experiences of the various traditions can't all be *ultima facie* veridical; while all are *prima facie* veridical, some aren't veridical in fact.

We are faced with three alternatives: (1) All these diverse religious experiences are delusive (and hence not *ultima facie* verdical). (2) Some are delusive and some are not. (3) None are delusive. Hick rejects the first because he is convinced that religion is not a "purely human projection."[12] He also rejects the second. The great traditions must be judged by their moral and spiritual fruits, and these are "more or less on a par." "Salvation or liberation . . . consists" in a "transformation from self-centredness to Reality-centredness," and this process takes place "to a more or less equal extent within" all "the great traditions."[13] "Salvific transformation is most readily observed by its moral fruits, which can be identified by means of the ethical ideal, common to all the great traditions, of *agape/karunā* (love/compassion)."[14] When we apply this test, we find that the major traditions are equally successful in meeting it. We are left, then, with the third alternative.

Yet how can experiences of Yahweh, of Nirvāna, and of the nirguna Brahman be equally veridical? Hick's suggestion is this. We must distinguish "between the Real in itself and the Real as humanly thought and experienced."[15] Jews and Buddhists, for example, experience the same thing, but they do so from "different historical and cultural standpoints."[16] The experiences of Muslims, Jews, Christians, and theistic Hindus are structured by the concept of "deity" (God). The experiences of Buddhists, Taoists, and nontheistic Hindus are structured by the concept of a nonpersonal "absolute." Deity takes concrete form as Allah, Yahweh, Shiva, Vishnu, and so on. The absolute takes concrete form as Nirvāna, śūnyatā (emptiness), the Tao, or the nirguna Brahman. (Hick calls these "concretizations" of deity the absolute, "divine personae" and "metaphysical impersonae," respectively.) Hick's view, then, is this. Religion is the joint product of a transforming experience of the Real and culturally created concepts such as the concepts of God, the absolute, Yahweh, or Nirvānathat structure and interpret the experience.

Our concepts of the divine are thus partly human projections and partly not. Behind our all too human theologies lies a religious *ding an sich* (thing in itself) which guarantees that our religious concepts aren't *mere* projections, and which grounds the saving transformation from self-centeredness to reality centeredness.

Hick calls his position "pluralism," and distinguishes it from both "exclusivism" and "inclusivism." A Christian or Muslim *exclusivist,* for example, maintains that there is no salvation outside Christianity or Islam, respectively. Thus, in 1302, Pope Boniface VIII declared:

> We are required by faith to believe and hold that there is one holy, catholic and apostolic church; . . . outside it there is neither salvation nor remission of sins. . . . Further, we declare, say, define and proclaim that to submit to the Roman Pontiff is, for every human creature, an utter necessity of salvation.[17]

The position taken by the vast majority of Catholic, Protestant, Jewish, Hindu, and Buddhist theologians today, however, is *inclusivism.* Even though one's own religion is regarded as intellectually and salvifically superior, salvation is believed to be possible outside its boundaries. Thus, in his first encyclical (*Redemptor Hominis*), Pope John Paul II asserted:

> Man—every man without any exception whatever—has been redeemed by Christ, and . . . with each man without any exception whatever, Christ is in a way united, even when man is unaware of it.[18]

Some Christian inclusivists believe that the faithful in other traditions who do not encounter Christ in this life will encounter him in the next, and there respond to him as Lord and savior. Other Christian inclusivists think that Hinduism and other non-Christian traditions can themselves be salvifically efficacious but only because Christ is "secretly at work" within them. Contemporary Advaita Vedānta provides another example of inclusivism. All the major religions point to the truth, and salvation is possible within any of them. But the truths pointed to are that distinctions are unreal and that we are the nirguna Brahman, and a tradition's salvific efficacy is measured by its ability to foster the spiritual realization of these truths in its adherents' lives. *Pluralism,* by contrast, is the view that while all the great traditions are valid encounters with the Real, and all are salvifically efficacious, none is truer or salvifically more efficacious than the others.

What consequences would an adoption of the pluralistic hypothesis have for Buddhism, say, or Christianity? At one level, none. Hick isn't suggesting that religions like Judaism or Hinduism should be replaced by some all-embracing world religion. If the religions were to lose "their particularity [their distinctive scriptures, symbols, devotional practices, and so on], they would lose their life and their power to nourish." The "different traditions . . . with their associated forms of worship and life-styles" should therefore be retained.[19] But adopting the pluralistic hypothesis *would* have a major effect on Jewish or Hindu or Christian *beliefs.* For one would have to excise those beliefs which imply that one's own religion is truer than, or salvifically superior to, another. Thus, Hick thinks that Christians who adopt the pluralistic hypothesis should abandon the doctrine of the Incarnation (that God was "made man" in Jesus Christ), since the doctrine of the Incarnation implies the salvific superiority of Christianity. They must also revise traditional Christian conceptions of salvation. For if salvation consist in union with the Trinity, or redemption through the atoning death of Christ, then the religions aren't *equally* salvific.

Hick's response to the problem of religious diversity is persuasive and influential. How should we evaluate it? Among the most frequently offered criticisms are these. (1) In Hick's view, we have no substantive knowledge of the Real and hence can't know which responses to it are appropriate and which are not. (2) Hick has not shown that the spiritual transformations effected by the great traditions are equally valuable. (3) Hick's pluralistic hypothesis is just one more religious worldview and, as such, deserves to be taken neither more nor less seriously than Christian exclusivism, say, or Hīnāyana Buddhism. We will discuss these objections in turn.

No Substantive Knowledge of the Real

Hick thinks that "divine personae" such as Vishnu or Yahweh, "metaphysical impersonae" like Nirvāna or the nirguna Brahman, and even the more abstract concepts of deity and the absolute, are human and culturally conditioned ways of conceptualizing the Real. They are mere appearances of a reality lying being them that cannot be directly experienced. Since we lack direct access to it, we have no substantive knowledge of the Real in itself. As a result, the only attributes that we can literally ascribe to the Real are "formal properties" like "being a referent of a term" (that is, being the referent of "the Real") or "being such that our substantial concepts do not apply" to it. We cannot apply "substantial properties" to the Real "such as 'being good,' 'being powerful,' 'having knowledge,'" and so on.[20] The upshot is that the Real can't be truly and literally described as personal or nonpersonal, substance or process, conscious or nonconscious, good or evil. This view is subject to at least three objections.

First, Hick himself seems to make substantive claims about the Real. As we saw, Hick believes that we veridically experience the Real. Now "*x* veridically experiences *y*" entails "*y* is a cause of *x*'s experience of *y*." So if we veridically experience the Real, the Real is the cause or ground of our experience of it, "that which there must be if religious experience, in its diversity of forms, is not purely imaginative projection but is also a response to a transcendent reality."[21] Yet *being a cause or ground of religious experience* is not a formal property.

It is also significant that, in Hick's view, the Real is experienced in some ways and not others. Hick suggests that "these two very different ways of conceiving and experiencing the Real, as personal and non-personal [that is, as deity or absolute], is perhaps a complementarity analogous . . . to that between the two ways of conceiving and registering light, namely as waves and as particles."[22] Suppose that it is. That light sometimes "appears to behave like a shower of particles" and, at other times, "like a succession of waves" surely tells us something substantive about light itself. To know that a thing behaves in only some of the logically possible ways in which something could behave is to know something substantive about *it,* and not just about its modes and manifestations. Consider now the divine personae and metaphysical impersonae, and the concepts of deity and of the absolute that they instantiate. The major theistic traditions apprehend the Real as deity, and typically experience it as powerful and intelligent—not as weak or foolish. The nontheistic traditions that apprehend the Real as the absolute never experience it as powerless or defective. *All* the great traditions experience the Real as good, and as the immediate ground of "salvation/liberation." They do not experience it as evil, or as the immediate ground of damnation/enslavement. The Real in itself, in other words, does not manifest itself in all the logically possible ways something could manifest itself. Why doesn't this tell us something substantive about it?

The second objection is this. It isn't immediately obvious why, in Hick's own view, the Real can't be characterized as good. If one tradition veridically experiences the Real as personal or as substance and another equally valid tradition veridically experiences it as impersonal or as process, then the Real can't literally be either. (For nothing can literally be both personal and nonpersonal, both substance and process.) But *all* the great traditions experience the Real as good. So why can't we say that it *is* (literally) good? Hick's reason appears to be this. The variety of verdical but conflicting religious experiences and conceptualizations leads us to postulate a Real in itself that transcends human thought and experience. Having done so, we are forced to accept our postulate's consequences. Since the Real transcends *all* human concepts, it transcends the concepts of good and evil. So even if the religions agree that the Real is (literally) good, we must deny that it is. The Real is good only in the sense that it is the ground of the change from self-centeredness to blessedness. That is, it is good only in the sense that it "causes," or is the ground of, goodness.[23] But this doesn't square well with other things Hick says. Hick believes that "Love and compassion are appropriate responses to the Real" is validated by the fact that all the great religious traditions teach it. Why then, isn't "The Real is (literally) good" validated by the fact that all the great traditions say that it is?

Hick's denial that we have substantive knowledge of the Real is the basis for a third objection. If we know nothing substantive about the Real, not even that it is good, then how do we know that a loving and Reality-centered life is an appropriate response to the Real? Hick's answer in *An Interpretation of Religion* is that, given that the various divine personae and metaphysical impersonae "are indeed manifestations of the ultimately Real, an appropriate human response to any one of them will also be an appropriate response to the Real."[24] For example, if our responses would be appropriate to Yahweh or to śūnyatā (emptiness) if there literally were such things, they will also be appropriate to the Real. But this won't do.

Hick's argument hinges on the following claim: "If an experience of x is a veridical experience of y, then an appropriate response to x is also an appropriate response to y." Now this claim can be taken in two ways. It might mean "If a person who is experiencing y as x is really experiencing y, then an appropriate response to x is an appropriate response to y." Taken this way, the claim is false. Suppose that, in the dark, I mistake a sheet hanging on a line for a ghost, and react with terror. Terror is an appropriate response to ghosts. It is not an appropriate response to the sheet that I am really experiencing. Hick's claim can be taken in another way, however. For it might mean "If a person is *veridically experiencing y as x*, then an appropriate response to *x* is an appropriate response to *y*." Taken in this way, the claim seems true. If I veridically experience the white shape on the line as a sheet, then responses appropriate to sheets are also appropriate to that white shape. So if the Real is *veridically experienced as Vishnu* or *as the nirguna Brahman*, appropriate responses to the latter are appropriate responses to the former. Yet this won't do either. For if *y* is to be veridically experienced *as x*, then *y* must *be x* or bear a significant likeness or analogy to *x*. (Responses to sheets are appropriate responses to the white shape because the white shape *is* a sheet. Terror wasn't an appropriate response to the sheet because the sheet isn't a ghost or significantly like one.) But in Hick's view, the Real isn't Vishnu or the nirguna Brahman. Nor (in the absence of substantive knowledge of the Real) do we have any reason to think that Vishnu or the nirguna Brahman is *like* the Real.[25] When language about the Real is emptied of all but formal content, no basis remains for saying that the Real is veridically experienced as one thing rather than another (as divine, for example, and not demonic). And so no basis remains for saying that one response to the Real is more appropriate than another.

Perhaps as a result of these difficulties, Hick has recently shifted to another position—that we know these responses to be appropriate because "all the great traditions teach" that they are, and we are simply *assuming* that these traditions are "authentic responses to the Real." That religion isn't a purely human projection or an inauthentic response to reality is now said to be an article of *faith*. It cannot be established by reason.[26]

Are the Great Traditions Equally Salvific?

Hick thinks that the transformations effected by the great traditions are fundamentally the same. Committing oneself in faith to Christ, transcendence of the ego to attain Nirvāna, and so on "are variations within different conceptual schemes" on a common theme; "the transformation of human existence from self-centredness to Reality-centredness" is the same. Religions effect this transformation to the degree that their members succeed in embodying "the ethical ideal, common to all the great traditions, of *agape/karunā* (love/compassion)." In principle, one tradition might do this more effectively than others. In fact, "no one tradition stands out as more productive of sainthood than another."[27]

Hick assumes that both the transformations from self-centeredness to reality-centeredness, and the traditions' ethical ideals, are the same. These assumptions may be doubted. John Wesley (1703–91) was a founder of Methodism. D. T. Suzuki (1870–1966) was an influential spokesperson for Zen Buddhism. Were their spiritual transformations the same? Only if the specifically Christian or Buddhist content of their religious lives are accidental to them. It is difficult to believe that they are. Wesley, for example, *might* have led much the same kind of religious life if he had been a Scotch Presbyterian. He wouldn't have if he had been a Theravadin or Zen monk.

One can raise similar questions about the agape/karuna ideal. The golden rule is (as Hick says) a common denominator in the great traditions, but how it is fleshed out varies. Even when ethical and spiritual ideals of love or compassion appear most alike, their content or flavor seems different. It isn't clear, for example, that the love of a Saint Francis who believes that others are made in God's image, and the compassion of a bodhisattva who believes that people are "empty" (that is, devoid of self), are the same in all important respects. (For more on this point, see Chapter 7.) Hick seems to be abstracting from real differences.

Why does Hick think these differences are unimportant? Because he believes that the great traditions are equally authentic responses to the Real? But that they *are* equally authentic responses to the Real presupposes that the differences in question are unimportant or nonessential. And *that* is precisely the issue.

Is Pluralism Just One More Religious Hypothesis?

Peter Byrne (1950–) makes an important point. If Hick thinks that religious pluralism expresses a religious truth that is only imperfectly understood by the traditions, then pluralism, too, it a religious worldview. Furthermore, it is a religious worldview that is incompatible with the worldviews of traditional Christianity, Buddhism, and so on. (If any of the latter are true, then not all the divine personae and metaphysical impersonae are fictions, and not all religions are equally salvific. But in that case, pluralism is false. Conversely, if pluralism is true, the worldviews of Christianity, Buddhism, and so on, are false.[28]) So if Hick continues to insist on the truth of his own theory, he hasn't transcended exclusivism and inclusivism. One religious worldview (namely, his own) *is* truer than—and therefore superior to—others. Religious pluralism is thus ultimately incoherent. In insisting that it is superior to Christian, or Muslim, or Buddhist exclusivism or inclusivism, religious pluralism implies the *denial* of what it wishes to profess, namely, that all the major religious worldviews are equally appropriate responses to the Real.[29]

Hick's response is to deny that religious pluralism is a religious worldview. It is, rather, a *meta*-religious explanation of the great religious traditions—namely, that they are "different [and equally authentic] human responses to the Real."[30] The pluralistic hypothesis is not a *religious* hypothesis but a higher-level explanation of the major traditions that leaves them more or less as they are. Since religious pluralism is *not* a religious worldview, there is no inconsistency in asserting *both* that it is superior to Muslim exclusivism or Christian inclusivism, say, *and* that the major religious worldviews are more or less equally true or authentic.

The trouble is that Hick's hypothesis *doesn't* leave things as they are. Christians or Muslims or Buddhists who accept the pluralistic hypothesis will have to alter their understanding of Christianity or Islam or Buddhism. Hick thinks that as a result of these altered understandings, each tradition will continue as it is with only those modifications required "to de-emphasize [that is, reject!] that aspect of its teaching which entails its own unique superiority."[31] Yet in the case of Christianity, at least, this aspect seems essential to it. If Christ is God incarnate, then salvation is ultimately through Christ alone. So pluralism implies that one of the central doctrines of Christianity (namely, the Incarnation) is false. Other traditions, too, include core doctrines that imply their salvific superiority. Hence, these doctrines will also have to be rejected. It looks, then, as if Hick's pluralistic hypothesis *is* in direct competition with traditional religious worldviews and is not just a higher-level explanation that leaves them intact.

This might not matter if the pluralistic hypothesis were better supported than its exclusivist or inclusivist rivals. But is it? Even if pluralism provides a better explanation of religious diversity, it doesn't follow that it is a better hypothesis, all things considered. Inclusivism may be an essential part of a more comprehensive hypothesis such as traditional Christian theism which has more explanatory power than either the plualistic hypothesis or a Christianity that has been modified to conform to it. For example, traditional Christianity can explain the existence of contingent being. But the pluralistic hypothesis cannot and isn't designed to. Nor can a Christian theism that has been modified to fit the pluralistic hypothesis explain it. For an essential component of the explanation is the contingent will of a necessarily existing omnipotent and omniscient being (see Chapter 2), and the pluralistic hypothesis denies that the Real has either mind or will. If pluralism is true, the Christian stories are "myths" or "symbols," and "myths" or "symbols" explain nothing.

Conclusion

Let us summarize our discussion. Two things lead Hick to postulate a Real in itself: (1) the *prima facie* verdicality of (for example) Christian, Buddhist, and Jewish experiences, together with the absence of relevant epistemic differences between them, and (2) the (alleged) fact that the major traditions are equally salvific. In Hick's view, the Real in itself is conceptualized and experienced differently, but equally authentically, in all the great traditions.

Hick's religious pluralism is an impressive attempt to come to terms with the diversity of human religious life and experience. But it is subject to at least three difficulties. (1) If we lack substantive knowledge of the Real, it is difficult to see how we can know which responses are appropriate to it and which are not. (2) Hick's claim that the transformation from self-centeredness to Reality-centeredness is the same in all the great traditions appears to abstract from real differences. (3) On the face of it, Hick's pluralism appears to be a religious worldview that is in direct competition with the Christian, Jewish, Muslim, or Hindu exclusivism or inclusivism it wishes to displace. If it is, then at least one religious worldview (namely, pluralism) is superior to others. But in that case, pluralism (which implies that *no* viable religious worldview is superior to others) is false.

So where do we stand? Chapter 7 examined criteria for assessing explanatory theories and applied them to some disputes between theists and nontheists. This chapter has discussed three responses to the possibility that any comparison of religious worldviews that is guided by these criteria will result in a standoff. It has argued that each is problematic.

A fourth response is possible, however. Even if a decision between Judaism, say, and Buddhism can't be made on the basis of reason, perhaps it *can* be made on the basis of revelation. We will discuss this possibility in the next section.

REVELATION AND RIVAL RELIGIOUS SYSTEMS

The intellectual aspect of a traditional religion is a worldview—a comprehensive picture of the nature of things. But it also purports to be a revelation. Christians think that their doctrines articulate a divinely revealed vision of reality and our place in it. While Vedāntists believe that reason can remove obstacles to belief and expose errors in competing traditions, Vedānta's truth is ultimately thought to rest on scripture (the Vedas). Buddhists maintain that their teachings express the wisdom of the Buddha. If we achieve enlightenment, we will see the truth of his teachings for ourselves. Initially, however, they must be accepted on faith.

If this is right, a proper response to the plurality of religions may be faith, not reason. Perhaps a final decision can't, or shouldn't, be reached either by applying our criteria or on the basis of other intellectual considerations. Ultimately, one may simply have to bend one's knee—accepting the tradition that he or she perceives as revealed.

There is undoubtedly truth in this. Religious worldviews *are* regarded as revelations. Furthermore, many of them contain teachings such as the doctrine of the Trinity or the absolute unity of Brahman that are believed to transcend (though not contradict) reason. Nor is the proper response to revelation mere intellectual assent. It is faith—a total submission of one's mind and heart to the reality disclosed in the tradition. Still, this isn't the whole truth. To see why, we must examine the concept of revelation.

The concept is interpreted in three different ways. Some theologians use "revelation" for moments of religious discovery and insight. The "bearers of revelation" are those who "perceive something new and introduce it into man's religious outlook."[32] Other theologians apply the term to encounters in which God actively thrusts His mind and purposes into ours. In this view, God doesn't reveal the truth of scriptural or dogmatic propositions but reveals *Himself*. Classical theists disagree. In their opinion, revelation consists in God's communicating truths about Himself and the world. Some of these truths can be confirmed by reason. Others cannot. In either case, one should believe them since the person who communicates them is necessarily truthful.[33]

The first view is clearly stated by C. H. Dodd (1884–1973). Dodd compares scriptural authority to authority in science or art. The authority of the prophets and saints who speak to us through scripture is that "which belongs intrinsically to genius." Newton's authority is based on his superior scientific insight. Tolstoy's is based on his understanding of human nature. Similarly, the prophets' and saints' authority is based on an experience of divine reality that is "fuller, deeper and more compelling than" our own.

Authorities see more deeply than we do. Nevertheless, their insights are mixed with error. Hence, while they provide "stimulus, support and direction," they don't absolve us of responsibility for our own judgment. The prophets' apprehension of the "thought of God," for example, was mediated through their historically conditioned and morally imperfect personalities. We should not, therefore, "submit to them blindly, or expect them to be infallible" but follow their guidance to see if what they say can be confirmed by our own experience.[34]

Traditional theologians fault this conception. In their view, the content of revelation isn't *discovered* but disclosed by God Himself. Revealed knowledge exceeds human capacities—even the capacities of genius. In equating revelation with scientific or artistic discovery, Dodd neglects God's active role in the process of revelation and thus empties the concept of most of its content.

The second conception is more traditional. Divine revelation is analogous to cases in which people reveal themselves to others, not to cases in which they disclose information. According to H. H. Farmer (1892–1981), revelation is a personal relationship in which God approaches men and women in their immediate situation as an "active personal will" that poses an "absolute demand" and offers "final succor." God takes the initiative, "thrusting" His mind and will into ours, His "values and purposes among" ours. The "essential content of revelation" is thus "God Himself, and not general truths about God," although Farmer admits that truths about God "are implicit in the divine self-giving," and will be articulated once one begins to reflect on one's encounter.[35]

The first two accounts have a common feature. In both views, scripture and theology are essentially *human* products. If they are, then the worldviews they express should presumably be assessed in the way we assess others.

Newton's theory was revolutionary. Nevertheless, it was assessed by the same scientific standards used to evaluate other scientific theories. Although Tolstoy's novels introduced new perspectives on human nature, they were subject to the same critical norms as other works of literature.[36] The discovery of a religious worldview may also be an act of genius. But if it is only that, its adequacy should be judged by the appropriate human criteria.

The second account has similar implications. In this view, God doesn't communicate general truths but reveals Himself. The words of scripture and theology are human attempts to articulate these encounters and their implications for human life. Christian or Muslim worldviews differ from systems of belief that aren't based on revelation because their primary data are the events through which God allegedly reveals Himself. Interpretations of the history of Jesus or the proclamation of Mohammed provide the key for interpreting reality as a whole. But even though God may encounter us in the life of Christ or the words of Mohammed, scriptural and theological interpretations of these facts are human and fallible. We should therefore assess them by the standards we use to assess other interpretations and explanations.

But suppose God reveals not only Himself but also truths about Himself. After all, people usually reveal themselves to others by *telling* them about themselves. Perhaps, then, God not only reveals Himself but also guides the process of interpretation. This, of course, is the traditional view. The biblical God, for example, not only encounters Moses but also informs him of His plans and purposes. According to this conception, the worldview, or at least its key features, is divinely communicated. How does this affect the process of assessment?

If a worldview is divinely communicated, then it is true no matter how plausible or implausible it may seem. Hence, if we have good reasons for thinking that the Christian or Hindu worldview has been revealed by God, we should accept it even if it doesn't fare well when assessed by our criteria. What is crucial is the views *origins,* not the inherent plausibility of its contents. It doesn't follow, however, that reason shouldn't play a role in assessing an alleged revelation's credentials.

The classical traditions contain a number of criteria for distinguishing between true and false revelations. For example, Advaita argues that the Vedas are reliable because they teach us about right, wrong, and other "things which are highly useful . . . and are not known otherwise" and because they aren't contradicted by other sources of knowledge. Ultimately, though, "the Veda is its own witness and proof." As the sun not only illumines other things but shines by its own light, so the Vedas establish their "own reliability as well as the reliability of other things."[37]

Christians have traditionally appealed to the trustworthiness of the biblical witnesses, the miracles that allegedly accompanied Christianity's promulgation, the gospel's apparent fulfillment of Old Testament prophecies, and the growth of the church. They claim that the gospel contains nothing that is contradictory or clearly erroneous and point to its beneficial effect on people's lives as well as its "power to meet even the highest aspirations" of humanity. Christians also appeal to "the internal conviction felt by the soul as to the truth of the doctrine"—a sense of its splendor and appropriateness to the human situation.[38]

Criteria like these specify the features that a divine revelation would allegedly have. They presuppose certain conceptions of ultimate reality and the human situation and are reasonable if those conceptions are reasonable. For example, that a revealed doctrine would improve people's lives and be free from error presupposes ultimate reality's goodness and truth. The appeal to miracles presupposes that God can perform them and would attest to the truth of His communications by doing so. A revelation's "intrinsic luminosity" or the "soul's internal conviction of its truth" is relevant only if a genuine revelation would be likely to exhibit this quality or have this effect.

The criteria for assessing revelations thus rest on conceptions of ultimate reality and its relation to human life. Hence, if appeals to the criteria aren't to be circular, these conceptions must be independently plausible. For example, the religions agree that ultimate reality is the Good and the True. They therefore agree that a divine revelation will be beneficial and truthful. Hence, a Christian who is arguing with a Vedāntin, or a Vedāntin who is arguing with a Christian, can appeal to these criteria without begging the question in favor of his or her own system. If one can independently justify the claim that ultimate reality is personal, one can also employ criteria shaped by a theistic understanding of the transcendent without falling into circularity.

But what sort of independent justification of the claim that ultimate reality is good and true, or personal, is possible? The most obvious answer is arguments like those discussed in Chapter 2 or an appeal to the successful fulfillment of the criteria discussed in Chapter 7.

Let us summarize our results. The intellectual aspect of a religion seems to be a worldview. If it is, the plausibility of a set of religious doctrines should presumably be assessed by the standards we use to assess other comprehensive metaphysical systems. Many believers are uneasy with this, however, because it seems insensitive to the fact that traditional religious worldviews purport to be revealed. Is it really appropriate to judge alleged revelations by purely rational criteria?

If religious worldviews are the creations of religious genius or human attempts to articulate divine-human encounters, then the answer is "yes." If the worldview is *itself* revealed, the situation is more complicated. If God is indeed the view's author, we should believe it whether or not it is independently plausible. Nevertheless, we must use reason to determine whether the view *has* a divine origin. We are confronted with a plurality of alleged revelations and need to sort them out. There are criteria for doing so. Many of these criteria, however, are purely rational (for example, "The doctrine mustn't contain contradictions" or "The witnesses must be trustworthy"). The others seem to presuppose metaphysical claims that require rational justification.

CONCLUSION

Is reason, then, the ultimate test after all? John Locke thought so. Propositions shouldn't be accepted as divinely revealed unless there is good evidence that God has revealed them. Reason must test revelation. A person who stifles reason to make room for revelation is like someone who blinds himself or herself "the better to receive the remote light of an invisible star by a telescope." Locke thinks that Christianity is credible but only because it is confirmed by miracles. Revelation, he concludes, is simply "natural reason enlarged."[39]

Locke is making two claims—that the rational evidence for a particular revelation (Christianity) is sufficient and that, if it weren't, it would be wrong to believe it. Both may be doubted.

Reason may be capable of provisionally eliminating some alternatives, and there may be better reasons for some views than others. For example, we have argued that there are plausible arguments for theism (Chapter 2), that the major objection to it is inconclusive (Chapter 3), and that theism might provide a better overall explanation than either naturalism or (at least some) nontheistic religious systems (see Chapter 7). But even if reason manages to *reduce* the number of alternatives, it may fail to eliminate all but one. For example, it may be unable to discover good reasons for deciding between rival theistic revelations. And even if rational investigation *should* find a (slight?) probability in favor of one alternative, the evidence is too complex and ambiguous to *compel* assent.

If this is correct, reason can't fully resolve the problem of choosing between worldviews. To embrace a religion with firm conviction, one may ultimately have to venture beyond the evidence or rely on one's immediate impression that the gospels, or the Vedas, or the teachings of the Buddha, contain the "words of life." This decision or impression *may* have a theological explanation. It might be explained as an expression of one's kinship with Brahman, for example, or by the indwelling of the Holy Spirit. These doctrines may make the decision or impression intelligible and also provide a kind of retrospective warrant for it. Still, one can't use them to justify one's adoption of the system of teachings in which they are embedded without falling into circularity.

The evidence may, then, support (some) religious beliefs. But it doesn't seem strong enough to justify a firm and steady commitment to a religious tradition. If it isn't that strong, faith's certainty must, at least partly, rest on other foundations.

The major traditions have usually recognized this. Advaita, for example, believes that reason supports the authority of the Vedas but can't establish it. If one is to grasp their truth, one's eyes must be opened to their intrinsic luminosity. John Calvin said, "Profane men . . . desire to have it proved by reason that Moses and the prophets were divinely inspired. But I answer . . . these words will not obtain full credit in the hearts of men until they are sealed by the inward testimony of the Spirit. The same spirit . . . who spoke by the mouths of the prophets, must penetrate our hearts, in order to convince us that they faithfully delivered the message with which they were divinely intrusted."[40] Thomas Aquinas thought there was good evidence for the divine origin of Christian teaching but didn't think it was sufficient to compel assent. "Of those who see the same miracle, or . . . hear the same sermon, some believe and some do not. Hence, we must assert another internal cause, which moves man inwardly to assent to matters of faith." This cause is a movement of the will that embraces the truths proposed for belief because it seems "good or fitting" or "useful" to believe. One's will, however, must be moved by God through grace. The free act by which one embraces revealed truths is thus grounded in a "supernatural principle."[41]

Are firm and steady religious beliefs improper when one's evidence isn't fully compelling? Locke thought so. The strength of a person's belief should be proportioned to the strength of his or her evidence. But Locke was an evidentialist, and evidentialism is controversial. (See Chapter 6.) There is also another consideration.

To suppose that the strength of one's belief should never exceed the strength of one's evidence may beg the question against theism and other religious outlooks. For the following might be true: (1) Human beings are capable of sharing in God's life or in some other way participating in supernatural reality. (2) One can't adopt the proper attitude toward the divine, however, if one doubts its reality or is ignorant of its nature. A firm belief in its reality, goodness, and so on, is necessary if one is to share in it. Finally, (3) our intellectual faculties are instruments for acquiring as many important truths as possible, and the most important truths are about the transcendent.

Suppose these claims are true. Knowing divine truths might be better than simply believing them. (Aquinas thought so.) Disbelief might be better than irrational belief—that is, a belief for which one has *no* good reasons, or is such that one has (or should have) good reasons for thinking it false. But is it improper to firmly hold a *true* religious belief that isn't *fully* supported by the evidence at one's disposal? It isn't obvious that the answer is "yes." If the belief happens to be true, one securely holds correct beliefs about the most important matters and has met a necessary condition for sharing in an overwhelming good.

Once believers encounter serious objections to their convictions or begin to doubt them, they may no longer be rationally entitled to them unless they think that at least as strong a case can be made for their beliefs as against them. It doesn't follow that the firmness of their beliefs should be determined only by the evidence at their disposal and thus fluctuate with their changing views of its strength.

This book has implicitly contended that reason can, and should, play an important role in the formation and retention of the religious beliefs of intellectually sophisticated people. Nothing that has been said, however, implies that faith doesn't have an equally significant part to play in the proper use of our cognitive faculties.

Notes

1. William James, *The Varieties of Religious Experience* (New York: The Modern Library, c1902), 475.

2. Although Śaṅkara may provide a better account of some things and Aquinas or Calvin of others.

3. Peter Winch, "Understanding a Primitive Society," *American Philosophical Quarterly* 1 (1964): 307–24.

4. John Watt, "Winch and Rationality in Religion," *Sophia* XIII (1974): 19–29.

5. Robin Horton, "Tradition and Modernity Revisited," in *Rationality and Relativism*, ed. Martin Hollis and Steven Lukes (Cambridge, Mass.: MIT Press, 1982). Horton argues that what was lacking wasn't so much an *awareness* of alternative worldviews as the presence of alternatives that "are being aggressively projected into" the thinker's mind "by other thinkers who wish to obliterate his own preferred theory." (227) In the absence of "critical assaults of other thinkers

committed to rival frameworks" (241), there was no pressure to develop and apply comparative criteria.

6. Mādhyamika and Zen *may* be genuine exceptions. If *no* claims are made (as they maintain), then no truth claims are made that purport to be objectively valid. Whether this strand of Mahāyāna Buddhism really avoids espousing a worldview, and making universal claims, is a moot point.

7. Wilfred Cantwell Smith, *Towards a World Theology* (Philadelphia: Westminster Press, 1981), 187.

8. ———, *The Meaning and End of Religion* (New York: New American Library, 1962), 161.

9. See George Mavrodes, "Real and More Real," *International Philosophical Quarterly* 4 (1964): 554–61, and James Ross, *Philosophical Theology* (Indianapolis, Ind., and New York: Bobbs-Merrill, 1969), chapter 6.

10. It should be noted that, in this view, the truly real isn't something over and above the space-time world such as God or the Brahman. It is the space-time world itself viewed without attachment or conceptualization. Since the truly real isn't conceptualized, its conceptualization isn't contradictory or incoherent.

11. There is another possibility. One can equate reality with value. God or Nirvāna are most real because they are most valuable. But a thing's value depends upon its other properties. Thus, the truth of "That's a good automobile" depends upon the truth of such propositions as "It gets good mileage to the gallon," "It seldom needs repairs," "It has the latest safety features," and so on. Similarly, the truth of "God (or Nirvāna) is most valuable" depends upon the truth of *other* statements about God (or Nirvāna). Questions of propositional truth can't be avoided.

12. John Hick, *A Christian Theology of Religions* (Louisville, Ky.: Westminster John Knox Press, 1995), 28.

13. Ibid., 18, 14.

14. John Hick, *An Interpretation of Religion* (New Haven, Conn.: Yale University Press, 1989), 14.

15. Ibid., 14.

16. John Hick, *God and the Universe of Faiths* (London: Macmillan, 1973), 141.

17. Quoted in John Hick, *God Has Many Names* (Philadelphia: Westminster, 1980), 29.

18. Quoted in Hick, *A Christian Theology of Religions*, 19.

19. Hick, *God Has Many Names*, 21.

20. Hick, *An Interpretation of Religion*, 239.

21. Hick, *A Christian Theology of Religions*, 60.

22. Hick, *An Interpretation of Religion*, 245.

23. Note that "causing goodness" appears to be another substantive property of the Real.

24. Hick, *An Interpretation of Religion*, 350.

25. Hick sees this. On page 251 of *An Interpretation of Religion,* he explicitly denies that analogical predications ("*x* is like so and so") apply to the Real.

26. Hick, *A Christian Theology of Religions*, 77.

27. Hick, *An Interpretation of Religion,* 36, 14, 307.

28. Or, in any case, less true.

29. Peter Byrne, "A Religious Theory of Religion," *Religious Studies* 27 (1991): 121–32.

30. Hick, *A Christian Theology of Religions,* 42.

31. Ibid., 30.

32. H. H. Farmer, *The World and God* (London: Nisbet, 1942), 82.

33. Revelation can be understood impersonally. For example, Advaita thinks that the Vedas are revealed although there isn't any revealer. There are, however, nontheistic parallels to the positions described in the text. The Vedas can be regarded as discoveries of religious genius, as expressions of mystical encounters with Brahman, or (more traditionally) as a set of supernatural truths.

34. C. H. Dodd, *The Authority of the Bible* (Glasgow: William Collins Sons, 1978), chapter 1.

35. Farmer, *The World and God,* chapter 5.

36. This is a bit oversimplified. The works of genius sometimes cause us to modify our standards. For example, the paintings of Picasso and Matisse altered our conception of what constitutes a good painting.

37. K. Satchidananda Murty, *Revelation and Reason in Advaita Vedānta* (New York: Columbia University Press, 1959), 27–33.

38. George H. Joyce, "Revelation," *The Catholic Encyclopedia,* vol. 13 (New York: Robert Appleton, 1907–12).

39. John Locke, *An Essay Concerning Human Understanding,* vol. 2 (New York: Dover, 1959), book 4, chapters 18 and 19.

40. John Calvin, *Institutes of the Christian Religion,* vol. 1, trans. Henry Beveridge (Grand Rapids, Mich.: Eerdman's, 1957), book 1, chapter 7, section 4.

41. Thomas Aquinas, *The Summa Theologica,* vol. 2, trans. Fathers of the English Dominican Province (New York: Benziger Bros., 1947), part II, question 6, article 1, and *The Disputed Questions on Truth,* vol. 2, trans. James V. McGlynn (Chicago: Henry Regnery, 1953), question 14, article 1.

For Further Reading

Other important defenses of religious pluralism include Wilfred Cantwell Smith, *Towards a World Theology* (Philadelphia: Westminster Press, 1981); John Cobb, *Beyond Dialogue* (Philadelphia: Fortress Press, 1982); and Peter Byrne, *Prolegomena to Religious Pluralism* (New York: St. Martin's Press, 1995). For critiques of Smith, Hick, and the doctrine of pluralism see William J. Wainwright, "Wilfred Cantwell Smith on Faith and Belief," *Religious Studies* 20 (1984): 353–66, and Peter Byrne, "A Religious Theory of Religion," *Religious Studies* 27 (1991): 121–32. See also George Mavrodes, "Polytheism," and Alvin Plantinga, "Pluralism: A Defense of Religious Exclusivism," both in *The Rationality of Belief and the Plurality of Faith,* ed. Thomas D. Senor (Ithaca, N.Y.: Cornell University Press, 1995). Keith Yandell, "Some Varieties of Religious Pluralism," in *Inter-religious Models and Dialogue,* ed. J. Kellenberger (New

York: St. Martin's Press, 1993) is a helpful overview of possible positions on religious diversity. William Christian, *Oppositions of Religious Doctrines* (New York: Herder and Herder, 1972) is an excellent analysis of the nature of inter-religious disagreement.

For the classical Western view of revelation see Thomas Aquinas, *On the Truth of the Catholic Faith*, vol. 1, trans. Anton Pegis (Garden City, N.Y.: Doubleday Image, 1955), chapters 3–8. The traditional concept of revelation has recently been defended by Richard Swinburne, *Faith and Reason* (Oxford: Clarendon Press, 1981).

For other views of revelation see C. H. Dodd, *The Authority of the Bible* (Glasgow: William Collins Sons, 1978); H. H. Farmer, *The Word and God* (London: Nisbet, 1942); Emil Brunner, *Revelation and Reason*, trans. Olive Wyon (Philadelphia: The Westminster Press, 1946); John Baillie, *The Idea of Revelation in Recent Thought* (New York: Columbia University Press, 1956); and Paul Tillich, *Systematic Theology*, vol. 1 (Chicago: The University of Chicago Press, 1951), 71–159.

Advaitin and other Hindu conceptions of revelation are discussed in K. Satchidananda Murty, *Revelation and Reason in Advaita Vedānta* (New York: Columbia University Press, 1959). Also useful is A. J. Arberry, *Revelation and Reason in Islam* (London: George Allen and Unwin, 1957).

Conclusion

THIS BOOK HAS EXAMINED the major problems in the philosophy of religion. Can we draw any general conclusions?

Chapter 1 suggested that a maximally perfect reality is the proper object of mature religious attitudes. Although some philosophers doubt whether the concept is coherent, none has proved that a maximally perfect being is impossible. The significant dispute is, instead, over *what* properties a maximally perfect reality would have. One's opinions on this matter are determined by what one thinks is a perfection. For example, those who believe that knowledge, power, and moral goodness are better than any properties with which they are incompatible will attribute them to the ultimate and interpret maximal perfection theistically. Those who believe that any kind of duality is an imperfection will construe the ultimate as an absolute unity that transcends all distinctions and therefore *isn't* personal.

Chapter 2 considered the three historically most important arguments for God's existence. Chapter 3 discussed the principal reason for doubting that He exists (the reality and pervasiveness of evil). Chapter 4 examined the doctrine of immortality, and Chapter 5 discussed religious experience.

The results of our discussion were these:

1. The three arguments for God's existence may be sound. Their premises are plausible or at least not obviously false, and they support their conclusions.

2. The argument from evil isn't conclusive since the theist has several ways of defusing the problem.

3. A belief in immortality is probably reasonable if a religious worldview is true.

4. A case can be made for the validity of some religious experiences.

But the situation isn't as straightforward as this suggests. Even if the arguments discussed in the first five chapters are plausible, they employ controversial premises and make controversial assumptions. For example, the belief that a maximally perfect reality is personal implicitly assumes that knowledge and rational agency are pure perfections. The ontological argument rests on the claim that a maximally perfect reality is possible. The cosmological argument depends on the principle of sufficient reason. Design arguments employ premises like "The world resembles an artifact" and "The probability of a nondesigned world exhibiting apparent design is low." One's assessment of the problem of evil reflects one's general sense of the plausibility of the theist's explanations of evil, and one's estimate of the likelihood of our grasping God's reasons for permitting evil if He did exist and had reasons for permitting it. The strength of the presumption of immortality created by our kinship to the divine or the demands of justice is a matter of dispute, and the religious views these arguments presuppose are themselves controversial. The case for the validity of mystical experience depends on the principle of credulity, and not everyone accepts it.

One's evaluation of the arguments discussed in the first five chapters thus depends on one's sense of the plausibility of a number of controversial claims. These claims aren't obviously false, and many of us think they are true. But they aren't self-evident like "A whole is greater than its proper parts." Nor can we conclusively prove them in the way we can conclusively prove that the angles of a Euclidian triangle equal 180 degrees or that arsenic is a poison. The arguments' controversial premises and assumptions *can* sometimes be supported. Chapter 2, for example, offered reasons for thinking that a maximally perfect reality is possible and that some form of the principle of sufficient reason is true. But some of us will find this support convincing and others won't. People's judgments about the arguments' premises and presuppositions thus differ. Nor is there any conclusive way of settling the matter.

This suggests two things. Our assessment of the evidence for and against religious claims may be unavoidably affected by experiential and passional factors—by our having or not having apparent experiences of the divine, for example, by our need for meaning (James), or by our love of God or lack of it (Pascal). A person's assessment of things like our alleged kinship with the divine or the greater goods defense may also be a function of his or her evaluation of the comparative plausibility of worldviews or comprehensive explanatory systems that include them as parts. Philosophers of religion should therefore examine our "passional nature" and other nonevidential bases of religious belief and the problem of assessing worldviews.

Chapters 6, 7, and 8 discussed these issues and came to the following conclusions:

1. Although nonevidential factors may play a legitimate and even necessary role in the formation of religious belief, they don't make evidence irrelevant.

2. There are criteria for assessing worldviews, and one can employ them to make a case for the overall superiority of theism. The case isn't, however, conclusive.

In the end, one's judgment concerning the truth or falsity of theism, pantheism, or naturalism is the result of a complex interplay between one's evaluation of particular arguments such as the design argument, one's sense of the comparative plausibility of different worldviews, and nonevidential factors. It isn't surprising, then, that philosophers haven't been able to reach a consensus on these matters.

What implications does this have for the rationality of religious belief?

We must distinguish between a strong and a weak sense of "rational belief." Someone's belief is weakly rational if and only if he or she violates no epistemic duties in holding it. Whether a person does so depends on his or her circumstances. A small child can't be epistemically faulted for believing whatever its parents tell it, but an uncritical trust in one's parents' opinions is a fault in adults.

The interesting question is, "What are the epistemic duties with respect to religious belief of intelligent and adequately informed men and women who are familiar with what has been thought on the matter—who are aware of what can be said for and against religious belief, are acquainted with the history of religion, and so on?" It seems clear that they violate an epistemic duty if they hold religious beliefs for which they have no grounds of any kind or continue to hold them in the face of what seem decisive objections. It isn't clear that they violate an epistemic duty if they hold religious beliefs that they don't think are more probable than not on the evidence or hold them more firmly than the evidence alone appears to warrant.[1] While evidence is never irrelevant, there are reasons for thinking that properly formed religious beliefs can have other sources. They may be properly basic (Plantinga), appropriate expressions of our passional nature (James), or of hearts touched by grace (Pascal).

A belief can be weakly rational, however, without being strongly rational. Someone's belief is strongly rational if and only if he or she violates no epistemic duties in holding it and *either* the belief is properly basic for an epistemic agent whose faculties are functioning properly in an appropriate epistemic environment *or* the available evidence supports it. If claims about God, the Brahman, and so on, are "evidence-essential," however, and so require evidence (see Chapter 6), then whether a person's religious beliefs are strongly rational depends on the strength of the case for religious beliefs that we have discussed in this book. Those of us who think that the evidence favors religious belief should conclude that religious beliefs can be, and sometimes are, strongly rational. Those of us who doubt that the case is that strong should conclude that religious beliefs can't be strongly rational.

But suppose the evidence does favor religious belief. Is disbelief irrational? Not necessarily. If the evidence supports religious belief, disbelief can't be *strongly* rational. It can, however, be weakly rational, for there are reasons for disbelief, and the case for religious belief isn't fully compelling. *Irrational* beliefs are those that any informed, intelligent, and fair-minded person who carefully considered the matter would reject. While the evidence for (some) religious beliefs may be stronger than many think, it isn't strong enough to make the rejection of religious beliefs irrational or to prevent disbelief from being weakly rational.[2] Those who think that the evidence favors *dis*belief should draw analogous conclusions. If they are right, belief can't be strongly rational. Nevertheless, there *are* reasons for belief, and the case for disbelief isn't conclusive. Skeptics should therefore concede that the religious beliefs of their intellectual equals can at least be weakly rational.

Intelligent and informed men and women differ over the truth of religious opinions. Only one side's assessment of the evidence can be correct, but neither is entitled to deny the other's rationality.

Notes

1. By "evidence," in this context, I mean any intellectual consideration bearing on the truth or falsity of the belief in question—that is, anything that can be legitimately offered as a reason for or against it.

2. These aren't the same. A belief can fail to be weakly rational without being irrational. I may believe that Trigger will win the race even though I haven't any grounds for thinking he will do so; I may just think that Trigger will run faster than the other horses. Since my belief is groundless, it isn't weakly rational. Nevertheless, it isn't *irrational*. "Trigger will win the race" wouldn't be rejected as *false* by every informed and fair-minded person who considered his chances. (Note that properly formed basic beliefs or beliefs rooted in the demands of our passional nature aren't *groundless* although they aren't inferred from a body of evidence.)

INDEX

A

action, timeless, 17–18
Adams, Marilyn, 103 n. 38
Advaita Vedānta, 91, 146, 183, 202
  sensus divinitatis and, 169
  conception of the self (ātman), 115
  inclusivism and, 208
  inexpressibility of reality in, 188
  karma doctrine, 116
  rejection of theism, 10–12
  religious experience in, 124, 125
  space-time world, 192–195, 198 n. 26
  true reality, 206
  true/false revelation, 216
agape, *vs.* karunā, 190–192, 207
Al-Ghazzali, 22
Alston, William, 126–128, 137, 206
Anselm, 13, 20–21
apparent design, 52–55
  theism on, 186
  universe general features in, 53
Aquinas, Thomas, 91, 92, 218
  on Gods's anger and sorrow, 21,
    32 n. 32
  on proofs of God's existence, 43–44
Arhat ideal, 190
atheism, 166–167, 168
ātman (true self), 193
Augustine, 13, 91, 117
autonomy of religion, 152–156
Averroës, 201
Avicenna, 201
Avidy (ignorance), 192–194
Azande practices, rationality of, 202–203

B

Bacon, Francis, 99
beginningless series, contingent exist-
    ence, 46–47

Benedict XIV, 61
Bertocci, Peter, 71
Bodhisattva, 190
Boniface VIII, Pope, 208
Brahman
  absolute unity, 10–12
  as experience of the Real, 211
  knowledge (jnāna), 192–195
  theistic mystical consciousness,
    124–125
Broad, C. D., 112
Bucke, Richard, 121
Buddhism
  historical accuracy, 188
  mysticism and, 123, 124, 137, 194
  pluralistic hypothesis applied to,
    212–213
  ultimate concern in, 2
Byrne, Peter, 212

C

Calvin, John, 91, 218
  sensus divinitatis concept, 168
Ch'an, 203
chance hypothesis, design argument, 57
Christianity, 155. *See also* Kierkegaard,
    Søren; Pascal, Blaise
  afterlife in, 106
  beliefs and pluralistic hypothesis,
    208–209
  mystical experiences in, 127–128, 137
  pluralistic hypothesis applied to,
    212–213
  religious experiences in, 121, 124
  revelation in, 216
  ultimate concern in, 2
Clairvaux, Bernard de, 20–21
Clarke, Samuel, 44, 50, 116, 117
Clifford, William, 142, 159–160

commitment, 147–152
compassion
  evil and, 76
  impassibility and God's, 19–22
contingent state of affairs, 5. *See also*
    Sufficient Reason, Principle of (PSR)
  beginningless series, 46–47
  argument for God's existence from,
    44–45
  God's knowledge of future, 25–27
  theism *vs.* naturalism on, 186
cosmological argument, existence of God,
    42–51, 224
creation myths, 195
credulity, principle of, 138
Crittendon, Charles, 6

D

design argument
  apparent design in, 52–55
  inference from apparent design, 55–60
determinism, 161, 180
  freedom and, 85–88
  God's foreknowledge and, 32 n. 40
divine, concept of, 1–4, 207
Dodd, C. H., 215
Dore, Clement, 37
Dvaita Vedānta, 114

E

Edwards, Jonathan, 75, 87, 89
Edwards, Paul, 46–47
eternity, 149–151
evidentialism/anti-evidentialism, 142
  disagreements on beliefs, 170–173
evil
  gratuitous, 95–100
  incompatibility of existence of God
    and, 70–75
  moral good and necessity of, 75–78
  natural order and necessity of, 78–80
  naturalist account of, 186
evolutionary processes, 54, 57–58,
    67 n. 33
Ewing, A. C., 60
exclusivism, 208
existence of God. *See also* Kierkegaard,
    Søren
  cosmological argument, 42–51

design argument, 51–60
  evil compatible with, 70–75, 102 n. 18
  ontological argument, 35–42

F

faith
  beliefs and, 205
  plurality of religions and, 214
  relation between reason and, 146–147.
    See also Kierkegaard, Søren;
    Pascal, Blaise
  religious truths and religious, 171
Farmer, H. H., 215
Ferre, Frederick, 185
fideism. *See also* Kierkegaard, Søren;
    Pascal, Blaise; Phillips, D. Z.
  comparison between Kierkegaard's,
    Pascal's, and Phillips's attitudes,
    156–158
  definition, 143
Flew, Antony, 112
foreknowledge, 25
  human freedom and, 27–29
  problems with, 25–27
foundationalism/classical founda-
    tionalism, criterion, 164
free will defense, 82–91
  determinism's compatibility with
    freedom, 85–88
  limitation of God's power and, 89–91
Freud, Sigmund, 190–191

G

Gale, Richard, 103 n. 41
Gaskell, Elizabeth, 1
God. *See also* existence of God; maximally
    perfect reality; Pascal, Blaise;
    revelation
  metaphysical attributes, 12–14
  omnipotence of 23–25
  omniscience of, 25–29
  perfection of, 6
  power/sovereignty and freedom,
    89–90
  timelessness of, 15–18
greater goods defense, 75–82
  moral good, natural order, and neces-
    sity of evil, 75–78
  value of the goods, 81–82

Gregory of Nyssa, 82
guilt, 17
  happiness and, 149
  self-hatred *vs.*, 198 n. 23
Gutting, Gary, 166–167

H

happiness, 8–9, 81
  immortality and desire for, 116–117
  Kierkegaard on, 148–150
Hartshorne, Charles, 14, 19–20, 25, 36
  maximally perfect reality, 9
  Principle of Sufficient Reason (PSR)
    and, 48
Hick, John, 96, 202
  claim about the Real, 209–211
  factual necessity of God, 44–45
  response to problem of religious diver-
    sity, 206–209
Hīnāyana Buddhism, 155, 202
  interpretation of reality, 189
  rejection of theism, 11
  vs. Mahāyāna Buddhism, 190–191
Hinduism, 110. *See also* Vedānta
  beliefs and pluralistic hypothesis, 208
Horton, Robin, 219 n. 5
Hügel, Friedrich von, 20
human freedom. *See also* Kierkegaard,
    Søren
  free will defense and, 83–85
  God's desire to respect, 145
  God's foreknowledge and, 19, 27–29,
    31 n. 27
  God's omnipotence/sovereignty and,
    89–90
  God's triumph and, 90–91
Hume, David, 50, 52, 56, 61, 63–64, 70

I

immortality
  argument from the soul's simplicity,
    112–113
  arguments for, 111–112
  desire for happiness argument, 116–117
  divine justice argument, 115–116
  kinship with the divine argument,
    114–115
  moral argument for the soul's, 113–114
  possibility of, 107–111

immutability, 7, 13
impassibility, 13
  doctrine of, 18–22
inclusivism, 208
inference to the best explanation,
    181–182
infinite temporal regresses, 43–44
Islam, 188
  afterlife in, 106
  pluralistic hypothesis applied to, 213
  proof of God's existence in, 43
  theistic mystical experiences, 124

J

James, William, 1, 120, 175 n. 25–26,
    185
  on religious hypothesis, 187
  on universality of religion's three
    beliefs, 201
  on will to believe, 159–164
Jesus, 215–216
jīva, 194, 199 n. 32
jnāna (knowledge), 192–195, 199 n. 29
John of the Cross, mystical experience,
    122–123
John-Paul II, Pope, 208
Jordan, Jeff, 135
Joyce, George, 94
Judaism, 91, 188
  afterlife in, 106
  beliefs and pluralistic hypothesis, 208
  visionary experiences, 121

K

Kant, Immanuel, 36
  moral argument for the soul's immor-
    tality, 113–114
karma, Indian doctrine of, 116
karunā, agape *vs.*, 190–192
Keats, John, 77
Kierkegaard, Søren, 156–158, 171–173
  on religious commitment, 147–152
  vs. Pascal's fideism, 152
knowledge, God's future contingent's
    and, 25–27
  impassibility and, 18–19
  timelessness and, 15–17
Krishna, 188
Kuhn, Thomas, 180

L

Leibniz, Gottfried, 50
Lewis, C. S., 78
Locke, John, 142, 217
    on personal identity, 108
logically possible/impossible world, 4–5,
    30 n. 4
love, 30 n.10. *See also* agape
    between God and His creatures, 82
Luther, Martin, 91, 190

M

Madhva, 114
Māchyamika Buddhism, 183, 188, 203,
    220 n. 6
Mahāyāna Buddhism, 203
    visionary experiences, 121
    vs. Hīnāyana Buddhism, 190–191
Maimonides, 201
Mansel, Henry, 70–71
Martin, C. B., 128–129
Mavrodes, George, 186
maximally perfect reality
    coherence of, 6–12
    concept of, 5–9
    ontological argument, 35–36
    properties of, 9–12, 30 n. 3
McTaggart, J. M. E., 112
mediumistic phenomena, immortality
    and, 111–112
metaphysical systems. *See also* religious
    systems; worldviews
    criteria for assessment, 182–185, 204
Mill, John Stuart, 61
mind/body problem, 107
miracles, 61–64
Mitchell, Basil, 179, 182
Mohammed, 215–216
moral evils, 70
moral good, necessity of evil and, 75–78
morality, 53, 103 n. 41
More, Henry, 38
mystical experiences. *See also* religious
    experiences
    absence of independent justification,
        131–133
    dissimilarities with sense perception,
        128–131
    veridical character, 122–123

N

natural evils, 70
natural order
    God's choice of best, 91–95
    necessity of evil and, 78–80
naturalism
    on natural world, 198 n. 17
    theism and, 185–187
Nelson, Kenneth, 54, 55
Neoplatonism, 106, 110
Newman, John Henry, 178, 181
Newton, 99, 180
Nirvāna, 189, 202
noetic experiences, 123, 125
numinous experiences, 121, 123

O

omnipotence, 23–25
    freedom and, 89–90
omniscience, 25–29
ontological argument
    assumptions, 41–42
    proof, 35–37, 223–224
    objections, 37–41
Origen, 76
Otto, Rudolf, 121

P

pain, 17
    incarnation and, 31 n. 22
Paley, William, 51, 56
paradigms, 180–181
Pascal, Blaise, 156–158, 171–173
    sense of the heart, 143–147
perceptual experience
    doxastic practices and, 126–127
    vs. mystical experience, 124–125
perfections
    degreed properties, 8–9
    incompatibility of, 7–8
personal identity, nature of, 107–111
Phillips, D. Z., 171–173
    autonomy of religion, 152–156
    comparison of Pascal/Kierkegaard's
        fideism with, 156–158
Pike, Nelson, 24
Plantinga, Alvin, 83, 171–173, 178, 185
    freewill defense and, 82–85
    properly basic beliefs and, 164–170

Plato, 106, 191
    kinship with the divine argument, 114–115
    on transcendent good, 116–117
pragmatic argument, God's existence, 65 n. 10
prayer, 1
probability argument
    application to miracles, 63
    application to design hypothesis, 58–60

Q

Quran, compassion in the, 20

R

Rama, 188
Ramanuja, 3, 195, 204
reason
    broadening of conception, 172
    faith *vs.*, 146–147, 214. *See also* Kierkegaard, Søren; Pascal, Blaise
    revelation and, 217–219
relativism, 202–205
religions, diversity of, 201–202
religious beliefs, 1–3, 226 n. 2. *See also* James, William
    D. Z. Phillips on, 153–154
    devaluation of propositional truth and, 205–206
    foundationalism/classical foundationalism views on, 164–166
religious experiences
    prima facie vs. ultima facie veridical, 206–207
    cognitive value, 125–128, 138
    conflicting claims about, 135–138
    natural explanations of, 133–135
    nature of, 121–125
religious pluralism, 206–214
    as a religious hypothesis, 212–213
religious systems
    criteria for, 182–185
    illumination criterion, 192–196
    pragmatic criterion, 189–192
resurrection, 106
revelation, 214–217
    reason and, 217–219
Rowe, William, 97, 99

S

Śaiva Siddhānta, theist mystical experiences, 124
salvation, 106, 115, 207. *See also* immortality
Śamkara
    mystical experience and, 122–123
    on space-time world, 192–193
Schlesinger, George, 92
Schoen, Edward, 184
secularization, 186
simplicity, doctrine of God's, 12–13, 22, 32 n. 33
Smith, Wilfred Cantwell, 205
soul
    kinship to the divine, 115
    moral argument for immortality, 113–114
    relationship to body, 106–107
    simplicity and immortality argument, 112–113
Sterry, Peter, 54
Sufficient Reason, Principle of (PSR), 47–51
Suzuki, D. T., 211
Swinburne, Richard, 62, 79–80, 125

T

Tennant, F. R., 53, 55
Teresa of Avila, mystical experience, 122–123
theism
    cumulative arguments for, 178–182
    western *vs.* Indian, 195–196
Tillich, Paul, 2, 185
timeless nature of God, 13, 15–18, 22
transcendental ego, 110
true self, 106, 192
truth, 149–150
    devaluation of belief and propositional, 205–206
    religious hypothesis, 161
    theistic beliefs, 167

U

ultimate concern, religious life, 2–3

V

Vaisnavas, 188

Vaisnavism, theist mystical experiences, 124

Vedas, 216

Vedānta, 106. *See also* Advaita Vedānta; Dvaita Vedānta; Viśistādvaita Vedānta

Vishnu, 188, 207, 209
  as experience of the Real, 211

visions, 122–123, 140 n. 20

Viśistādvaita Vedānta, 91, 195, 204

W

Wesley, John, 211–212

Winch, Peter, 202–203

worldviews. *See also* religious systems
  comparison of religious, 188–189
  revelation and, 215–217

Wykstra, Stephen, 99, 169

Y

Yahweh, 207, 209

Yoga, monistic mystical consciousness, 124, 194

Z

Zen Buddhism, 211